EVERYDAY JIHAD

EVERYDAY JIHAD

The Rise of Militant Islam
among Palestinians in Lebanon

BERNARD ROUGIER

Translated by Pascale Ghazaleh

Harvard University Press

Cambridge, Massachusetts

London, England

2007

First published as *Le Jihad au quotidien*
Copyright © 2004 by Presses Universitaires de France

Library of Congress Cataloging-in-Publication Data

Rougier, Bernard.
[Jihad au quotidien. English]
Everyday jihad : the rise of militant Islam among Palestinians
in Lebanon / Bernard Rougier ; translated
by Pascale Ghazaleh.
p. cm.
"First published as Le Jihad au quotidien (Paris : Presses
Universitaires de France, 2004)."
Includes bibliographical references and index.
ISBN-13: 978-0-674-02529-5 (alk. paper)
ISBN-10: 0-674-02529-6 (alk. paper)
1. Islam and world politics. 2. Jihad.   3. Religion and
politics. 4. Islamic fundamentalism—Lebanon. I. Title.
BP173.5.R6813   2007
320.5′57089927405692—dc22   2006102855

To the memory of my father,
Yves Rougier

Contents

Guide to Political and Religious Groups

Palestinian Organizations

Palestine Liberation Organization (PLO): secular Palestinian organization

Major factions:
—Fatah (core organization)
—Popular Front for the Liberation of Palestine (PFLP)
—Democratic Front for the Liberation of Palestine (DFLP)

Hamas (Islamic Resistance Movement): Islamist Palestinian group

Islamic Jihad Movement in Palestine

Dissident Palestinian Groups Linked to Syria

Sa'iqa (Vanguards of Popular Liberation War Organization)

Fatah-Intifada

Popular Front for the Liberation of Palestine—General Command (PF—GC)

Islamist Political Parties in Lebanon

Lebanese Muslim Brotherhood (al-Jama'a al-Islamiyya)

Islamic Society for Charitable Works, known as al-Ahbash ("the Ethiopians" in Arabic)

Islamic Unification Movement (Harakat al-Tawhid al-Islamiyya, better known as al-Tawhid)

Hezbollah ("Party of God"):
Shi'a organization that is both a party, with
deputies in the Lebanese Parliament, and an
armed militia that struggled against Israel

Islamist Networks in Lebanon

Association for Guidance and Goodwill (Jam'iyyat al-Hidaya wal-Ihsan): salafist educational network

Liberation Party (Hizb al-Tahrir): clandestine network that seeks to reestablish the caliphate in the Muslim world

Congregation of Muslim Ulema (Tajammu' al-Ulama al-Muslimin): group formed to bring together Sunni and Shi'a clerics

Clandestine Islamist Networks Active
in the Ain al-Helweh Palestinian Camp

Partisan's League (Usbat al-Ansar): main salafi-jihadist network; consolidated its presence in the camp at the beginning of the 1990s

Combatant Islamic Movement (al-Haraka al-Islamiyya al-Mujahida): group founded to fight the PLO's influence in the Palestinian camps

Diniyeh Group: network of young jihadists who escaped the Lebanese army in the wake of fighting in January 2000 in the Diniyeh Mountain in North Lebanon

EVERYDAY JIHAD

Introduction

Roughly 370,000 Palestinian refugees currently live in Lebanon. That figure represents 12 percent of the country's population, and almost 10 percent of all Palestinian refugees officially registered with the United Nations Relief and Works Agency (UNRWA).[1] In 1948, nearly 100,000 Palestinians left northern Galilee, where they were cultivators, and went to seek refuge in Lebanon. Today, most of these refugees have only mythical ties to their country of origin: three or even four generations after the *nakba* (disaster) of 1948, only one out of ten Palestinians was actually born in Mandate Palestine, while 40 percent of the inhabitants of Lebanon's refugee camps are under fifteen years of age.[2] More than half of all refugees live in a dozen camps near the country's main coastal cities. The most densely populated camps are on the outskirts of Beirut (Burj al-Barajneh), Tripoli (Nahr al-Barid), Saida (Ain al-Helweh), and Tyre (Rashidiyyeh and Burj al-Shamali).

This book traces the path of jihadist militants who, from the alleyways of the Palestinian camps, waged a religious, global war for the victory of Islam against unbelief.

These militant Islamists situate themselves within the international jihadist network and identify with the rhetoric of al-Qa'ida. They have capitalized on the Israeli-Syrian conflict to take control of places—specifically, the refugee camps in Lebanon—that the

1

Lebanese army cannot enter without the permission of Syria's leaders. They have set up bases in the most populated camps bordering the eastern Mediterranean, in Ain al-Helweh, in southern Lebanon, and in Nahr al-Barid, in the north of the country.

This book, based on four years of research in the camps, focuses specifically on the jihadist networks that operate in Ain al-Helweh. With more than 35,000 inhabitants, the camp is home to the highest concentration of Palestinian refugees in Lebanon. By staying very close to the key figures, their rhetoric, perceptions, and means of persuasion, I have tried to show how a new religious ideology took root in this Palestinian environment. Combining a literal interpretation of the sacred texts of Islam with emulation of the first Muslim communities *(salaf)* and a warlike cult of jihad, an active minority of Palestinian refugees were led into the global space of jihadist Islamism. How this minority managed to create a salafist-jihadist sanctuary in Ain al-Helweh is recounted here.[3] By exploring its ideological references, production of Islamic knowledge, internal and external enemies, religious figures, and mechanisms of socialization and mobilization, I hope to provide an interpretive model for an unprecedented phenomenon. This model might also capture similar realities in other contexts.

The Ain al-Helweh camp has become a recruitment site for young enthusiasts and a retreat for militants hunted down in their countries of origin. The camp now belongs to the global geography of jihadist Islamism: its extraterritoriality, justified by the absence of a solution to the problem of Palestinian refugees at the regional and international level, has become a resource for religious militants who seek to escape the control of the Lebanese state and its "impious" institutions. For these activists, the camp constitutes a peripheral urban space that, though similar to the outskirts of major Arab cities, is closed off to the legal authorities.

These Islamists did not settle in Ain al-Helweh unobstructed and unopposed. Since the jihadist networks first appeared in the early

1990s, the camp has been the site of an embryonic civil war, punctuated with violent confrontations between partisans of globalized jihad, on one hand, and militants for the nationalist Palestinian cause, on the other. The Islamic salafist movement managed to find a powerful means of mobilization by establishing its opposition, first to the Madrid Conference (October 1991), which brought Arabs and Israelis together for the first time, and second to the Palestinian-Israeli peace process that resulted from the Oslo Accords in 1993. Each time, religious militants sought to capture the Palestinian question, even if that meant modifying its significance radically, neglecting its national history, and redefining its values.

The battle described in this book is fundamentally a battle for identity. In that sense, all the camp's inhabitants, even the poorest, are involved in the struggle. When faced with uncertainty and vulnerability, displaced people search for something with which to identify. In this respect the camp is less a marginal area than a site of significant expression, at the intersection of local, regional, and transnational space. In this perspective, mobilization entails creating identities that modify the way individuals represent and interpret their social and political universe.

After the Israeli government and the PLO (Palestine Liberation Organization) signed the Oslo Accords in September 1993, the conflict took an increasingly violent turn, with a face-to-face confrontation between two opposed processes—one leading to the construction of a transnational salafist identity, the other built on Palestinian Authority (PA) efforts to justify the peace agreement and its state's promises to the Palestinian diaspora.

Today, it is no longer possible to speak of a Palestinian society in Lebanon's camps, so deep is the fracture between the PLO and its hard core (Fatah), on one hand, and the salafist militants, on the other. The latter will use all means available to reduce the influence of the Palestinian national movement. The second Intifada, triggered in September 2000, did nothing to attenuate the faultline separating these two groups of people, who, even if they live in the same space, now evolve in different worlds. The nationalist Palestinian organizations, including Hamas and Islamic Jihad, despite their often profound divergences regarding the means and ultimate objectives of the struggle to liberate Palestine, still locate themselves primarily within national space, while the jihadists have moved into the realm of global Islamism.

This confrontation in Lebanon's Palestinian refugee camps was one of the first experiences of jihadist Islamism's rise to power in an Arab, Muslim context deeply marked by a nationalist tradition. Even though it remains localized, this religious dynamic reveals that a considerable part of the population has freed itself from the national Palestinian framework and is no longer governed by a nationalist universe. Before explaining how this new identity was constructed in places that were once, in the late 1960s, the crucible of Palestinian national consciousness, we might do well to present the issues at stake in the Palestinians' presence in Lebanon. This will allow us to reach a better understanding of the way the salafist-jihadist networks integrated regional limitations in relations with their internal and external environment. Here, we will reject commonplace statements about the apocalyptic logic attributed to the jihadists, and emphasize the fact that they are capable of combining their ideological commitment with a sharp sense of power relations. Untangling the complex skein that is the Palestinian question in Lebanon is a prerequisite to understanding the logic that guides these militants, and the way they have been able to exploit the regional and national situation to keep their networks alive.

Palestinians at the Heart of Lebanon's Contradictions

In 1948, less than two years after the French mandatory power had departed from Lebanon, tens of thousands of Palestinians from Galilee arrived, posing one of the first challenges to the country's national identity. In Lebanon, these refugees, the vast majority of whom were Sunni Muslims, were seen through an exclusively communitarian prism: under the presidency of Camille Chamoun (1952–1958), naturalization was granted to a few Palestinian Christian refugees but not to the overwhelming majority of Sunni Muslim Palestinians. The presence of a Sunni Arab population challenged the internal equilibrium in a country in which the different religious communities coexisted on the basis of political and administrative power sharing.

The Maronite Christian leaders who held the main offices in Lebanon's security apparatus at that time set up a policy forbidding any militant activity. They also applied a common-law system to the job market that led, in practice, to the socioeconomic exclusion of Palestinians in Lebanon. Most of these Palestinians, who were originally peasants, constituted a cheap labor force employed on the margins of the Lebanese economy, mainly in building and agriculture. Political surveillance was intended to prevent encounters between a population of refugees sensitive to the Nasserist propaganda Cairo was sending out via the "Voice of the Arabs" radio station, and a Muslim street enthusiastic about the Egyptian president's pan-Arab discourse and alienated by President Camille Chamoun's authoritarian political practices and adherence to the Eisenhower doctrine (1957).

Summoned to power after the mini–civil war of 1958, which pitted Chamoun against all his opponents—and in which the Palestinians did not participate in any way—the new president, Fouad Chehab (1958–1964), led a foreign policy aligned with Egypt's. He thus managed to satisfy Sunni Muslims while strengthening the state's control over Palestinian refugees. The Lebanese army's "second bureau" (intelligence service) was given the task of managing the refugee issue; it posted guards inside the camps and, at times, required the refugees to obtain special authorization for domestic travel.

The Palestinian community's increasing militarization, and the emergence of a new militant ideal represented by the PLO after Israel defeated the Arab armies in 1967, exacerbated tensions within Lebanese society.[4] The Cairo Accords, signed on November 3, 1969, confirmed the extent to which military and civilian spheres overlapped: the refugee population received social rights, recognition of its autonomy inside the camps, and the right to armed resistance against Israel "in coordination with the Lebanese army." The Palestinian question was thus plunged into the heart of Lebanon's contradictions, often with the assent of the Palestinian leadership itself. Rival parties invoked the Palestinians' cause to promote their own claims. The Lebanese left wing, carried along by the Druze leader Kamal Jumblatt's National Movement, demanded that the political system be stripped of sectarian power sharing and society secularized. Conservative Muslim leaders called for better political representation and the diffusion of executive power, which had been given to the Maronites at independence. All those who wanted partial reform or a wholesale overhaul of the Lebanese political system trumpeted their solidarity with the Palestinian cause. They accused the Lebanese army—whose commander in chief, like the majority of the officers, was Christian—of fighting the Palestinian organizations instead of acting first and foremost against Israeli incursions. Massive Israeli strikes, in retaliation against the fedayin infiltrating the Lebanese-Israeli border, intentionally increased domestic tension, hoping to force the army to crack down on Palestinian armed factions. As for the Christian "Lebanists," they made preserving Lebanon's integrity in the face of the "foreign invasion" an absolute priority and refused to consider domestic political changes under threat from Palestinian military forces. Some were willing to replace a state that they judged a failure, even at the risk of weakening its authority by creating private militias to defend "the real Lebanon" against the Palestinians and their Lebanese allies.

Palestinian organizations, traumatized by the precedent of Black September in Jordan (1970), sought to build a sanctuary in Lebanon.[5] They "worked on" different opposition groups, from the extreme left wing to the Islamists, thereby running the risk of losing all communication with the Christian elites and of justifying the accusations those elites leveled against them. Left-wing Palestinian militias like the Popular Front for the Liberation of Palestine (PFLP) and the Democratic Front for the Liberation of Palestine (DFLP) would have liked nothing more than the creation of a socialist republic in Lebanon, which they saw as a North Vietnam–like sanctuary from which they would be able to free Palestine. They pressured Fatah, under the leadership of Yasir Arafat, to increase its support for Kamal Jumblatt's National Movement. Jumblatt, for his part, blocked any possibility of rapprochement between the PLO president and "sheikh" Pierre Gemayyel, the head of the Kata'ib Party, the leading Christian group in Lebanon.

The fear that the Palestinians would settle permanently in Lebanon reflected an emotional identification between Lebanon's Maronite Christians and a sectarian regime that had given them a degree of political preeminence since the 1943 National Pact between Christians and Muslims. A single logic now merged the defense of Lebanon's sovereignty and political regime with the defense of the Maronite community, which had contributed historically to the construction of the Lebanese state. From this perspective, the Palestinian presence was seen as a threat to the current order. This perception was implicitly contained in denunciations of a permanent settlement, as rendered by the Arabic term *tawtin*, which conveys the idea that Lebanon could serve as a "spare home" for the Palestinian refugees. The vagueness of the term—which confuses legal stay and naturalization—and the emotional charge it bore (the word is a derivative of the root *watan*, which signifies homeland in a sentimental sense) implies that there would be a zero-sum game between Christians and Palestinians. According to this dramatic view, were the Palestinians to stay for good, Christians would either be forced to leave Lebanon or be subjected to political and cultural subordination. In the few years preceding the 1975 war, Christian leaders—like the Maronite president Sulayman Franjiyyeh, who was one of the first figures to provide some paramilitary groups with weapons in anticipation of a confrontation with the Palestinians— exploited that threat, as did the Muslim elites, who used that fear among the Christians to back up their desire to transform the Lebanese political system to their own advantage by demanding greater participation.

The militarization of Lebanese society and the corresponding increase in insecurity and vulnerability thus changed the balance of power within each camp in favor of the most radical forces. In April 1975, this situation resulted in a civil war with unpredictable consequences. Against a background of rising sectarianism, the collapse of progressive ideals, social recomposition within each of the communities, the development of war economies, and the nationwide consolidation of the militia phenomenon, another conflict emerged inside the war. This time the PLO, headed by Yasir Arafat, was pitted against Hafiz al-Asad's Syrian regime.

The Conflict between the Syrian Regime and the PLO

The permanent character of the confrontation between Syria and the PLO is remarkable in a conflict where shifting alliances have been the norm rather than the exception. From the early 1970s, the emergence of an independent Palestinian organization known on the international scene (the PLO) represented a danger for Damascus. It weakened Syria's legitimacy in the Arab world as well as its regional capabilities, by showing that a Palestinian-Israeli peace was possible outside its sphere of influence, and perhaps even to its detriment. The first confrontation between Syria and the PLO took place in June 1976, when Syrian troops entered Lebanon. By preventing a military victory of the National Movement and the PLO over Christian forces, the Syrian president managed to justify to the United States his intervention on Lebanese territory and to forestall the possibility of Israeli interference. This last occurrence would have been inevitable had the Syrians fallen in behind the "Islamo-progressists" they were supporting before they intervened in Lebanon. The second direct confrontation took place in 1983, when Palestinian dissidents backed by the Syrian army attacked the Palestinian camps in the north. Under siege in the Nahr al-Barid camp, near Tripoli, since September 1983, Arafat and loyalist PLO militants were able to escape by sea on December 20, thanks to French military protection, but to the great chagrin of Syrian leaders who wanted the Palestinian chief physically eliminated.

At other points in the war, the conflict between the two was more latent but no less real, as each of the parties eagerly offered political and logistical support to the other's absolute enemy. During the virtual civil war (1976–1982), which pitted the Muslim Brothers against Hafiz al-Asad's regime in Syria, the PLO's main component, Yasir Arafat's Fatah organization, gave financial and military assistance to the various Islamist movements located in Tripoli, northern Lebanon's "Sunni capital." They did so with the intention of helping to topple a regime that had never recognized the principle of "independent Palestinian decision-making" *(istiqlal al-qarar al-falastini)*.

Between 1985 and 1988, during the deadly "camp war" episode, Amal, the Shi'ite militia, was encouraged by its Syrian sponsor to take control of the camps in Beirut and the south. Less than three years after the 1982 Israeli invasion and the Sabra and Shatila massacres, Amal surrounded and bombarded the Palestinian camps in Lebanon's capital. These clashes closed a cycle of Lebanese-Palestinian violence that had begun ten years earlier, at the start of the Lebanese war, when Christian militas, with assistance from Syria's artillery forces, had razed the Palestinian camps of Tal al-Za'tar and

Quarantine on Beirut's outskirts in August 1976. In the Lebanese phase of their history, therefore, the Palestinians have already paid the price several times over for Syria's regional agenda coinciding with that of local Lebanese militias.

Under a shared threat from Syria, former enemies—Lebanese Christians and Palestinians—drew closer in the 1980s, in the name of a common defense of their political autonomy. During the "liberation war" *(harb al-tahrir)* launched by General Aoun against the Syrian army in March 1989, Fatah officer Fuad al-Shubki provided the Lebanese army with intelligence information and logistical support. At this time an anti-Syrian Arab axis was forming, made up most notably of Iraq under Saddam Hussein, the PLO, and Lebanon's Christians.

Finally, in summer 1991, the Lebanese army, purged and restored to Syrian influence after General Aoun's ouster on October 13, 1990, managed, after a brief struggle in Saida, to seize the PLO's heavy armaments in a region where the Syrian army could not penetrate without violating the "red lines" tacitly negotiated with Israel at the start of the war.[6] As a whole, the refugee camps have always been involved in the many phases of the Syrian-Palestinian conflict, and in post-war Lebanon, the Syrian-Lebanese security forces in charge of the Palestinian question made no distinction between civilian and military interests.

Indeed, the Syrian-Palestinian conflict continued after the creation of an autonomous political authority in the Palestinian territories in 1993. Each time an agreement was signed or negotiations were undertaken between the PLO and the Israeli government, Yasir Arafat was accused of encouraging the permanent settlement of Palestinians in Lebanon. Syrian and Lebanese critics assumed that the (still very hypothetical) creation of a state in the West Bank and Gaza would imply that the refugees had given up their right of return and were staying in Lebanon for good. Throughout the 1990s, the ups and downs of the Palestinian-Israeli peace process were unfavorably compared with the heroic saga of Hezbollah's military resistance in southern Lebanon. The latter's armed struggle was seen as the only way to regain territories occupied by the Israeli enemy. In Syria and Lebanon, the Palestinian leaders who signed the Oslo Accords were accused of collaborating with Israel. The Syrian goal was to prevent the Palestinian Authority from consolidating its influence and control over the camps as a whole, by encouraging inter-Palestinian rifts and by blocking any possibility of direct negotiation between the Lebanese government and the PA's local representatives. An extreme example of this policy was provided by the death sentence, passed in absentia in December 1999, against the PA representative in Lebanon, Sultan Abul-Aynayn, for "illegal constitution of an armed group." This decision, which was more political than legal, was a way for the Syrian regime to punish Abul-Aynayn's diplomatic activity (following instructions from Yasir Arafat, he had undertaken a series of discussions with public figures from Lebanon's main communities), and to defeat the PA's attempt to establish itself as the representative body for all Palestinians on Lebanese territory.

Since it was established in 1970, in the wake of the coup carried out by Hafiz al-Asad, the Syrian regime therefore strove to segment and control the political activity of the Palestinians. Ironically, this repressive policy was aimed at a Sunni population that, thanks to its family ties throughout the region and its attachment to Arab nationalist causes, was the best human example of "Greater Syria" (Bilad al-Sham)—a geographical entity that served to justify the Asad family's regional ambitions.

The struggle against Arafat's Fatah was also directly linked to the Syrian regime's policy in Lebanon. The Palestinian organization had existed in tandem with the Muslim sectors of Lebanese society in the early 1970s, and Syria's leadership understood, correctly, that the main threats to its interests would emerge from that environment, and especially from within the Sunni community.

Echoing the clashes of the war's first years, during which the Syrian army fought the pro-Palestinian Lebanese left wing, former loyalties could be reactivated to serve in a new context. Subsequently, Yasir Arafat's support of the Syrian Muslim Brothers in their struggle against the Asad regime between 1978 and 1982 illustrated the threat's continuity despite the change in ideology. As the Syrian vise grew tighter around Lebanon, progressive intellectuals, Islamist activists, and Palestinian independence fighters looked to the Palestinian camps for the experience and fighting manpower necessary for their political survival. As soon as they returned to Beirut in 1987, the Syrians were therefore careful to silence all those who were opposed to their tutelage in Lebanon's Sunni communities. When necessary, they resorted to local allies for petty police work.

The Palestinian Population since the End of the War

The end of the war in Lebanon led to the demobilization of combatants, who constituted at least 50 percent of the male labor force.[7] Meanwhile, the financial impact of the Gulf War (1991) resulted in a welfare crisis for the refugee population: the many types of assistance (pensions, scholarships, salaries) provided by the PLO's social institutions were cut off or drastically reduced. Excluded from the Lebanese job market and deprived of a share of the resources generated by the "Palestinian economy" in Lebanon, the Palestinians continue to face chronic underemployment and survive through recourse to the informal economy, private foreign aid, and the safety net provided by NGOs and charity organizations.[8]

At the regional level, the Palestinian question has served to illustrate the "united destiny" shared by Lebanon and Syria, to quote the Ba'thist slogan used by the two countries' leaders at the end of the 1990s. From the Syrian perspective, the goal has been to prevent Palestinian refugees from becoming integrated into Lebanese society, by submitting them to a system of exclusion that applies to their legal, geographical, and social situation. Successful integration of the Palestinians into Lebanese society would satisfy the Israeli side, which would like to see the refugees settle permanently in the host states, thus precluding their right of return as stipulated in U.N. General Assembly Resolution 194. Syria must do everything in its power to prevent such a development as well as the transfer of the "refugee" question to the Palestinian Authority or any other external political body. Permanent settlement would deprive Syrian negotiators of a powerful bargaining chip in their dealings with Israel: the ability to wield a threat that ultimately touches on the legitimacy of a Jewish state in Palestine.

At the end of the Gulf War, in April 1991, a ministerial committee headed by two members of the Lebanese government, Abdallah al-Amin and Chawqi Fakhuri, met with a Palestinian delegation to establish the terms and conditions of the Palestinians' rights and duties in Lebanon. The Madrid Conference, which opened in October 1991, and the constitution of a multilateral commission on refugees, boycotted by both Syria and Lebanon, brutally interrupted these efforts. As a result, the Palestinian question has been frozen until the hypothetical resumption of Syrian-Israeli talks. Such talks would allow the Syrian government to retrieve the Golan Heights, which Lebanon occupied in 1967. The Syrian regime cannot allow the Palestinian question in Lebanon to be internationalized, as long as its regional usefulness has not been exhausted.

In the context of an imminent Israeli withdrawal from southern Lebanon in 2000, the Syrian regime needed the Palestinians in Lebanon once again, this time to show its Israeli adversaries that it still had leverage to force the Israelis to negotiate. On March 8, 2000—the anniversary of the coup that brought the Ba'th Party to power in Syria in 1963—Lebanon's president Lahoud intervened for the first time in writing, to inform international public opinion that Lebanon would not guarantee the security of international borders in the case of unilateral withdrawal. He warned that no one would be able to prevent camp inhabitants from infiltrating the surrounding areas. The Syrian government was thus brandishing the threat of a "historical repeat" if the withdrawal was not followed by a regional peace settlement; in other words, the camps could become what they had been in the 1970s, the bases of a Palestinian resistance movement embodied this time around by the descendants of the 1948 refugees. This position was reaffirmed forcefully in a memorandum of April 5, 2000, from the Lebanese president's office to U.N. Secretary-General Kofi Annan, who had just been informed that the Israeli government intended to apply Resolution 425, mandating its withdrawal from southern Lebanon. Lebanon's refusal to deploy its army in the liberated southern region after Israeli troops withdrew in May 2000, and its demand that the Chebaa Farms (a zone of fifteen square miles that includes a dozen hamlets south of Chebaa, a Lebanese village on the foothills of Mount Hermon) be restored unconditionally, were also part of a strategy that kept every possibility open, at least on the level of rhetoric.

With the approach of negotiations that were intended to be "final," according to the long-postponed schedule of the Palestinian-Israeli peace process, the reinforcement of Fatah's military capabilities partially neutralized the credibility of references to a Middle Eastern apocalypse. By providing a military presence in the southern camps, the Palestinian Authority was demonstrating that it sought to prevent opponents of the peace process from using the camps to launch military operations against Israel. Such attacks would have weakened the Palestinian negotiators' position and their claim to speak in the name of all Palestinian refugees in the Middle East. In Lebanese and Syrian circles of power, Arafat was accused of playing into Israel's hands and "weakening the resistance camp." By way of response, during the Camp David negotiations that took place in summer 2000, the Palestinian delegation did all it could to counter Syria's claims (in equal measures directed against Arafat and addressing the international community and Israel) by giving priority to the return of Lebanon's older Palestinian refugees to Israel, and of the others to a new Palestinian state—even if this implied compromising the principle for all remaining Palestinian refugees.

On another level, Syria's refusal to consider the social rights of the Palestinian refugees was also a way for Damascus to regain the support of Lebanon's Christian leaders. At the request of the Christians, the rejection of a permanent settlement had been enshrined in the peace accords signed at Taif in September 1989, and was subsequently integrated into the new Lebanese constitution the following year. When General Lahoud reached power in 1998, the question of *tawtin* was immediately placed at the top of the official political agenda, so as to address a dual concern—preventing Syria's regional isolation, on one hand, and reconstituting an alliance between the Christians and Damascus, on the other. This strategy, designed to detract from the Christian opposition's anti-Syrian stance, presented Syria as the only power capable of guaranteeing the existential security of Lebanon's Christians—at the expense of Lebanon's independence—by preventing the permanent settlement of Palestinian refugees in the country. Pushing the Palestinians aside also fulfilled the aspirations of Syria's greatest ally in Shi'ite circles, the immutable president of the Lebanese parliament, Nabih Berri, whose Amal militia waged a particularly ferocious anti-Palestinian campaign during the siege of the refugee camps in the south and the capital.

For the Syrian rulers, until a Syrian-Israeli agreement is reached, the refugees must be isolated from Lebanese society and artificially maintained in the original time of the Arab-Israeli conflict. The existence of "security-free islands" *(juzur amniyya)* symbolized by the camps and the survival, within them, of a "Palestinian armed struggle" offer three benefits: they feed anti-Palestinian sentiment in Lebanese public opinion, which Damascus exploits in its relations with Beirut's new elites; abroad, they constitute a warning to the Israeli leaders after the unilateral withdrawal from southern Lebanon in

May 2000; and, finally, they force the international community to face its historical responsibilities with regard to the Palestinian problem.[9]

The Political Geography of Palestinian Camps in Lebanon

When the war in Lebanon ended in 1990, the country's Palestinian camps were subjected to restrictive measures that perpetuated the Syrian regime's policy toward the Palestinian leadership during the war. The Palestinian camp diaspora was fragmented spatially, both to limit the camps' ability to coordinate and to weaken their political leadership. Just as some Maronite Lebanese leaders from the Beqaa (in Zahleh) and from the north (in Zghorta) tied their political destiny to that of the Syrian leadership, some Palestinians in the north benefited from relatively privileged living conditions compared with their compatriots in other parts of the country. They owed this special treatment to the fact that their local leaders declared their allegiance to Syria during the confrontations of 1983. The camps in the north were cut off from those of Beirut and the south, thanks to a policy that cleverly mixed material advantages and armed repression. Their inhabitants, who in post-war Lebanon enjoyed almost total freedom of movement (unlike the camps in the south, Nahr al-Barid and Baddawi were not circled by military barricades), have been able to take control of their physical environment. They were allowed to bring building materials into the camps without facing military or legal constraints. They thus managed to increase their habitable space without ever incurring the slightest charge of *tawtin* from a political class that was otherwise always quick to brandish the accusation. This material freedom came at a cost, however: the popular committees were made up exclusively of Abu Mussa's Fatah-Intifada militants, linked to the Syrian agents delegated to the Akkar region, in the north and in Tripoli.

After the beginning of the second Intifada, portraits of Yasir

Arafat could be seen in the street markets, which would have been impossible before September 2000, when the only portraits that could decorate the camp's alleyways were those of Hafiz al-Asad and his son, Bashar (the camp's main thoroughfares bore the names of these two representatives of the Syrian ruling dynasty). After Yasir Arafat and Bashar al-Asad met in Amman on March 27, 2001, Fatah, which had been banned from organizing since 1983, began to enjoy a marginal degree of tolerance and a certain visibility, though the organization is still unable to open an office. Some Fatah leaders exercise clandestine influence in the camp, by handing out social benefits and scholarships to students. From the Syrian perspective, the ideal Palestinian refugee camp is one without pro-Arafat activists, with a local police force totally loyal to Syria, and preachers keen to maintain the best possible relations with Damascus.

Further south, Syrian constraints relax gradually, even though they do not disappear entirely. In the camp of Ain al-Helweh, less than a mile and a half east of Saida, every religious and political sensitivity can be expressed, whether through bureaus, mosques, schools, meeting houses, sports clubs, or armed militias.

This political pluralism is due to the median position Ain al-Helweh occupies in the constellation of Palestinian camps in Lebanon. Until May 2000, the camp was less than twenty-four miles from the so-called security zone Israel occupied in southern Lebanon. This geographical proximity to Israel's "red lines"—and, consequently, the camp's relative distance from the Syrian army's positions in Lebanon—paradoxically gave all the different groups operating in the camp the possibility of benefiting from a minimal right to free expression in a space of more than three hundred square miles. Israel's withdrawal in May 2000 did not fundamentally change this situation, since the Syrian troops are still situated below the Awali River, which marks the geographical beginning of southern Lebanon.

Finally, in the extreme south of Lebanese territory, the camp of Rashidiyyeh, near Tyre, is entirely controlled by Fatah. Even though all the Palestinian organizations are represented there—including Hamas and Islamic Jihad—Fatah forces are the only ones bearing weapons. This exceptional situation has led to tight control at the checkpoints that command access to Rashidiyyeh. The Lebanese army does not hesitate to stop anyone bringing in building materials, as a way to "punish" the camp for its pro-Fatah and pro-Arafat orientation.

Eliminated from Lebanese politics in 1990, Yasir Arafat's Fatah, which played a key role in constructing the nationalist Palestinian movement in the 1960s, lost control of its last territorial bases in the Middle East when the Lebanese civil war ended and Syrian hegemony was established in the country. After Fatah returned to Palestine in 1993, thanks to a subsequently defunct Palestinian-Israeli peace process, it was unable to effect a massive reentry into the camps, where the movement was historically constituted, because of the veto imposed by Damascus.

By exploiting such political divisions, as well as Syria's passive opposition to the Palestinian-Israeli negotiations, various religious groups took over this space, seeking to capture the allegiance of a population that was struggling to survive economically, had no clear prospects for the future, had been pushed to the margins of society, and was being forced by post-war Lebanon's political elites to bear the guilt for the supposedly exclusive role played by Palestinian leaders in triggering the civil war in 1975.

Islamist Jihadism in Ain al-Helweh

The Ain al-Helweh camp was built in 1949, on the initiative of the International Committee of the Red Cross, before coming under UNRWA administration in 1951. Its "official" size is 290,000 square meters (roughly 181 miles), but demographic pressure has extended the camp's limits to their current size of 500,000 square meters, or more than 300 miles. In 1997, the number of inhabitants was estimated at 32,645, 30,557 of whom lived within the camp's official borders, while the others were spread between the areas of *al-sikka,* so called in reference to the abandoned railway line that runs along the camp's entire western flank, and *baraksat,* at the northernmost tip of Ain al-Helweh. There are eight UNRWA schools in the camp, attended by 6,529 students (more than 50 percent of girls are enrolled in school, and the number continues to increase). More than 95 percent of the camp's inhabitants are originally from the *kaza* of Safad and the surrounding area, in northern Palestine; the others are originally from the *kazas* of Haifa, Ramleh, and Jenin.

Until the Israeli invasion of 1982, Fatah, locally headed by its security officer in the South, Hajj Isma'il, who was later made responsible for Lebanon within the Palestinian Authority, effectively governed the city of Saida. Local relationships with Lebanese allies in Saida were anything but easy, since Fatah forces clashed frequently with Mustafa Saad's Nasserist Lebanese militia. During the 1982 invasion, the camp resisted fiercely, forcing the Israeli armored vehicles to go around Ain al-Helweh on their way to Beirut. The camp had been evacuated earlier by Palestinian factions, which then retreated further north, and Islamists from Ain al-Helweh organized the camp's defense. The Islamists, virtually unknown until that point, thereby provided some of the inhabitants with blood-soaked proof of their resistance.

After it had been evacuated and partially destroyed by the Israeli army's bulldozers, Ain al-Helweh was rebuilt and reoccupied by refugees, who arrived in ever-greater numbers as perceptions of the Palestinian cause changed in Lebanese society. One of the reasons for this change, notably, was the sectarian mobilization of the Shi'ite community in the late 1970s. Outside the camps, in the south, the Amal militia had become the instrument of an internal reconquest benefiting the local Shi'ite population, which was tired of Palestinian exactions and Israeli bombs targeting its villages. Inside the camps, the groups close to Iran under Ayatollah Khomeini sought to exploit the political and military vacuum caused by the 1982 Israeli invasion in order to build support bases in religious circles. This intervention was aimed less at destroying Palestinian identity than at influencing the PLO's policy, by subjecting it to the demands of the new power in Tehran, which at one point wished to use the PLO as its foreign policy arm in the Middle East, before choosing the Lebanese Shi'ite community instead. But such involvement proved decisive nonetheless, since it was taken up inside the camps by religious figures who expended most of their energy dissolving the national political community the PLO had worked to crystallize since its creation.

Today, the camps of Beirut, Tripoli, and Saida are no longer part of Middle Eastern political history. They now belong to Lebanon's urban geography. They have become ungovernable zones of poverty and delinquency that have driven down real estate prices in the surrounding areas. The reconstruction plans of the 1990s have passed them by.

During the 1980s and 1990s, social isolation and the closure of a distinct period of Palestinian history in Lebanon provided the context in which preachers were able to transfer to Ain al-Helweh the ideological universe of Peshawar, Pakistan, which for several years was the gathering place of Arab volunteers fighting the Soviet Union in Afghanistan. This ideological transplant led to a rejection of the PLO and to the de-nationalization of Palestinian history. For some groups, that history ceased to be an experience of national dispossession and became instead one more link in the chain of Muslim peoples victimized by the *kuffar* (unbelievers) since Mustafa Kemal abolished the Muslim caliphate in 1924. Ain al-Helweh thus became a receptacle for every variety of radical Islamism, and the confined space within which the ingredients of a new religious ideology were tried out: salafist jihadism, born in Peshawar among international jihadists and developed autonomously thereafter by groups that saw themselves as the "vanguard" of Islam. The camp was was no longer a player in the area—as soon as the Lebanese war ended, the southern front of its struggle against Israel was locked up by Hezbollah, the Shi'ite militia—but the ideological resonance it lost within Lebanon was compensated by its insertion in the field of global Islamism.

Subsequently, the main challenge was how to sustain mobilization of new recruits, when the Afghan jihad was coming to an end amid internal struggles that were difficult to decipher for those who had enthusiastically supported the *mujahidin*'s heroic fight against "infidel Communism." In order to understand how jihadism, though alien to the Palestinian world and unknown in the occupied territories, was able to maintain itself and expand, it is necessary to consider the role played by places of worship and Islamic educational institutions in transmitting new religious norms, both inside and outside the camp.[10] Religious centers located in the large Sunni cities of the coast—Beirut, Tripoli, and Saida—have attracted Sunni Muslim students of various nationalities, seeking a new and improved self-image (there, one can meet alienated young intellectuals of Lebanese, Palestinian, Syrian, or Kurdish origin). In the camp mosques, young men and their shaykhs, who generally emphasize the importance of jihad as an individual duty, re-create an Islamic sense of belonging in a closed society.

By looking closely at the jihadist networks in the Ain al-Helweh camp, it becomes possible to understand the real-time production of salafist-jihadist ideology, the way preachers played a decisive role in reframing social reality exclusively in religious categories, and the deep changes that those networks effect in perceptions of self and other. References to early Muslim heroes have played an essential role in creating a charismatic community. By emulating the earliest Muslim societies, militant salafists have been able to denounce all the practices that adulterated the original message, from the various brotherhoods of Sufi Islam to "Shi'ite heresy," via the main schools of Sunni jurisprudence. Indeed, there is a close connection between this production of meaning and the different calls to violence it has borne, for one needs to fight innumerable enemies to remain mobilized for the defense of "true Islam." Assassinations—of magistrates in the middle of a hearing, "deviant" preachers, nationalist Palestinian militants, or alcohol vendors on the outskirts of Saida or Tripoli—are part of a religious vision where belief must be validated by a morality of action. In every case, rhetorical violence has paved the way for physical violence, whose legitimacy is trumpeted through the teaching and preaching networks that gradually spread in the camps of Tripoli and Saida during the 1990s.

Fighters without a territory to defend, Palestinian salafist militants have devoted themselves to defending the imaginary borders of identity, declaring themselves the protectors and guardians of the cause of Sunni Islam worldwide. The struggle against the transnational Ahbash sect was a particularly important element in preserving salafist-jihadist mobilization. The assassination of the sect's leader in August 1995 by Palestinian and Lebanese salafists was the equivalent of a symbolic takeover. By eliminating the leader of a sect they judged as heterodox, they were affirming their status as "defenders of the faith" in the Middle East. Their actions won them the support and gratitude of those who, inside and outside Lebanon, saw the Ahbash's existence as a heresy that threatened orthodox Islam and needed to be eliminated by any means possible. The struggle against the Ahbash thus accelerated the process of detachment from the Palestinian national cause, by provoking an exaggeration of Sunni identity and giving birth to global solidarities that transcended national affiliation. It was no accident that a video aired by al-Qa'ida in September 2006 showed a young Saudi—one of the nineteen operatives who died on September 11—dedicating a poem to "Abu Mahjin the Palestinian," the main leader of the Ain al-Helweh jihadist network studied in this book.

*   *   *

Shortly after the terrorist attacks of September 11, 2001, Western audiences were shocked by broadcast images of Arab people rejoicing in the streets. In one such image I recognized the alleyways of Ain al-Helweh refugee camp, which I had walked down so many times. A Palestinian friend of mine, while condemning such demonstrations of joy, sought to explain that this behavior was the irrational expression of revenge: throughout their history, the Palestinian refugees had suffered through many bombardments by the Israeli army, the most recent in 1996, during Israel's "Grapes of Wrath" operation. They now rejoiced in the knowledge that they were no longer the only ones to experience such destruction and grief. The global superpower that was at least partly to blame for their misery could bear similar blows.

My hope is that this book will make it easier to understand the conditions that facilitated the creation of jihadist networks in a Palestinian environment that might have seemed immune to such militant ideologies. Only by examining how individuals gradually moved to new forms of violence in the name of global jihadism can we hope to understand acts of monumental destruction such as those of September 11, 2001. At stake is not only the future of Islam but also that of the West's relations with the Arab world.

PART I

THE SALAFIST DYNAMIC

CHAPTER 1

From Iranian Influence
to Sunni Affirmation

Links between Fatah, the Palestinian organization, and Iranian Shi'ite Islam date back to the mid-1960s, when Ayatollah Ruhollah Khomeini denounced the regime of Muhammad Reza Shah Pahlavi for its close cooperation with Israel. Shortly before Khomeini was expelled from Iran in 1963, the man who was to become the leader of the Islamic Republic blamed the shah's secular reforms on Israeli influence and warned against Israel "seizing" the country's economy, culture, and institutions, as it was already doing in some areas of the military.[1]

By linking the regime in Tehran to Israeli encroachment in the region, and by issuing numerous fatwas, or legal pronouncements, that declared the Palestinian cause to be sacred for Muslims worldwide, the exiled Shi'ite ulema (scholar) fed a revolutionary dynamic that mingled Islam with Iranian national pride. His call for a total liberation of Palestine from "Zionist usurpation" was a means of declaring the Pahlavi monarchy illegitimate, compromised as it was by its privileged relations with the United States and Israel. In 1965, a PLO delegation visiting Najaf in Iraq was welcomed enthusiastically by Arab and Iranian students. One Shi'ite spiritual leader of the time, the Iraqi Grand Ayatollah Muhsin al-Hakim, issued fatwas in support of Fatah so that the funds raised through *khums* might be used to benefit the Palestinian cause.[2] In 1968, Khomeini

27

told Muslims that it was necessary "to help Fatah's men, who are *mujahidin* [warriors] in the path of God, by every possible means, by devoting part of the legal alms [*zakat*] to them, so as to help them fight unbelieving and inhuman Zionism."[3] In his sermons and communiqués, the Iranian imam continually reminded every Muslim that "even if he is at the very end of the Islamic world," he has a duty to devote his energies to liberating Palestine.[4]

Many future leaders of the Iranian Islamic Republic and their close associates—like Ayatollah Ali Janati, the representative in Lebanon of Ayatollah Ruhollah Khomeini; Khomeini's sons, Mustafa and Ahmad; and Muhammad Montazeri, Ayatollah Montazeri's son—received military training in Lebanon's Palestinian camps in the 1970s. According to Waddah Sharara, a Lebanese sociologist, "until 1976, Fatah members trained no fewer than 700 members of the Da'wa Party *(Hizb al-Da'wa)*. As for Yasir Arafat, he visited Khomeini in Najaf at least twice."[5] Fatah's support reached its apogee in Iran at the end of 1978, when Hani al-Hasan, a member of the group's central committee and a political adviser to Yasir Arafat, helped organize the mass demonstrations that brought down the shah's regime. He later became the PLO's first representative in post-revolutionary Iran, where he set up the Palestinian headquarters in the offices of the former Israeli Embassy in Tehran.[6]

Besides its interest in weakening a regime that enjoyed close ties with Israel, and the possibility of political and financial support should the revolution in Iran succeed, Fatah sought to obtain something else from the Shi'ite ulema: the religious legitimation of its military actions in southern Lebanon. It hoped such legitimation would appease the local population, which had grown weary of the massive reprisals of the Israeli air force that followed every Palestinian attack.[7] To ease the growing resentment among Shi'ites at the end of the 1970s, the PLO drew on the authority of Khomeini, and began to cover the walls of West Beirut with his portraits.[8] Very early on, one of the first Lebanese Shi'ite ulema to support the Palestinian cause, Sayyid Muhammad Hasan al-Amin, realized the extent of the "excesses" *(tajawuzat)* committed by the Palestinian factions in the south:

> In 1974, I talked with Yasir Arafat and Abu Jihad about the need to put an end to these excesses. They were aware of the danger. With Abu Jihad, we tried to smooth over the difficulties, but we were unsuccessful. The Lebanese War could have been avoided, on two conditions: it would have been necessary to place the Palestinian Revolution outside the Lebanese political game—many Lebanese political forces have sought to use the Palestinian apparatus to their own benefit—and it would also have been necessary to secure Arab support for a Palestinian presence in Lebanon. This was not the case.[9]

Tension between the Lebanese population in the south and the Palestinian movements gave rise to a specifically Shi'ite organization increasingly hostile to the PLO—Musa Sadr's Amal movement (though Sadr himself, like all the opposition groups in pre-war Lebanon, had benefited from the Palestinian organization's military expertise).

As early as 1973, Imam Musa Sadr was one of the first Muslim religious leaders to criticize the PLO for its military action in southern Lebanon. He displayed his hostility toward Palestinians by publicly proclaiming that he did not consider launching rockets and grenades to be revolutionary fedayin action.[10] As Syrian troops entered Lebanon in June 1976 to oppose the Lebanese Left and the PLO, Musa Sadr precipitously left PLO-controlled Jabal Amel for the Beqaa, along the Syrian border, where he sided with the Syrians against the Lebanese National Movement and its Palestinian allies. In August 1976, when the Palestinian camp of Tal al-Za'tar fell to the Phalangists (the Lebanese Christian party) backed by Syrian artillery forces, he refused to send in his militias to defend the popular Shi'ite quarter of Nab'a, near the camp, although his organization, which ran a hospital in the neighborhood, had established a significant presence there.[11]

This growing distrust of the PLO on the part of a figure who had been emblematic of the Lebanese Shi'ite community's restructuring in the 1970s was echoed within the Iranian leadership. Mustafa Shamran, who helped create the Amal movement before he was appointed minister of defense for the Iranian Republic in August 1979, believed that Iran had to establish ties with the Lebanese Shi'ite community rather than with the PLO. By contrast, under the influence of Muhammad Montazeri, the members of the Revolutionary Council favored the PLO, even as they attempted to Islamicize the significance of the Palestinian struggle: in the earliest days of the new regime, they organized the deployment of Iranian "volunteers" to fight alongside the fedayin in southern Lebanon. In Tehran, the PLO lost an unconditional ally on the Iranian domestic scene in 1980, when the People's Mujahidin organization was eliminated. The PLO's influence on Ayatollah Khomeini was decreasing. When American diplomats were taken hostage at the American Embassy in Tehran, a high-level Palestinian delegation led by Abu Jihad offered to mediate, but Khomeini refused to meet with them.

In 1980, the Iran-Iraq War precipitated a break between the former allies. According to Muhammad Hasan al-Amin, the first Gulf War was responsible for the Iranian-Palestinian crisis:

> This war was a catastrophe. I even went to Iran by car to try and re-establish Iranian-Palestinian relations. The Iranians wanted absolute support for their cause, which the PLO could not give them. Subsequently, I distanced myself from the Iranian regime. They wanted to set up an Iranian party in Lebanon—later the Hezbollah. Such a thing was not acceptable. I disagreed with the idea of creating a partisan structure heavily dependent on Iran.[12]

On July 16, 1980, the leader of the Iranian revolution made a speech in which he stated that the PLO leadership should "stop paying visits and coming and going, but rather mobilize their people on God's path, by turning their weapons toward Israel to fight until the death. With these visits, fighting peoples lose the hope they had in their leaders."

In the wider Muslim world, Iran's leaders tried to affirm their ideological preeminence by adopting the rhetoric of religious mobilization and encouraging believers from all the Muslim countries to rally the Islamic revolution against their fearful, conservative regimes. After the Fahd Plan—proposed by the future king of Saudi Arabia at the Fez Summit in November 1981, and accepted by Yasir Arafat, who was directly involved in drawing it up—implicitly recognized Israel, the Iranian regime accused Saudi Arabia, and all the Gulf regimes with ties to the United States, of treason.[13] Iran's policy goals were, among others, geopolitical (control of the Persian Gulf) and sectarian (support for the Shi'ite minority in Saudi Arabia's Hasa province, and for the Shi'ite majority in Bahrain). The Palestinian leadership refused to place itself under Iranian tutelage. In Iran, this defection led some leaders, including Defense Minister Mustafa Shamran, to argue that the new Islamic Republic should choose a Lebanese constituency deprived of true leadership, such as the Shi'ites, rather than trying to help the unpredictable Palestinians. Hence the empowerment of Lebanese Shi'ites capable of filling the military and political vacuum left by the PLO in southern Lebanon after the Israeli invasion of 1982. This final decision did not, however, preclude the formation of religious networks that remained close to Iran and were inspired by preachers who were determined to destroy PLO influence in the camps.

Islamist Preaching for Iranian Interests

In the region of Saida, Iran's influence among Sunnis was manifest in the early 1980s in the creation of a network of preachers responsible for spreading a revolutionary vision of Islam in line with Khomeini's message. These religious figures of Lebanese and Palestinian origin were co-opted in a pro-Iranian organization known as the Congregation of Muslim Ulema (Tajammu' al-Ulama al-Muslimin). The congregation had been set up in 1982 by the Iranian ambassador to Lebanon, Shaykh Ruhani, and had two objectives: to weaken the role of Lebanon's traditional notables *(zu'ama)* so as to give the religious elites authority over the country's political affairs, and to unify the Muslim religious communities in order to reduce sectarian antagonism between Sunnis and Shi'ites. According to members of the organization, Lebanon's religious institutions had been carefully divided along sectarian lines, in such a way that "citizens always found refuge with their community elites for their minor or major concerns," and thereby "moved away from their religious elites."[14] For the Congregation of Muslim Ulema, this separation between politics and religion led to a split between community and religious elites, with catastrophic results for Lebanon, as demonstrated by the Israeli-Lebanese peace accords of May 17, 1983, signed by Lebanese deputies and violently opposed by members of the Tajammu'. According to the ulema, the failure of the accords gave the clerics an opportunity to restore their supremacy over the politicians, and to take up, within Lebanese Islam, a role similar to that which the "Christian Church" supposedly enjoyed among Christian politicians, "whom [the Church] long ago forced to submit to its authority and respect its opinion."[15] Moreover, the victory of Iran's Islamic revolution, led by Imam Khomeini, had demonstrated that the ulema could successfully lead a political movement.

Shaykh Muharram al-Arifi, an autodidact and a member of the Congregation of Muslim Ulema, was one of the first Lebanese clerics to preach in the southern Palestinian camps in the mid-1980s. The Israeli army arrested him in 1982 for preaching civil disobedience in al-Batah Mosque, in the heart of Saida's old city, and kept him in detention camps at Ansar, then at Atlit, until 1985. According to Shaykh al-Arifi, Muslim solidarity among the prisoners made it possible for them to transcend the sectarian tension encouraged by the Israelis, who broadcast the earliest images of the "war of the camps" in the hope of provoking internal clashes between Sunnis and Shi'ites. Accounts like Muharram al-Arifi's are intended to show that inter-Muslim divisions are a product of Israeli military strategy. Such narratives are fairly common among Sunni shaykhs who were imprisoned in Israeli jails before being integrated into networks close to revolutionary Iran upon their release. Muharram al-Arifi was freed shortly after Israeli troops left Saida on February 16, 1985, and took up the cause of "spreading Islam in the Palestinian camps of the south" so as to combat the influence of the PLO, which he opposed fiercely.[16]

That same year, Muharram al-Arifi became secretary-general of an "Islamic front" *(al-jabha al-islamiyya)* headed by Shaykh Maher Hammud, and was admitted to the Congregation of Muslim Ulema. During the war of the camps, he built up his popularity among Palestinians by embarking on a forty-day hunger strike in the Rashidiyyeh camp, which was then under siege by Shi'ite Amal militias, to denounce the absurd "war of discord" *(harb al-fitna)* that prevented Sunnis and Shi'ites from joining together on the Lebanese scene. Clashes with the Lebanese forces east of Saida in 1985 provided al-Arifi with an opportunity to give religion classes to young fighters, and to preach jihad against the Christian militia acting on Israel's behalf. According to his official biography, al-Arifi donned military garb and went to the front, "Kalashnikov in hand."[17] He did not see the end of the Lebanese war in 1990 as a return to civil peace, because Lebanon, as he saw it, would and should always be at war. In a 1992 sermon, Muhammad al-Arifi denounced American pressure on Lebanon, Syria, and Iran:

As I have already told you in the past weeks, [Americans] fear the Islamic Republic more every day. They fear the geographical base of its influence, which is extended and continues to grow. They know that Iran is the spine *(al-amud al-fiqari)* of the Islamic resistance, embodied in Hezbollah . . . And it is also a message to the slumbering *(mutaqa'isat)* Arab countries: "You must remain timid, and you must slumber on! For we strike all those who awake through jihad, as we struck Galilee, as we struck the south, Saida . . ." As they will eliminate all those who rise up against what they call the new world order.

Until his death in 2000, Shaykh al-Arifi rephrased, in his own terms, the clichés of popular Islamic discourse in the Arab world. According to him, the Arab regimes that "made peace with the Jews" proved their "Qur'anic ignorance":

One cannot make peace with the Jews . . . Until now, the Arabs have made one concession after another. The Palestinian police force was created for the Jews. This force arrests, beats, imprisons, and tortures Palestinian martyrs, and receives nothing in return. Really, the only possible path is the one traced out by Shaykh Yasin and the martyr Yahya Ayyash.

Two themes with devastating implications for the reconstruction of a peaceful political order in post-war Lebanon emerge from Shaykh al-Arifi's preaching. The first touches on the presumed actions of an "internal enemy," identified as such owing to his opposition to the "Islamic Resistance" (by which al-Arifi means Hezbollah's military actions against the Israeli occupation of southern Lebanon). Taken to its logical extreme, this argument likens all those who question the need to maintain a military option after the Israeli retreat, and who demand that the Lebanese army be deployed in the region to guarantee the country's southern borders, to agents of Israeli influence. The shaykh condemns not only the "Christian opposition" of the time but all proponents of peace in the various Lebanese communities. The late Sunni prime minister Rafiq al-Hariri, for one, favored regional stability and saw the end of the state of war that prevailed between Israel and Lebanon as the necessary condition for economic and political development.

Shaykh al-Arifi maintained that those who adopted such a defeatist attitude should be charged with treason—an idea expressed in Arabic by the term *takhwin*. The expression, which promised to gain great currency in the post-war Lebanese political lexicon, was also applied to the Palestinian negotiators who signed the Oslo Accords in 1993. In the most radical circles, Eastern Christians are commonly portrayed as agents of the West who benefit from preferential treatment on the part of the Lebanese state, as illustrated by the relatively lenient sentences that Lebanese courts handed soldiers of the South Lebanon Army (SLA, financed by Israel) after Israel pulled out on May 22, 2000.

The accusation is reminiscent of the ideological climate that prevailed in the earliest days of the Lebanese civil war, when Palestinian resistance fighters were pitted against "isolationists," a term that at the time referred to the conservative Christian camp. According to the Lebanese analyst Joseph Maila, an isolationist is "someone from the interior who stands out and is set apart by behavior or ideas that cause some of his fellow citizens to consider him a foreigner to his environment."[18] A decade later the regime adopted the reasoning of a religious figure with no official responsibilities. At the time al-Arifi was speaking, in the early 1990s, Hezbollah's role in Lebanon and the weight of Iranian influence at the regional level had not been clearly defined, and were still being evaluated by the Syrian leaders engaged in the Madrid talks. Hezbollah had initially opposed the Taif Accords, signed in November 1989, because their implementation threatened both to dissolve all the militias and to end armed action in southern Lebanon. The shaykh, then, was speaking at a time when the new rules of the regional game had not yet been set by international and regional powers (the United States, Israel, Syria, and Iran) nor internalized by the various actors in Lebanese society. His talk of "Islamic resistance" anticipated new power relations in the offing, but did not reflect the status quo. Denunciations of the "Israeli border guards," which were very popular in Islamist pamphlets at the time, were taken up verbatim by Syrian-Lebanese policymakers to justify their refusal to deploy the Lebanese army in southern Lebanon after Israel pulled out in May 2000.

Shaykh al-Arifi did not simply defend Iran and Syria's interests in the region against the "American-Zionist" conspiracy and its domestic supporters; he also insisted that it was necessary to defend Islamic morality in Saida against hedonistic temptations. According to the shaykh, fighting Zionist enemies and defending an Islamic order in the city of Saida were two facets of a single struggle:

> We do not live in a time of pleasure and love. It is unacceptable, utterly unacceptable, that the owners of recreational facilities, cinemas, video stores, or any other such business spread corruption *(fasad)* in the city of Saida through dancing and songs! To all of these I say: "You live in Saida; you don't live in Paris or London! . . . Saida belongs to Islam, and to the Resistance!"

These last words go beyond moral sermonizing to incite action: in this case, a series of attacks on alcohol vendors and owners of gaming rooms and cinemas in the region of Saida and Tripoli in the 1990s. By linking the legitimacy of resistance in the south to the defense of religious values in "Muslim Saida," the shaykh was demonstrating that it is difficult—if not impossible—to maintain a religious understanding of the Israeli-Arab conflict without applying it to other issues at stake in collective life. While Hezbollah later made successful efforts to convert images of "Islamic resistance" into "national resistance"—the price of its integration within the Lebanese political system—by keeping most of its religious demands hidden, the Sunni shaykhs, who played no role in the armed struggle, were all the more vigilant about social behavior. Today, they continue to pressure Dar al-Fatwa, the highest Sunni religious authority, to censor certain forms of entertainment. When the public authorities fail to respond to their grievances, they incite believers to take independent action when they deem it necessary.

Another Sunni religious leader with close ties to Iran gave the Palestinian camps a special place in his organizational and religious activities. Shaykh Ahmad al-Zayn is the religious judge *(qadi)* of Saida and the administrative region of southern Lebanon. Just before Syria intervened militarily on October 13, 1990, the event that marked the official end of the war, Shaykh Ahmad al-Zayn was interviewed for a publication run by young Islamist Palestinians from Ain al-Helweh. In that interview he openly challenged the political identity of the Lebanese state as it was formulated in the Taif Accords. The publication's op-ed piece condemned the accords for confirming sectarianism by merely renewing the "political privileges" of the Maronites. Here Shaykh Ahmad al-Zayn brought his religious authority to bear:

It is necessary to clarify an essential point immediately: Lebanon's Muslims were unable to obtain their rights in the Taif Accord for two reasons. First, Taif guarantees that Maronite Christians will continue to hold the presidency, although Islam forbids Muslims to be ruled by or subjected to the authority of a non-Muslim; second, by reserving the presidency of the republic for the Maronite community, the presidency of the council for the Sunni community, and the leadership of Parliament for the Shi'ite community, the accord contravenes an elementary principle of democracy (or what they call democracy), in that this form of power-sharing deprives the majority of the population of its right to popular expression in the matter of electing its leaders . . . The Maronites are the main winners. The Muslims are outside the political game, as long as the conflict is just about knowing that this Maronite rather than that one will become president. If the Muslims want to stop being nothing more than an auxiliary force in the conflicts of others, if they want to play a real part in the political and military game, as active protagonists, above all they will have to adhere to a complete Islamic project, whereby the government will be run by Muslims and by no one else. This will bring about an obvious and natural thing, which only a Muslim leader can accomplish: the establishment of Islamic law. Only in this case will they have the power to decide freely, without having to follow others. But that is not what emerges from the Taif Accord and the constitutional arrangements it contains.[19]

In his first, strictly sectarian argument, Shaykh Ahmad al-Zayn disregards the content of the reforms and limits his analysis to the formal reality of the Lebanese political system: if the presidency is reserved for a Maronite, then Muslims have no power. This position is particularly dogmatic because the Taif Accord in fact transferred to a council of ministers, headed by a Sunni prime minister, most of the prerogatives formerly held by the president of the republic. Furthermore, Shaykh al-Zayn's comment, made in 1990, cannot have been based on an empirical analysis of the Accord's implementation: by definition, it could not take into account the way in which two successive presidents sought Syrian support to improve the presidency's status vis-à-vis other institutions. The majority argument is both more subtle and more dangerous to the long-term viability of the Lebanese political pact, which, by distributing political offices on a sectarian basis, violates the rights of the popular majority and thus conflicts with democratic majoritarian principles. Shaykh Zayn offers a reductive, populist definition of democracy, which he likens to the reckless exercise of majority rule. Demography is thus called upon, not to buttress the "desectarianization" of the state, but rather to defend the idea of an Islamic state, "led by Muslims and governed according to Shari'a." During the Gulf War, Shaykh Ahmad al-Zayn strongly criticized "shaykhists"—that is, those religious clerics who choose to worship the Saud family instead of worshiping God.[20] He continued:

> The raid on the land of the Hijaz by American and European forces perpetuates the pillage of the Islamic nation's resources, this time manifestly and insolently, while before this pillage was carried out indirectly, through the intermediary of these kings, princes, and

shaykhs, to end up in the banks of America and Europe. Over there, the enemies of Islam, and Israel in particular, can use it as they wish, while in Asia and Africa, the peoples of the Muslim nation are dying of hunger, and the crusading Vatican *(al-fatikan al-salibi)* takes advantage of the situation to convert them . . . The only clear position that results from the Book and the *Sunna* is to support the Islamic policy that uses Muslims' money and jihad expenses against those who covet Muslim land and wealth. We cannot accept the presence of an American and European army on the land of Mecca and Madina. Muslims must unify their ranks and their economic, political, and military energy to confront this new raid, which follows that on Palestine. He who reads the book of God must know that it is not permitted to submit to unbelievers and to make them the protectors of Muslims.[21]

Though Iranian propaganda as transmitted by Shaykh al-Zayn found support for its favorite themes in the 1991 Gulf War, the conflict failed to strengthen the clerics' allegiance to Iran and its policies. Rather, Sunni preachers of Lebanese or Palestinian origin recycled anti-Saudi rhetoric to reaffirm their Sunni identity through increased hostility toward Shi'ite Islam. This situation confirmed the limits of a strategy for Islamic unity among Sunnis in Lebanon.

In Shaykh Ahmad al-Zayn's worldview, Palestinian refugees are part of the "Muslim people" persecuted because of their religion. It is no coincidence that many of Ain al-Helweh's inhabitants leave the camp on Friday to pray in the mosque of Shaykh al-Zayn or that of Shaykh Maher Hammud in Saida, which conveys a similar philosophy. Certainly they could hear the same message in the camp of Ain al-Helweh, but by going to Saida they are making the statement that their religious identity supersedes their national identity. Imperceptibly, a change is occurring in the way camp residents identify themselves. Some of them are increasingly adopting a religious classification scheme that rejects the categories of the Lebanese state and, more generally, the values of the world order. Lebanon's preachers, who owe their authority in part to their position in the Sunni religious establishment of Dar al-Fatwa, contribute significantly to this change, since many of those who choose to pray outside the camp are seeking a qualified religious authority.[22]

To the Lebanese preachers, the camp is a kind of "social vacuum" that escapes the authority of the Lebanese state and its representatives.[23] By addressing a Palestinian audience that lives in isolation from the outside world, the Lebanese preachers can freely criticize the region's governments and their efforts to bring about regional peace. Moreover, the camps' extraterritorial status allows these preachers to express themselves outside the constraints of the national political game and some of its taboos, especially with regard to relations between religious communities and the rules of coexistence *(al-aysh al-mushtarak)* between Christians and Muslims.

Shaykh Abdallah Hallaq

Integrated into this environment and known to have links with Hezbollah, the Palestinian shaykh Abdallah Hallaq has been one of the PLO's main enemies in the Palestinian camps since the beginning of the 1980s. The son of a construction worker, Abdallah Hallaq followed the religious lectures given by Shaykh Ghunaym (see below) in the al-Nur Mosque in Ain al-Helweh. After receiving his baccalaureate (the equivalent of a high school diploma) in the late 1970s, he began attending classes at Beirut Arab University's Arabic literature department, in the heart of the Fakahani neighborhood where the PLO had most of its offices and committee rooms. In class, he found his professors' enthusiasm for erotic poetry *(ghazal)* and odes to wine *(khamriyyat)* intolerable, so he left to devote himself exclusively to the more austere study of "religious sciences." When former professors from the Arab University set up Imam al-Awza'i's religious institute in 1979 (see Chapter 6), he decided to join the movement, registered at the institute, and was in the first graduating class. In 1983, he received his master's degree and started his career as a preacher by joining the Congregation of Muslim Ulema. Along with other members of the congregation like Mahir Hammud, Ahmad al-Zayn, and Muharram al-Arifi, he was one of the main proponents of Iranian interests in the Palestinian refugee camps. During the war of the camps, he called for the creation of an "Islamic operations room in Lebanon and in the camps" in which all the "Islamic fighting forces" would be united in a common jihad against Israel, the enemy, and coordinated with "the Islamic resistance in Palestine."[24]

In a 1985 pamphlet titled *Jihad and Change,* Abdallah Hallaq attributed responsibility for the civil war to Lebanon's Christians, "who have always oscillated between the creation of a little separate Lebanon and the preservation of a greater Lebanon under Maronite domination," and who seek Israeli support to that end. He wholeheartedly supported the Islamic resistance in the form of Hezbollah, because he saw the Shi'ite organization as "a model that Muslims will imitate on a wider scale to eliminate the Israeli presence."[25] According to the shaykh, Hezbollah successfully substituted itself for the Palestinian resistance, "constituting the most convincing example in current times of popular resistance against the Zionist enemy," because it was able to bring to light "the existential nature of the conflict between Muslims and Jews, revealed by Qur'an verses and the Prophet's *hadiths* on this topic."[26] During battles that broke out between Palestinian Fatah fighters and Hezbollah forces in Iqlim al-Tuffah, in southern Lebanon, in July 1990, Abdallah Hallaq and other Palestinian shaykhs of the Ain al-Helweh camp declared their support for the "Islamic resistance"— in other words, for Hezbollah—and their refusal to tolerate any "Palestinian involvement" in the region:

> The first thing that we need to understand is that the conflict is a religious one. The unbelievers have allied against Islam: from Algeria, where they are trying to strike a blow against Islam through a bloody coup d'état, to the occupied territories, where they are trying

to repress the Islamic Intifada, to Lebanon, where they are trying to surround Islam and God's fighters. The second thing that must be understood is that since 1948 the Palestinian people have never stopped suffering, from Dayr Yassin to the massacres in Amman, Tal al-Za'tar, then Sabra and Shatila, and then the war of the camps . . . By involving themselves in Iqlim al-Tuffah, do they want to expose our people, yet again, to renewed suffering and renewed pain? They [Fatah's leaders] pretended to be a buffer force [between Amal and Hezbollah], and now, in fact, they are taking sides . . . The third thing you have to understand is that there is a global plot to divide Lebanon into a multitude of security zones, to the benefit of Israel (Shi'ite, Sunni, Druze, and Maronite zones). It seems that this plan requires the Palestinians to establish themselves in Iqlim al-Tuffah. We must fight against the establishment plot and cooperate with the forces of jihad to keep the southern door open, in order to liberate Palestine and link up with the holy Islamic Intifada. For this reason, we advise the Palestinian leadership to abandon such a policy.[27]

This declaration underscores the impact of defeat on the rhetoric and behavior of many Islamist militants of Palestinian origin. Although it evokes tragic trials undergone in the past, it does not thereby seek to rally the group around a common memory, as is usually the case in national commemorations. The function of this recollection, rather, is to remind listeners that every time the Palestinians have affirmed their national existence as a collective body—which they have been able to do only by linking their fate to a unified political leadership—they have exposed themselves to massacres and repression, as if defeat were inevitably associated with the existence of a Palestinian national structure in the region. Shaykh Hallaq's funereal litany ("Tal al-Za'tar, Sabra and Shatila, the war of the camps") recapitulates, in chronological order, the three defeats the Palestinians suffered in Lebanon: at the hands first of the Christian Lebanese forces, then of the Israelis and their auxiliaries in Beirut in 1982, and finally of the Amal movement's Shi'ite combatants. Even though Shaykh Hallaq does not explicitly say so, the examples he cites all refer to Syria, which played a considerable military role during the fall of Tal al-Za'tar in August 1976, just as it offered logistical support to Amal militias in their struggle against the Palestinians during the war of the camps.

Paradoxically, a habitus of defeat can coexist with the preaching of violence, for in this case, violence is inscribed within the "political-ideological system Syria set up in Lebanon," as Samir Kassir wrote, and is directed against the Palestinian leadership.[28] Though refugees who deliberately place themselves under Hezbollah's protection by paying the group allegiance do not forego their national identity, they refuse to link that identity with any obligation of political loyalty. In other words, their identity is not negated, as is the case with the salafists, who take their "de-Palestinianization" to extremes by refusing any kind of nationalism; but it is neutralized, as if Palestine were a *watan* only in the sentimental sense of the word, a homeland that has powerful religious and symbolic value but has been stripped of territorial and national relevance.

Furthermore, Shaykh Hallaq denounces Palestinian nationalism, the symbol of the Arabs' rediscovered dignity after the 1967 defeat, as a form of weakness, the equivalent of a divisive force at the level of the Muslim *umma*:

> After this cause was the primary cause of Muslims worldwide, it became, first, the Arabs' cause, and then it shrank to become the Palestinians' cause, since the decision became even smaller, a strictly Palestinian decision! This choice led to the division of the Muslim *umma* [Islamic nation] in general, and then of the Arabs in particular, and finally of the Palestinians even more specifically. On the political level, this division . . . led to capitulation before the Jews and submission to their conditions.[29]

Today, Shaykh Abdallah Hallaq, whose wife is Lebanese, lives in the Abra neighborhood on the outskirts of Saida. While performing his duties as the *khatib* (preacher) of the Batah Mosque in the old city, for which he receives a salary from Dar al-Fatwa, he continues to carry out the *da'wa* (spreading of the word of Islam) in the Palestinian camps, because, according to him, a propitious religious climate reigns there that "does not exist in the rest of Lebanese society."[30] Shaykh Hallaq also works at the Hezbollah center Dar al-Wihda in southern Beirut. In the camps, he has specialized in denouncing the Palestinian Authority, which he describes as an entity hostile to Islam, entirely subject to Israel, and essentially concerned with arresting religious figures and closing down mosques in the territories it controls.[31]

The Birth of Palestinian Islamism in Ain al-Helweh

The Israeli invasion of Lebanon in June 1982 revealed the existence of Islamist networks inside the Ain al-Helweh camp. Absent the PLO factions, which had retreated north to defend Beirut, Ain al-Helweh's resistance against the Israeli army—the "Palestinian Masada," according to Israeli observers—lasted for about twenty days.[32] It is said to have given rise to the invasion's most ferocious fighting.[33] The Islamist militants who provided the camp's principal defense were almost all students of the Palestinian shaykh Ibrahim Ghunaym, who was visiting Iran during the clashes but lost a son in the siege of the camp.

Some people consider Shaykh Ghunaym to be the "spiritual father of all Palestinian men of religion." His biography sheds light on the various metamorphoses that Islamism has undergone in Ain al-Helweh over the past fifteen years or so. Ibrahim Ghunaym was born into a peasant family in 1924 in the village of Safuriyya, in the *kaza* of Nazareth. Forced to flee Palestine in 1948 with his young, illiterate wife, he settled in a shantytown east of Beirut known as the "Abattoirs" *(Masalikh)*, where he worked as a manual laborer in a cement factory. In the early 1950s he joined the Naqshabandiyya, a Sufi brotherhood, through a student of Muhammad Ahmad Junayd, the brotherhood's guide, a Syrian shaykh of Kurdish origin who had set up a lodge *(zawiya)* in the neighborhood. Ibrahim Ghunaym met the guide in Aleppo in 1953 and was later responsible for teaching religion in a small village of Akkar, in northern Lebanon. In 1963, Shaykh Ghunaym set up house in the Palestinian camp of Ain al-Helweh, which became one of the focal points of the Sufi brotherhood in Saida. He started teaching at al-Nur Mosque, and his students from that time—originally Palestinians like Jamal Khattab and Abdallah Hallaq, or Lebanese like Shaykh Muharram al-Arifi—subsequently became the main figures of radical Islamism in the camp and in Saida.

During the 1982 Israeli invasion, Shaykh Ghunaym was in Tehran attending an "international conference of the dispossessed" organized by the Iranian government, and he later returned to the Nahr al-Barid camp, near Tripoli. That same year, he was jailed in Damascus's Mazzeh Prison for two months for his alleged links to the Syrian Muslim Brotherhood, which was locked in a confrontation with the regime. After he was freed, he asked the Iranian government for protection. In 1984, he helped create a small clandestine group, the "Combatant Islamic Movement" (al-Haraka al-Islamiyya al-Mujahida), led by Shaykhs Jamal Khattab and Abdallah Hallaq. Shaykh Ghunaym arranged for the al-Quds (Jerusalem) Mosque to be built in the camp of Nahr al-Barid with funding from the Iranian Embassy. In the 1990s, he made sure to participate in all the Hezbollah-organized events on Palestine's political future.[34] In 1992, he helped set up a military training center for the IJMP (Islamic Jihad Movement in Palestine) at Khan al-Abdeh, on the road leading to Halba in the Akkar. He was close to Shaykh Sa'id Sha'ban, the head of Tripoli's main Islamist militia—the Tawhid, or "Islamic Unification Movement"—and served as a faithful link to the Khomeini regime among Lebanese Sunnis. Since Sha'ban's death, he has also maintained regular contact with his son, Bilal Sa'id Sha'ban, who has taken over the Tawhid leadership.

Shaykh Ghunaym's political involvement attests to the fact that there is no radical opposition between popular Islam, incarnated in Sufism, and radical Islamism. In the Sufi tradition, it is possible to carry out divine acts *(karamat)* in this world, as long as one respects the injunctions of the Shari'a—"otherwise, *karamat* become satanic."[35] The shaykh also insists on the importance of armed struggle, in which he makes "jihad against the Jews" a priority. It is important to note that the shaykh belongs to the Naqshabandiyya-Khalidiyya order—in other words, to a brotherhood that distinguishes itself from the other mystical orders by emphasizing a strict respect for Islamic law, by refusing to accept legal innovations, and by advocating a return to the model of perfection represented by the Prophet and his Companions. The shaykh's students have insisted on this last aspect and abandoned any reference to Sufi Islam.

In the mid-1980s, one of Shaykh Ghunaym's students in Ain al-Helweh, Hisham Abdallah Sharaydi, set up an Islamist militia called the Partisans' League (Usbat al-Ansar). In the early 1990s, the league became Ain al-Helweh's main salafist-jihadist militia.

Hisham Abdallah Sharaydi's family hails from Safsaf in Galilee; Sharaydi was born in 1957 in the Ain al-Helweh camp. Even as a teenager, he followed Shaykh Ibrahim Ghunaym's lessons at the al-Nur Mosque. After the camp fell to the Israelis, he was taken prisoner and placed in the al-Ansar jail for a year and a half.

When he was freed in a prisoner exchange, he returned to the camp and was appointed preacher at the "Martyrs' Mosque" (Masjid al-Shuhada), built on Ain al-Helweh's upper road, just past the camp's northern entrance. The resistance that Shaykh Ghunaym's students originally put up provided a durable foundation for the legitimacy of Islamism at Ain al-Helweh. Owing to exceptional circumstances, military feats on the battlefield, and time spent in an Israeli jail, a neighborhood *abaday* (strong man) like Hisham Sharaydi, who worked odd jobs such as butcher and petty tradesman until 1982, was able to acquire the charismatic qualities necessary to establish himself as one of Ain al-Helweh's foremost shaykhs. He compensated for the paucity of his religious education by advocating a cult of armed jihad, drawn from his own combat experience against the Israeli army.

Today, the members of Usbat al-Ansar trace the founding of their group to 1985, and Shaykh Sharaydi's initiative. At that time the militia did not yet bear its current name, and in fact was called "God's Partisans" (Ansar Allah). The difference was not only one of semantics: originally the group belonged to an Iranian network and carried out its military operations in cooperation with the Lebanese Shi'ite groups that went on to form the nucleus of Hezbollah. The battles waged in 1985 against the "crusader agents" to the east of Saida (the "Lebanese Forces," the main Christian militia), in which Sharaydi sustained wounds to the leg, were an opportunity for the camps' Palestinians to assert their shared Islamic identity against "the Maronite-Zionist plot."

At the end of the 1980s, hostility between Sharaydi's group and the local Fatah commander in Ain al-Helweh, Amin Kayyed, reached a point of no return. Besides the political antagonism that raged between them, the quarrel revolved around the struggle each side was waging to mobilize the allegiance of camp residents from the Palestinian village of Safsaf, the birthplace of both men. To strengthen his position, Sharaydi allied with a former PLO official, Jamal Sulayman, who had been excluded from Fatah after initiating closer ties with the organization of a pro-Syrian dissident, Ahmad Jibril, the leader of the Popular Front–General Command. In 1990, "God's Partisans" coordinated their military activities with the "Ain al-Helweh Phalange"—as Jamal Sulayman's local militia was called. A training camp was improvised in the region of Jabal Halib, to the east of Saida. The wording of the communiqués the two sides issued together after each military operation against the SLA in the "security zone" occupied by the Israeli army in southern Lebanon emphasized the group's dual nationalist and religious orientation; it was careful to inscribe its acts in the framework of "armed jihad against the despicable Zionist enemy." An attack on SLA positions in the area of Kafr Falus on June 18, 1990, was thus presented as a "natural response to the massacres carried out by the Zionist enemy on our families and our people in occupied Palestine."

During battles that started in January 1990 and pitted Palestinian Fatah against Lebanese Hezbollah in the Iqlim al-Tuffah region of south Lebanon, both Hisham Sharaydi and Jamal Sulayman sided with Hezbollah. Consequently, the conflict moved to the heart of Ain al-Helweh. In August 1990, after battles that left twenty dead and more than a hundred wounded, Jamal Sulayman was forced to leave the camp. Sharaydi did the same, only to return to Ain al-Helweh three months later, "acclaimed by thousands who were proclaiming God's glory." During a sermon he gave at the al-Nur Mosque on the occasion of the Prophet's birthday celebrations *(mulid)*, on September 19, 1991, Hisham Sharaydi radically questioned the legitimacy of "those who represent us or who speak in Palestine's name, when it is they who have betrayed religion and Palestine." The accusation was intended to discredit the PLO's diplomatic efforts on the eve of the Madrid Conference (October 1991), and was part of an Iranian strategy aimed at conflating Islam and Palestine in order to equate any PLO political initiative with a form of treason committed against religious faith. The Tehran Conference on Palestine, held in December 1990, had challenged the legitimacy of the Palestinian command, particularly Fatah's traditional "Palestine-centrism." This it did through the use of sensationalist rhetoric and the manipulation of suprapolitical categories.

As with the Islamic Jihad organization in Palestine, the ideology of Sharaydi's group must be analyzed as an exaggerated form of nationalism expressed in religious terms. It is as Palestinians that the group's members led military operations and claimed responsibility for their accomplishments on the battlefield. This orientation found confirmation in the target chosen for such operations: God's Partisans struck at the Israeli enemy (through its auxiliary militia, the SLA) on the ground, in the occupied zone, which was considered a passage to Palestine.

On December 15, 1991, Shaykh Sharaydi was assassinated. The hit was probably ordered by Amin Kayyed, and was carried out in front of the Martyrs' Mosque, which was later renamed Shaykh Hisham's Mosque. His body was taken to the burial site amid a large crowd that was shouting: "Abu Ammar [Yasir Arafat's nom de guerre] is God's enemy!"[36] During the funeral, the presence of shaykhs Mahir Hammud, Abdallah Hallaq, and Sa'id Barakat (the leader-in-exile of Islamic Jihad) provided a further indication that Iranian networks were responsible for the birth of Islamism in Ain al-Helweh: the funeral oration (ritha') was pronounced by the Lebanese shaykh Muharram al-Arifi, secretary-general of the "Islamic Front" led by Maher Hammud. Shaykh Sharaydi's sycophants may have wanted to remain faithful to the memory of the deceased by carrying on his work, but the new leaders changed the network's initial line by stamping it with a salafist character it did not originally have. They put an end to Iranian tutelage for reasons of sectarian incompatibility, and reoriented the group's operations far from the Lebanese-Israeli border.

Usbat al-Ansar and the End of Iranian Tutelage

Usbat al-Ansar was the first armed militia to claim a salafist-jihadist orientation in the camp at Ain al-Helweh. The salafist line was imposed by Shaykh Sharaydi's successor, Abd al-Karim Sa'di, otherwise known by his laqab (nickname), Abu Mahjin. When power passed to Abu Mahjin, a former student of Shaykh Sharaydi's, the group took a new name, the "Partisans' League" (Usbat al-Ansar). In all likelihood, a council (majlis) made up of Ghunaym's former students decided by consensus to give Abu Mahjin this responsibility, though he was only twenty-eight years old. Abu Mahjin's family, like that of his predecessor, was from the village of Safsaf, near Safad, and experienced a series of displacements and expulsions, almost all of which were provoked by the violence of war: in 1948, when the state of Israel was created, his parents were forced to leave Galilee and seek refuge in the West Bank (Abd al-Karim was born there in 1963); then, during the Six-Day War, in June 1967, the family was forced to flee again, this time to Jordan, before leaving for Lebanon in 1971 to escape Jordanian repression after the events of Black September. After a brief stay in the Nahr al-Barid camp, near Tripoli, the family settled permanently in Ain al-Helweh, where most of Safsaf's inhabitants have sought refuge in Lebanon (one of the camp's quarters is even named after their home village).

As a teenager, young Abd al-Karim attended Shaykh Ghunaym's religious lessons and was publicly involved in the shaykh's Naqshabandiyya order, although the members of Usbat al-Ansar, concerned with projecting an image of uncompromising salafism to their external supporters, later downplayed these activities. Abd al-Karim, like the great majority of the camp's young people, left school in ninth grade and survived by working odd jobs (he sold *shawarma* on the Saida Corniche), as his predecessor, Hisham Sharaydi, had done before him. Perhaps because he was from the same village as Shaykh Hisham—each village was dominated by one or two families tied together by marriage alliances—and because a struggle for supremacy over the Safsaf *asabiyya* (solidarity group) was being played out between the Fatah officer responsible for Sharaydi's murder (Amin Kayyed, also from Safsaf) and the Islamist movement, Abu Mahjin was elected head of the "League" just after Sharaydi was assassinated in November 1991. The promotion of one of Safsaf's "sons" also dovetailed with an upheaval in the balance of power between clans, to the detriment of Safuriyya, the village that had formerly ruled Ain al-Helweh. Many of Safuriyya's inhabitants, who were scattered among Ain al-Helweh, Nahr al-Barid, and the Yarmuk camp in Syria, emigrated to Europe (especially Denmark) or the Gulf after the Israeli invasion of 1982. Safsaf's inhabitants thus gained the upper hand; for example, they arranged for the food distributed by UNRWA to be given to them first, a benefit the people from Safuriyya had enjoyed until then. Designating Abu Mahjin the new leader, at that point, made it possible to limit Fatah's ability to recruit members from within Safsaf's family networks, which seemed especially urgent given that Amin Kayyed was the only Fatah representative with real tribal roots in Ain al-Helweh.

Abu Mahjin's appointment also indicated the rise of salafism-jihadism and the concomitant loss of influence suffered by Khomeini's brand of Islamism. Though Abu Mahjin's rise to power coincided with the fading of Iranian influence, it is nevertheless inaccurate to describe this change as a sudden break in the group's ideological make-up, since the seeds of jihadist salafism had already been sown when the camp became part of the Peshawar network.[37] Of course, it is impossible to know whether Shaykh Hisham's "Islamo-Palestinianism" corresponded to a deep-seated conviction, or whether he was projecting this image for tactical reasons (that is, to benefit from continued Iranian protection), since he knew he was under physical threat from the PLO within the camp. In this last hypothesis, the emphasis placed on Palestine would mainly have been the result of pressure from Iran. In fact, after Sharaydi's death, there would be no more military operations directed at Palestine from Ain al-Helweh. But the partisans of the salafist trend were probably a majority from the first, which would account for the ease with which they imposed themselves thereafter.

Hezbollah Outbids on Palestine

Hezbollah, the Lebanese Islamist militia, considered the defense of the Palestinian cause a key element of its regional strategy. Every year "World Jerusalem Day" gives rise to mass meetings organized by the Shi'ite militia in the outer boroughs south of Beirut.[38] The invention of this occasion allowed Ayatollah Khomeini to place the Palestinian question permanently on the agenda of Iran's foreign policy. Hezbollah has used this opportunity to make its presence known in Lebanon's Palestinian camps, and particularly in the region of Tyre. At each of these ritualistic demonstrations, participants focus their attacks on the threats posed by the peace process and the dangers of the "Arafatist-Zionist" plot for the region. Such verbal excesses were not exceptional in Syrian-controlled post-war Lebanon; on the contrary, they resonated with all those who saw the Palestinian Authority as an enemy on a par with Israel.

After the Wye Accords—which the Israeli government never implemented—were signed in September 1998, Hasan Nasrallah, Hezbollah's secretary-general, went so far as to call for the assassination of Yasir Arafat, wondering aloud: "Is there no other Khalid Islambulli among the Palestinian people?"[39]

According to Hezbollah's adjunct secretary, Shaykh Na'im Qasim, the president of the Palestinian Authority committed "further treason" by signing a text that "demolishes the rights of the Palestinian people":

> We know that the final solution that has been put forth will include only 40 percent of the surface of the West Bank and Gaza. This means that Arafat's Palestine will amount to no more than 12 percent of all occupied Palestine, with a security role for Arafat, [who will have become] the head of the Zionist police, an agent for the repression of the Palestinian people, and a tool for the realization of Zionist projects. This new phase will have negative effects on the region in the future, since henceforth Tel Aviv and Washington will be free to put pressure on Syria and Lebanon to exact concessions.[40]

According to Hezbollah's newspaper, the peace negotiations had one aim: to "guarantee the enemy's security, first and foremost," for the presence of the Palestinian police would be tolerated only to the extent that it fulfilled the condition of "collaborating with Israel."[41] The assassinations of two Lebanese police officers in Saida and of an Islamic Jihad leader were immediately seen as consequences of the cooperation accord between the "Zionist intelligence services, those of America, and those of the Palestinian Authority" in Lebanon.[42]

Those who sought to defend the Palestinian Authority's policies were placed on the defensive. They immediately denounced the "hate campaign against the PLO and Fatah in Lebanon" from the platform of *al-Quds,* the only newspaper to which they had access. According to *al-Quds,* which was published clandestinely from the Rashidiyyeh camp, "The accord has become a stake in a game of outbidding among all those who nurse a stubborn hatred in their hearts, who are thereby able to release their poison and who have found an opportunity to express their complacency and sycophancy toward certain regional parties, with which they move in tandem."[43] Many Fatah leaders denounced the permanent outbidding *(muzayadat)* engaged in by Hezbollah and Iran with regard to the policy the Palestinian leadership had adopted. In a message directed personally at Hasan Nasrallah, they evoked the precedence of the Palestinian struggle in south Lebanon and the former existence of ties with Lebanon's Shi'ites:

> You are the first to know the value of this resistance in the south, which is bending beneath the claws of the occupation, and you know how much of our martyrs' blood this dear south has seen spilled. You know that you are a student of this revolution, against which you now aim the arrows of your hatred; you sprang from its belly, even though it is true that the children who emerge from their mother's womb are not all good.[44]

Against this smear campaign, negotiations were presented as the only means by which the Palestinians could retrieve a territorial base and establish political independence before exercising state sovereignty. After the Wye Accords were signed, *al-Quds* set out a code of good conduct aimed at the Palestinian Islamists. The paper asked them to "move away from regional influences" and think of "the higher Palestinian interest" by refraining from any military action launched from within the zones controlled by the Palestinian Authority: "In the past, there have been Hamas operations outside the liberated territories, but the Authority made no arrests, since these operations were not launched from within its territory. When operations take place outside the liberated territories, and responsibility is claimed by external parties, the results are favorable to the Palestinians, because this challenges the occupation."[45]

After south Lebanon was "liberated" on May 24, 2000, a debate immediately began around the relevance of a "Hezbollah model" of armed struggle as the only means of ending the Israeli military occupation of the Palestinian territories. In the euphoria of "victory," the message conveyed by Hezbollah and its supporters in the state apparatus (including President Lahoud) was that armed struggle was the only means of obtaining results against the Israeli enemy. The evacuation of Israeli troops from occupied south Lebanon was soon exploited in Ain al-Helweh as an additional argument against a negotiated solution; in the camp's two main streets banners were hung with the message "Zionism in Palestine is null and void *(batil)*, signing and negotiating with it is null and void."

The debate over the consequences of May 24, 2000, not only pitted the opponents of the peace process against the Palestinian Authority but also cut through the ranks of the various Palestinian organizations. Militants gathered in one of the offices of the DFLP in Ain al-Helweh observed that this victory should serve as a model for Palestinians in the West Bank and Gaza, who needed to overcome the enemy by means of a new popular Intifada.[46] The refugees were far from united on the best course of action, however. Other analyses circulated among civilian members of Fatah who rejected any comparison between south Lebanon and the West Bank, arguing that what had taken place was not so much a victory for Hezbollah as it was a retreat on the part of Israel from a zone without the same strategic value as the West Bank. Moreover, they argued that Hezbollah's victory was less military than political, to the extent that Ehud Barak had mainly responded to pressure from Israeli society in ending an occupation that was no longer justified in security terms, and which was costly in terms of human lives. According to these observers, following the imprecations of Hezbollah's leaders and launching an armed Intifada in the territories would pose a mortal threat to the Palestinian cause.

Strategic Conflict and Sectarian War

Hezbollah's political exploitation of the Palestinian cause had ambiguous consequences within the camps. In nationalist circles Hezbollah's influence was contained by a support base that remained loyal to Yasir Arafat; in religious circles whose members shared Hezbollah's opposition, on principle, to the peace process, such exploitation was diffracted by the magnitude of the breach between Sunnis and Shi'ites, which had been provoked, in turn, by the exacerbation of Sunni identity.

For the Islamists, the goal, then, was to separate strategy from religion: they sought to associate themselves with Hezbollah's campaign against regional peace, while further developing a sectarian orientation that testified to their powerful distrust of Shi'ite Islam and their constant vigilance against its presumed proselytizing.

The militant Islamist Palestinians accused Lebanon's Shi'ites of planning to encircle the coastal Sunni cities one by one: "The city of Tyre used to be Sunni, and now it's been colonized. The same risk exists for Saida."[47] For them, Hezbollah's interest in the Palestinian camps since the war of the camps in the late 1980s could be attributed to its desire to use the camps as strategic bases from which to control the southern regions, to the detriment of Amal, the rival

Shi'ite organization. To resist this trend, they are campaigning to denounce all the Palestinian shayks who were on "Iran's payroll." According to a former Palestinian leader of the Jama'a Islamiyya, Hezbollah wanted to take advantage of Palestinian weakness in Lebanon to implement a three-part sectarian and political project:

> First of all, Palestine has a symbolic value that no religious movement can disregard; next, the point for them is to use the camps as strategic bases in their struggle against Amal for control of the southern regions; in the longer term, there is a purely religious objective, which aims to convert Sunni Palestinians progressively to Ja'fari [Shi'ite] Islam. A few years ago, they tried unsuccessfully to build a mosque in Ain al-Helweh camp. In the south, they are moving forward more easily. We are very worried about the future. We don't have the means to fight against this project. One of the greatest difficulties we face is related to the absence of an identifiable interlocutor with whom we could negotiate. There are many actors who are linked to Iran: the "Guardians of the Revolution," the Iranian Embassy, the Iranian cultural center *(mustashariyya)*, Hezbollah, Islamic Jihad, the Congregation of Muslim Ulema, some individuals . . .[48]

In 1994, Hamas sympathizers created an association called Sanabil, with the unstated aim of competing with Hezbollah in the area of humanitarian work. Immediately after Israel's "Grapes of Wrath" operation in 1996, Sanabil spent more than $100,000 on the inhabitants of the southern regions who had taken refuge in Saida, in a bid to avoid abandoning the monopoly on social work to Hezbollah as a Shi'ite organization.[49]

Obviously, Hezbollah does exert a some influence through its efforts to mobilize the Palestinian constituency against any move that could terminate the state of war with Israel. The party's direct involvement, however, has remained marginal in the largest Palestinian camps on the coast, from Tripoli to Saida. In Nahr al-Barid and

Ain al-Helweh alike, "God's Party" has been unable to open offices. It is significant that Hezbollah's closest Palestinian supporters—the members of Islamic Jihad—put up their posters at night, and that the posters, inscribed with quotes by Ayatollah Khomeini, are invariably in tatters by the next morning. Shaykh Ghunaym, who is known to have ties with the Iranian Embassy, found himself isolated in Nahr al-Barid after having allowed a Shi'ite preacher to evoke the death of al-Husayn, grandson of the Prophet Muhammad, during a Friday sermon early in 2002, at al-Quds Mosque, where he is the imam. According to the refugees, barely twenty individuals are on the Hezbollah payroll in Nahr al-Barid, and they are "hardly religious at all; they do it for the money."

Israel's withdrawal from southern Lebanon on May 24, 2000, and Hezbollah's subsequent victory, aroused mixed feelings of jealousy and admiration in salafist circles. The Shi'ite organization's success offered proof that religious faith guarantees victory; but victory was experienced painfully as that of Shi'ite Islam, in other words, of an Islamic form of unbelief. Sunni Muslims, while considering themselves "superior" in religious terms, were thus humiliated once again by better-organized and truly motivated adversaries: "Despite our religious disagreement, which is absolute, despite the fact that we hold opposite opinions on every point, despite their non-belief *(kufr)*, we have to admit that they won, because they fought for their faith. Here, a Palestinian would sell his mother for $20."[50]

This sectarian *(madhhabiyya)* tension translates into the Sunnis' violent rejection of Shi'ism and its exuberant religiosity. During the ceremony of Ashura, the faithful flagellate themselves until they bleed to commemorate the martyrdom of Imam al-Husayn in a passionate ritual reminiscent of Good Friday services held in certain Catholic countries. This ritual provides a pretext for the expression of confessional differences between Sunnis and Shi'ites. Shaykh Yusif, one of the preachers of Usbat al-Ansar, the salafist militia, denounced all those who "pretend to weep over him [al-Husayn] to-day, and who weep not because they are sad, but because they want to preserve confessional resentment and division *(na'arat)* and act as if they are persecuted and have nothing. How are we responsible for what happened? Why do these masses seethe so, when there were neither Sunnis nor Shi'ites at the time? The truth is that those who curse the Companions *(Sahaba)* are accursed themselves."[51]

The war in Afghanistan provided an additional motive for hatred of Iran, which Sunnis judged guilty of "involving itself in the country's domestic affairs" and accused of "continuously supporting Shi'ite Afghans and opposing the Taliban movement."[52] In such conditions, those who draw salaries from the Iranian Embassy or Hezbollah, in proportions that vary according to the means available at a given moment, must excel in the art of *taqiyya*—dissimulation—generally ascribed to Shi'ite Muslims.

Murshid and the Socialization of Young Palestinians

The Combatant Islamic Movement has a display case in a religious institute called Murshid—the Arabic acronym for the "Supervisory Council on Religious Affairs" (Majlis Ra'ayat al-Shu'un al-Diniyya). Under the honorary presidency of Shaykh Ibrahim Ghunaym and the educational guidance of his former student Shaykh Abdallah Hallaq, the institute was created in the mid-1980s as an instrument of socialization responsible for turning Palestinian refugees against their political leadership. (In the words of one of its directors, its role is to develop "a religious, intellectual, and political awareness" that will allow the refugees to "reject the peace formulas that concern the Palestinian cause.")[53]

The association is registered with Saida's Sunni religious court— "affiliated with the presidency of the Lebanese Republic's Council of Ministers," as the foreword to the introductory pamphlet specifies with an eye to legal conformity. It views its role as that of a ministry of *waqf*s (pious foundations) within the camps, supervising the management of mosques, the ulema's training, and the education of students.

The "department of instruction and education" *(da'irat al-tarbiyya wal-ta'lim)* plays a leading role in the "religious orientation of young generations, from primary school to additional and secondary education, up to university level."[54] Religious studies— Qur'an and *hadith* sciences, Islamic jurisprudence and history— make up the essential part of the three-year training program, while lay topics are restricted to languages (Arabic and English) and geography. Since 1986, Murshid has also offered scholarships to those who want to pursue religious studies at an Islamic university, where their expenses are covered from the first year until they receive their degree.[55] By supporting religious education, the network's organizers hope to achieve their goal of defending religion, which they believe is under threat within Lebanese society.

The institute's directors have built several Qur'anic schools, which students attend free of charge, in the camps and the popular quarters that surround them. The association has also set up a secondary school, inaugurated in 1986 under the aegis of Hasan Khalid, the mufti of the republic, in the Ain al-Helweh camp.

One would expect these efforts in the field of education to result in more efficient mobilization in the service of Islam. Weekly conferences are thus held in the Ain al-Helweh camp, "constituting a religious, cultural, and social sanctuary for young men and girls in our society, which has been tainted by corrupt cultural trends and moral deregulation." The conferences take place every Sunday (for men) and every Thursday (for women), immediately following the afternoon prayers. The brochure does not specify which themes will be addressed, but the booklet indicates, on the page devoted to religious celebrations, that "Murshid supports the cause of Muslims in the world," and this affirmation is backed up by a photograph of a solidarity gathering for Bosnian Muslims. One of the conferences held in September 1998 was on "the causes of the Islamic awakening *(sahwa)* in Algeria." The speakers are Palestinians or, just as often, Lebanese: the inauguration of a Qur'an school in the Rashidiyyeh camp provided Shaykh Ahmad al-Zayn with the opportunity to declare that "the only path back to Palestine and to holy Jerusalem *(al-Quds al-sharif)* is Islam; only Islam can mobilize the Islamic nation on purely religious bases." As the *qadi* of Saida, he welcomed the efforts made by Murshid, "which strives to protect Muslims in the camps in order to edify a new generation—the pious generation of liberation."[56]

In the framework provided by Murshid, too, Shaykh Hallaq intervened to condemn the Palestinian Authority's diplomatic activities. When the second Intifada broke out in September 2000, there was not the slightest hint of solidarity with the Palestinian leadership, for Shaykh Hallaq had found the Palestinian delegation guilty of having given way on every point raised in the Camp David and Taba negotiations (January 2001). To his students in Ain al-Helweh, he accused the Palestinian leadership of having accepted the humanitarian reunification program suggested by the Israeli negotiators and of having asked for the right of return for only 100,000 refugees:

> This means that the impact of Resolution 194 has been erased, and, as a result, that four and a half million Palestinians have been deprived of the right to return to their homes and their land. Such a surrender led to the problem of settlement *(tawtin),* which the Palestinians reject in any form . . . In the bitter heritage of peace with the Jews, we must also state the fact that Israel's sovereignty over West Jerusalem has been recognized, and that the Palestinian Authority has negotiated over East Jerusalem.[57]

Earlier in the same speech, Shaykh Hallaq had rejected the principle of land for peace on the grounds that "the recognition, by the Arabs and a few Palestinians, of international resolutions 242 and

338" meant the recognition of Israel and its supremacy over 80 percent of Palestine.

The "department for mosques" within Murshid contributes to the construction, renovation, and expansion of mosques in the camps of the north, the Beqaa, Beirut, Saida, and Tyre. It also pays a monthly salary "to all the imams, preachers, teachers, muezzins, and employees, which comes to over a hundred people employed by the department." In all, 27 teachers work in Murshid's three schools (located in the camps at Ain al-Helweh, Rashidiyyeh, and Nahr al-Barid). The Ain al-Helweh center organizes sessions for women every six months. It is noteworthy that Murshid places great importance on training women preachers *(da'iyyat)* and young people as part of its socialization work. According to the academic director, summer sessions bring in between 175 and 225 women students for two months a year. The classes, held twice a week, are divided into four ascending levels, each of which lasts for six months of the year: when they reach the highest level, women obtain the title of "preacher." Such activity is aimed especially at "private homes" *(buyut khassa),* in other words, mainly at the camps' residents. Abdallah Hallaq believes that the best way to reach society is through women, since a woman is always "surrounded by four men: the husband, the son, the father, and the brother," according to a *hadith* which states that a virtuous woman takes four men to paradise, while a loose one takes all four to hell.[58] More prosaically, by focusing part of their educational efforts on women, Murshid's organizers acknowledge the fact that men must first find a job to provide for their families. Social and economic constraints were probably at the root of the outreach to women, even if that approach was later justified in religious terms.[59]

In the religious schools, a young person is taught not "to see himself as one among many," but rather to see himself as *better than the others*—the others, in this case, being the rest of Lebanese and Palestinian society.[60]

Evidence suggests that some powerful figures in Iran have not given up the policy of influencing Palestinians in Lebanon, not exclusively via a partisan structure like Hezbollah, but by encouraging the emergence of a new religious elite from within camp society that would speak in that society's name. Within this framework, Murshid could appear as the main instrument of an Iranian strategy emphasizing covert, informal action on the part of local operatives integrated in a network covering all the Palestinian camps in Lebanon, from Rashidiyyeh in the south to Nahr al-Barid in the north. The need for discretion can be attributed to the magnitude of the confessional gap between Shi'ites and Sunnis, and the persistence, among Palestinians in the camps, of nationalist sensitivities that make any kind of foreign involvement suspect. A close examination of this network reveals the way some power centers in Tehran, in seeking to "edify the pious generation of liberation," have attempted to modify the way the Palestinians in the camps see the Arab-Israeli conflict. This was done by insisting on the conflict's religious dimension in order to mobilize the population against the peace process and the policies of the Palestinian Authority.

Many factors make Murshid a likely vehicle for the "re-Islamicization" of the Palestinian community in Lebanon, including the size of its networks extending through Lebanon's camps, the many circles in which those networks find a place, the vast wealth the association controls through its *waqf* assets, and the strong ties Murshid enjoys with representatives of Lebanese Islam. Moreover, it is clear that financing for Murshid's many social and educational projects, as indicated above, does not always come exclusively from private donors.[61]

Despite evidence of Iranian influence, Murshid's organizers have not lost all power to take the initiative; nor have they become a transmission belt for Iranian policies in the dispossessed environment of the Palestinian camps. On the contrary: Murshid officials do not hesitate to call upon other patrons, if they can benefit from such intervention, and they know how to move easily within the world of Islamist humanitarian assistance.

Religious Networks and Financial Pragmatism

The way religiosity and humanitarian action are articulated in Ain al-Helweh makes it possible to understand the role of external aid in the expression of identity and political positions, as well as the strategies that religious figures have invented to fulfill the donors' conditions.

Because several religious sensibilities coexist within the association's leadership, the Murshid network has the capacity to mobilize support in extremely diverse, not to mention rival, political and religious circles. Ibrahim Ghunaym and Abdallah Hallaq, Murshid's academic director, have close relations with Iran and Hezbollah, while other leaders, like Shaykh Jamal Khattab and Abu Dia', a young shaykh, are very close to the salafist group Usbat al-Ansar, the most zealous members of which detest Shi'ite Islam and its Iranian political incarnation. The elderly Shaykh Nawal Ahmad Abu As'ad, also known as Shaykh al-Ablini after his village in Palestine, still has ties to the PLO that date back to the time when Fatah funded small Islamist groups. Whereas the older generation—Shaykh Ghunaym and Shaykh Abu As'ad—belongs to the Naqshabandiyya brotherhood, the younger leaders, who are in their forties, consider Sufism to be a deviation from the pure faith.

This diversity serves a purpose, for it enables the association to gather funds from donors of very different backgrounds. An anecdote told by Shaykh Ghunaym sheds light on the way Murshid organizers circumvent constraints imposed by international Islamic assistance:

> There were funds that came from Kuwait. Salafist funds . . . When they found out I was a Sufi, they stopped the funding. So we set up a

committee, managed by Shaykh Jamal, separate from Murshid. And the money came back . . . We did this for the orphans' best interest, mind! . . . For the orphans' best interest . . .[62]

In Nahr al-Barid, on the walls of Murshid's primary school, which is adjacent to the mosque, a painting of Ashura (the martyrdom of Imam al-Husayn) can be seen. Ahmad Ghunaym admits that the Iranian Embassy partially finances Murshid, but he specifies that the association has other funding sources as well: "I was asked to fly a Hezbollah flag from the school that's next to the al-Quds Mosque; but if I do that, I lose the other subsidies!"

Murshid also receives money from an important pro-Wahhabi Islamist nongovernmental organization known as the "Good Works Organization" (Hay'at al-A'mal al-Khayriyya), which has its headquarters in Ajman, the most conservative of the United Arab Emirates. This link was established thanks to ties among "the Islamic forces of Ain al-Helweh"; the organization's representative in Lebanon, Ali Abbas, is the shaykh of the Khalid Ibn al-Walid Mosque, a short distance from the al-Nur Mosque, and he has close connections to the Lebanese Muslim Brothers.

By expanding networks that often bring together a limited number of individuals, and by giving them specific designations, religious leaders put up a protective screen between social work and militant activism, while channeling funds from one circle to the next. This practice increases opportunities for capturing the interest of external donors concerned about the religious orientation of aid recipients. A pragmatic way to broaden the scope of aid is thus to present each donor with the desired profile, "in the orphans' best interest." A network can benefit from a state-based source of funding, as with Murshid and Iran or Sanabil and Saudi Arabia, but state sponsorship is rarely avowed by local leaders, even if they avoid speaking out publicly against these states. In any case, state sponsorship does not preclude fund-raising activities that seek out additional donors.

Financial montages of this sort allow a veritable "Islamic economy" to function in the Palestinian camps. Religious figures are financially autonomous, since they have put together—and diversified—their own support systems. They no longer have any practical reason to identify with the discriminatory, depressing status of Palestinian refugees to gain access to public or private international aid.

This system works in a decentralized manner, not according to an authoritarian hierarchy; the people who make it work have privileged relationships with different funding sources. For example, despite his privileged connections with the Iranian Embassy, Shaykh Ghunaym has always made it a point to diversify his external contacts as much as possible, to avoid being identified definitively with any given group or alienating any party on the local religious scene. In this way he has been able to preserve his own space to maneuver. All the network's members are linked by a shared opposition to the peace process, and they publicly denounce its Arab and Palestinian supporters. Thus, they fulfill the role Iran wishes to see them play among the other refugees, but their attitude does not make them mere mouthpieces of Iranian policy, since, underground, many of Murshid's members are strongly influenced by salafist-jihadist themes.

A Jihadist Core

The network may be decentralized, but it is not fragmented: despite the nuances that distinguish them, members share an ideological core, a militant, jihadist conception of Islam that encompasses all Lebanese society. Those whose work is clandestine—like the Usbat al-Ansar militia in Ain al-Helweh—are thus able to receive some of the funds that are distributed, without the initial donor's necessarily realizing where the money has ended up. Once we move past the border that divides public activities from more discreet or even clandestine ones, jihad takes on a more subversive dimension. In relation to the outside world, jihad as the association's leaders preach it is essentially directed against Israel and corresponds to Hezbollah's discourse of mobilization.

In the publications and tracts that circulate among Murshid's young members, however, the authors emphasize the internal dimension of jihad, which applies primarily to Arab political systems and societies, starting with Lebanese society itself. Murshid's organizers, who are undertaking a veritable lesson in Islamist epistemology, see all modern humanist thought as a war machine turned against Islam.[63] Such knowledge is cast as "the natural heir to the Christian missionaries sent by the crusading states to our Islamic world." Clad in the garb of humanitarian intervention, Christian missionaries, in turn, are described as the continuation, on cultural terrain, of crusades led by an "aggressive West against the Islamic influence that had turned the Mediterranean into a crystal clear Islamic lake." As for "men of religion," they "must drive back this aggression, free Islam of laicism, which brought us tyranny and oppression, and return to teaching the Shari'a in all fields: political, economic, and social." In order to meet this objective, they must publicly denounce Lebanese school curricula, since they are "filled with calumny and encourage doubt in the service of Western thought," which is designed to "wash the minds of young Muslims of their Islamic beliefs," the better to strip them of their Muslim identity. Schoolbooks dealing with topics as diverse as "literature, history, philosophy, and science" are subject to "the influence of foreign cultures in considerable proportions"; as such, they are "filled with poison (mali'a bil-sumum) and specious arguments (shubuhat) that slander Islam and Muslims." For instance, Darwin's theory of evolution, "which claims that men are descended from monkeys, is still taught to our young people in most schools, although many scientists have refuted it and it is forbidden in certain countries."

Lebanese history as taught in textbooks is also subjected to a critical reexamination in the name of defending Islamic traditions, which have been distorted by the Lebanese school version of national historiography. According to an article in *al-Hidaya:*

> In most [Lebanese] history textbooks, the Islamic period is the victim of systematic distortion *(tashwih):* it is always a time of exploitation *(istighlal),* feudalism *(iqta'),* and oppression *(zulm).* Books that deal with Lebanese history, for example, describe France as a tender mother-figure and accuse the Islamic Ottoman Empire of despotism *(tughyan);* they misrepresent Sultan Abdul-Hamid II and describe the Muslim leader Jamal Pasha as a butcher *(jazzar),* and so on.[64] All of this is mendacious insinuation and baseless slander. Everything is designed to arouse doubt among young Muslims with regard to their beliefs, their history, and their glorious past.[65]

By showing the unequal treatment in Lebanese textbooks of two political entities—one (the Ottoman Empire) was founded on Islam, whereas the other is a collection of negative traits (foreign, Christian, secular, and imperialist) that have continued to undermine "Muslim personality"—the author of the article implicitly sought to illustrate the original illegitimacy of the Lebanese state (the traits of which are celebrated in school textbooks), which owes its existence to France's role in the region after the collapse of the Ottoman Empire.

The positive reference to Jamal Pasha is a good indication of how intensely the jihadist militants who wrote that text despise the Lebanese state: this Turkish general, who served as commander of the Ottoman army's fourth division in Syria-Palestine starting in 1915, is portrayed in particularly negative terms in local political culture and provides Lebanese and Arab historiography with a common target of abhorrence.[66] His name is associated pell-mell with the suppression of the autonomous status Mount Lebanon had enjoyed since 1861; the establishment of a food blockade, with murderous effects on the mountain's population, in 1914; and, most important, starting in 1916, with a series of executions by public hanging in Beirut and Damascus, of several dozen members of Arab secret societies who were accused of colluding with the enemy. The sacrifice made by the "first martyrs of independence" is celebrated with a national holiday, and, before the 1975 war, "Martyrs' Square," in the heart of Beirut's old city, was a rare site of collective memory with which Lebanese citizens, whatever their orientation—"Arabist" or "Lebanist"—could identify.

Defending the memory of the Ottoman Empire, with an emphasis on the reign of Sultan Abdul-Hamid II, who attempted to launch pan-Islamism anew against the European powers, is at odds with nationalist versions of the region's Arab past. The latter versions generally reject the Ottoman heritage, which is perceived as a Turkish occupation or, in religious terms, as the misappropriation of a legitimate religious attribute, since only an Arab could claim the office of the caliphate, as the reformer Rashid Rida believed, for example. The Ottoman Empire as the camp's Islamists see it never existed as a historical phenomenon—ironically, the real Lebanon is the Arab country that is no doubt closest to Ottoman political culture. The empire is, rather, the emblematic figure of a myth: that of a "pan-Islamic empire" stirred up by Sultan Abdul-Hamid's propaganda after 1876 and taken up unchanged by Ain al-Helweh's ideologues a century and a half later.

Today, the shaykhs who teach at UNRWA's schools warn their students about the contents of Lebanese history textbooks, which, they believe, present a narrow, sectarian vision of regional history. This new interpretation of Middle Eastern history is in close accord with the affirmation of a new Sunni identity within a Palestinian environment. In the past, the history curriculum as taught did not spark controversy.[67]

Ain al-Helweh may have been a favorite spot for intervention on the part of Yasir Arafat's Middle Eastern opponents, but the policy of taking over Palestinian camps had consequences that probably never entered the initial calculations of Syria's or Iran's leaders. The Iranian-Syrian axis, as it crystallized in Lebanon through constant condemnations of the Palestinian Authority and the systematic undermining of its representatives in the camps, opened up a space for autonomous religious figures who followed their own objectives in matters of policy and identity politics. These leaders expended most of their energy on dissolving the very idea of a Palestinian national community, which the PLO had managed to create and maintain over several decades of political and military struggle. These religious networks thus developed an identity-based dynamic that defines itself through exaggerated confessional affirmation; the rejection—at least in the most extreme forms this dynamic can take within certain groups—of any territorial affiliation; and the negation of Palestinian national history. These individuals and groups, which are more responsive to Islamism's evolution in the Indian subcontinent than to the routinization of the Iranian revolution, have transcended the opposition between political Shi'ism and Wahhabi religious conservatism by declaring themselves to be the vanguard of the "Sunni cause" in its most sectarian (and therefore anti-Shi'ite) dimension, while recycling some of the anti-Saudi propaganda that Khomeini deployed in the 1980s.

CHAPTER 2

Islamism from Peshawar
to Ain al-Helweh

In October 1991, a video of the life of the Palestinian "martyr" Abdallah Azzam was shown in Ain al-Helweh's main mosques. There the faithful saw a tribute to the leading proponent of jihad against the Soviet Union in Afghanistan, who was killed, along with two of his sons, in a car bomb in Peshawar, Pakistan, on November 24, 1989. The film was also shown to the younger students in the "Qur'an schools" run by Murshid. The screening was arranged by the Muslim Student Union (Ittihad al-Talaba al-Muslimin) led by young Islamists in the camp. *Al-Hidaya*, the group's newsletter, devoted several articles to the Palestinian shaykh's career, thereby offering the camp's young people a new hero.[1] The articles often reveal more about their authors than about the biography of Abdallah Azzam. For this reason we will follow the militant shaykh's life through his admirers' gaze, while offering critical additions to complete the silences and omissions that characterize all hagiographies.

Abdallah Azzam was born in 1941 in the village of Silat al-Harthiyyeh, Jenin province, in the northern West Bank. He came from a conservative rural background and attended high school in Tulkarm, then went on to agricultural college, where he specialized in agronomy. According to *al-Hidaya*, as a teenager he spent his time "praying or immersed in studying the Qur'an." His piety opened the door to academic excellence: he easily earned his high school diploma at the village school and, despite his youth, graduated "with merit" from the agricultural college. After Jordan annexed the West Bank in 1951, he was hired as a teacher in southern Jordan, in the Bedouin region of Karak, where he stood out among colleagues who "drank tea and ate sandwiches during their free time, while he sat alone to read the Qur'an, for he did not let a moment pass without using it to the full." He decided to pursue religious studies at Damascus University's department of Shari'a, where in 1966, at the age of twenty-five, he graduated with distinction.

After the 1967 War, Abdallah Azzam could not tolerate life under "Jewish occupation" and decided to move to the Jordan River's East Bank (today Jordan), so as to "undertake a period of preparation and training for the military profession." In late 1969, he joined the movements supporting the Palestinian cause and participated in guerrilla operations the fedayin were carrying out across the Jordanian border. His conversion took place at night, "when he heard the first fedayin leaving for Palestine." He then decided to quit his job as a teacher at a girls' school in Amman and leave his apartment in the middle-class neighborhood of Jabal Amman, in the western (and Westernized) part of the capital, to live in "one room" built of mud in a refugee camp in Amman. *Al-Hidaya*'s account goes on to present Azzam as a demiurge capable of single handedly changing the course of history: he mobilized "young Muslims," secured assistance from the "Islamic movement in Jordan," and formed a group of fighters in the Jordan Valley. Despite its members' "heroic actions against the Jews," this movement was eliminated by the Jordanian regime during the events of Black September in 1970.

In fact, Azzam received his military training in a camp set up by Fatah and the Muslim Brotherhood in northern Jordan, dubbed the "shaykhs' camp" because the Islamists from different Arab countries who joined it did not want to mix with, or be corrupted by, secularist PLO factions. By evoking military actions against Israel after the 1967 war, *al-Hidaya* was fulfilling two functions: first, it was showing that the "secularists" who took over the PLO two years later were not the only ones on the ground, as Islamist fedayin were also in the Jordan Valley; second, it was establishing continuity between jihad's two front lines, and responding indirectly to those who objected that Palestinians fighting in Afghanistan or elsewhere, far from Palestine, were at war with the wrong adversaries and were spreading themselves too thin, to the benefit of the Israeli enemy. Significantly, the *al-Hidaya* author is silent on an important point: the fact that Abdallah Azzam maintained a neutral attitude during Black September. His prudence allowed him to be appointed as a lecturer at Jordan University's Shari'a department, and thereby to slip past a possible veto by the Jordanian security services, which even today must approve the appointment of all new faculty. He was subsequently sent on a fellowship to al-Azhar University in Cairo, where he received his doctoral degree in Islamic jurisprudence *(usul al-fiqh)* in 1973.

On his return to the Jordanian capital, Azzam taught at Jordan University's Shari'a faculty. Although his salary had doubled and he was living in enviable material comfort, *al-Hidaya* tells us, his social success left him profoundly dissatisfied, for "his family had lost the blessing it had received when they lived in a single mud room and fought for Islam. For Abdallah Azzam, the metamorphosis into a university professor was not natural, for he had tasted the sweetness of jihad . . . And, just as a fish cannot live out of water, Islam's fighters *(mujahid)* cannot live without jihad." This marked a second break in the martyr's life: he decided to abandon his middle-class (as the author insists) but unfulfilling existence and return to the meaning of "true life." At Jordan University, where he occasionally lectured in combat fatigues, his enthusiasm for the ideas of Sayyid Qutb, combined with his influence on students who came from all the campus's faculties to hear him, were behind the decision of Amman's military governor to fire him from his job in 1980.[2] "He trained hundreds of young Muslims to bring them back to their Lord," *al-Hidaya* maintained, and "he prepared them to meet the enemy so as to free Palestine from the yoke of occupation, and together establish the state of the Qur'an." Since "the gates of jihad were closed on the land of Palestine" (the author conveniently forgets the Palestinian resistance that formed in southern Lebanon in the late 1960s, with which the Jordanian Muslim Brothers decided not to associate in order to preserve their special relationship with the Palace), Abdallah Azzam began to seek a place where he could devote himself to "the religious practice of warfare" *(ibadat al-qital)*.

In 1981, Azzam went to Saudi Arabia to teach at King Abd al-Aziz University, in Jeddah, where one of his students was a young civil engineering major named Osama bin Laden. In Saudi Arabia, he met a member of the Egyptian Muslim Brotherhood, Shaykh Kamal al-Sananiri, who explained the benefits of organizing a "jihad" in Afghanistan. Sananiri had been there just after the Soviet invasion of 1979, and had attempted to mediate among the different leaders of the Afghan opposition. Azzam, convinced by Sananiri's arguments, obtained a teaching position at Islamabad Islamic University, in Pakistan, through his international connections in the Muslim Brotherhood network. This position allowed him to establish contacts with Afghan combatants, before creating the Service Bureau for Arab Combatants (Maktab al-Khadamat) in the Peshawar Valley. On November 24, 1989, Azzam was killed, along with two of his sons, in a car bombing on Peshawar's main street.

This hagiographic account was intended for a readership with a low overall level of education, and it insists repeatedly on the link between religious studies and militant jihadist action. Young people seeking a concrete path toward political engagement in the service of Islam are thus encouraged to pursue a religious program of study. But religious education is not presented as an end in itself; it is not designed to produce university professors, despite all the material advantages that are associated with that position. Details regarding the spacious apartment Dr. Azzam occupied in Amman, seen in contrast with the single room built of mud, have great meaning for young people whose everyday lives are hampered by the camp's crowded conditions.[3] Those who have made a profession of their religious knowledge have frozen that knowledge (so the authors of Azzam's biography imply); they are condemned to suffer the monotony of teaching without ever knowing the joy of jihad. During his lifetime, Abdallah Azzam underwent three trials in which he had to choose between the "temptations of the profane world *(dunya)*" and those of jihad, interpreted as an "armed struggle in God's path"; each time, he unhesitatingly chose the path of jihad, indicating an order of priorities that corresponds to the definition of a "true Muslim." The moral of the story told by Ain al-Helweh's Islamists is crystal clear: religious studies are meaningful only if they lead to military and political struggle.

Al-Hidaya emphasizes not only the quality of Abdallah Azzam's academic career, but also his Syrian teachers at Damascus University's department of Islamic law: Sa'id Hawwa, Muhammad Sa'id Ramadan al-Buti, and Muhammad Adib Salih. The author also writes that, in the Syrian capital, Abdallah Azzam met "the warrior shaykh" *(al-shaykh al-mujahid)* Marwan Hadid. It is important to point out that this information, which is not at all central to Azzam's biography, conveys subversive coded messages to readers familiar with the experiences of the individuals cited: Sa'id Hawwa spent five years (1973–1978) in Damascus's Mazzeh Prison for having opposed the draft constitution proposed by Hafiz al-Asad in 1973, which failed to mention the state's Islamic character. Marwan Hadid, who introduced Sayyid Qutb's works in Syria, played an important role in the first insurrection against the Ba'th regime in Hama in 1964. On the eve of the second insurrection, in 1976, the

Syrian security services tortured him to death. Both these men were Syrian Muslim Brothers. References to these "martyrs" show that the memory of conflict with the Syrian regime is still vivid, that its content can be transmitted to other generations, and that the accounts of the past are far from being settled, at least as far as certain militants are concerned.

It was no coincidence that this panegyric to a martyr who did not die for Palestine was made in the heart of Lebanon's largest Palestinian refugee camp. Since the late 1980s, the Muslim Student Union had served as a communications network between Peshawar and Ain al-Helweh. The union had a center in Peshawar to welcome volunteers who had decided to join Shaykh Abdallah Azzam in Pakistan.[4] Azzam's goal was to cast his net in the pool of thousands of Arab students in Pakistani universities in order to create a support base for the Afghan *mujahidin*. With the help of Pakistani Islamist organizations, the Muslim Student Union managed to redirect Arab students from the PLO's student branch, the Palestinian Student Union, to a transnational structure that had a religious goal stripped of any national reference.

Thus by the late 1980s, some of Ain al-Helweh's refugees had already appropriated an imagined version of Peshawar, the Pakistani city that served as a point of reference for Arab volunteers on their way to wage jihad in Afghanistan. Myths forged thousands of miles away penetrated Ain al-Helweh, to the extent that several socialization networks—Murshid among them—adapted jihadist salafism to the camp's daily life. In the Palestinian environment, this religious ideology was able to achieve something that neither the Israeli government nor the Arab regimes had managed to accomplish: to introduce a division so deep into families and clans that at any moment it could trigger a civil war among the camp's "sons." Ain al-Helweh, once part of a revolutionary Palestinian ideology epitomized by the PLO, which had made the refugee camps the vanguard of its nationalist struggle, has been restored to an urban shantytown home to the Muslim world's most vivid expressions and contradictions. By exploring Peshawar, we can understand the conditions of this transformation, and the genesis of an ideology—salafism-jihadism—that appeared at an exceptional moment but was nonetheless able to take on meaning in the most diverse social contexts.

Peshawar and the Birth of Salafism-Jihadism

For dissatisfied Islamists who saw no way to take power in their countries of origin, or who objected to strategies of cooperation with the existing regimes, Peshawar in the 1980s was a site of radical Islamism. The Pakistani city was partially disconnected from the weight of national politics and the prudence that Islamist leaders had to demonstrate in managing their relations with authoritarian and unpredictable governments. Peshawar was run by religious figures who established Islamic centers, welcome centers, mosques, schools, and jihadist publications that brought together in one place all the different types of radical Islamism at work in the Muslim world.

This exceptional situation thus provided a pretext for summoning an imaginary landscape of jihad that had originated in the twelfth century in militant Sunni literature, but was now being reactivated, more than eight centuries later, to narrate a modern war that Ibn Taymiyya and his disciples could never have imagined. The theology of jihad, which until then had referred to medieval representations, thus found a new meaning in the Islamists' struggle against a Soviet army fighting to maintain Afghanistan's secular regime. To see Peshawar as a *ribat*—the term, which has several meanings, evokes a military fortress for fighters in the way of the faith—was to use language as a means of transforming young Arab volunteers into austere soldiers responsible for defending the *umma* against the enemies of Islam.[5]

The Service Bureau, founded in 1984 by Abdallah Azzam, was the first structure where these Arab volunteers, mobilized worldwide for the cause of jihad in Afghanistan, were greeted, lodged, and trained. At the time, Azzam received multifarious Saudi support; at his request, the kingdom's great ulema—Ibn Baz, Ibn Uthayimin—backed a struggle characterized as "jihad in God's path" *(al-jihad fi sabil Allah)*, while U.S. weapons, paid for by the Saudis, were distributed by the Pakistani Directorate of Inter-Services Intelligence (ISI). Public and private Saudi funds were invested in an international jihad that was closely monitored by the Saudi state: thus the Service Bureau received money from the emir Salman Ibn Abd al-Aziz, the governor of Riyadh. Osama bin Laden, who had taken Abdallah Azzam's classes in 1981 at King Abd al-Aziz University in Jeddah, had helped create the bureau and was among its most generous donors.

Besides logistical support and military training—the Service Bureau had two training sites: a camp at Sada and another at Khaldun, each of which prepared about 400 combatants—Azzam's work also entailed ensuring that this environment did not become the base for a jihad turned against the Saud family. A short time before, in 1979, the Sauds had faced an attack on the Great Mosque at Mecca. This religious uprising claimed to represent the "true" values of Wahhabism and denounced the royal family for its corruption and its alignment with U.S. policy. Despite a bond forged around common interests, relations between Abdallah Azzam and the Saudi regime soon deteriorated. At the end of 1986, the Saudis encouraged the creation of new guest houses *(madafat)* for Arab volunteers, which competed with and weakened the Service Bureau. The proliferation of *madafat* subsequently transformed Peshawar into a microcosm of all the clashes between different strands of radical Islam that the struggle against the Soviet enemy was supposed to unite. In October 1986, Osama bin Laden created his own guest house, the "Partisans' Den" *(ma'sadat al-ansar)*, which brought together Gulf nationals, most of them of Saudi or Yemeni origin. Bin Laden's Partisans had three training camps near the Afghan border: Abu Bakr al-Siddiq, al-Faruq, and al-Qa'ida (the Base). The last of these gave its name to the terrorist network that subsequently formed around Bin Laden.

The disagreement between Bin Laden and Azzam had to do with relations between the Arab volunteers and the Afghan resistance, which was divided along ethnic and regional lines into seven representative organizations. Bin Laden supported the creation of an independent Arab military structure, while Azzam felt that Arab volunteers should serve as an auxiliary force for the Afghans. Turki al-Faysal, who at the time was head of the Saudi intelligence services and mastermind of the anti-Soviet struggle in Afghanistan, had approved, if not requested, Bin Laden's initiative. According to the testimony of Uzaifa, one of Abdallah Azzam's sons, there was even a training camp for Bin Laden's *madafa* in Jeddah, in Saudi Arabia.[6] During this period, Turki al-Faysal made several personal visits to Partisans' Den and to another salafist guest house, Jamil al-Rahman.

The *madafa* of Jamil al-Rahman, also created under the auspices of the Saudi government, bore the name of a Wahhabi Afghan shaykh who was originally from the region of Kunar, in Afghanistan, and who had been assassinated in 1991 during a settling of accounts between Arab volunteers. Its eponym may have been Afghan, but the *madafa* hosted Arab volunteers almost exclusively. It incarnated a salafist trend that was radically opposed to the Muslim Brothers; the latter were gathered in the Service Bureau. According to several Arab jihad veterans, Jamil al-Rahman's preachers were famous for their doctrinal rigidity and their propensity for pronouncing *takfir* (excommunication or, more accurately, condemnation for apostasy) against anyone who failed to engage in behavior they considered to conform to that of the earliest Muslims. This is why they were called salafists: the term *salaf* designates the "pious forebears" in Arabic. Jamil al-Rahman's young volunteers were not to visit competing *madafat;* if they disobeyed, they faced exclusion and the cessation of their monthly stipend—which, thanks to Saudi financing, was far higher than the salaries paid to volunteers in other guest houses. Jamil al-Rahman's Saudi shaykhs had also condemned Sayyid Qutb, the Muslim Brotherhood's most prominent theoretician and Abdallah Azzam's favorite author, as an apostate. The *madafa's* views were published in *al-Mujahid* ("The Jihad Combatant"). The articles praised the Sauds as guardians of authentic Islam in the heart of the Arabian Peninsula. The publication's rare "forays" into Arab politics were put down by Saudi censorship, for it was forbidden to attack an Arab government. Still, criticisms of the Syrian and Egyptian regimes appear several times in the publication. For example, an article published in *al-Mujahid* in April–May 1989 mentioned a "believer" imprisoned by the "tyrant of Syria" *(taghut Suriyya):* Saudi officials demanded that the reference be removed immediately.[7] The same issue, which included a special dossier devoted to guerrilla techniques in an urban environment, was pulled off the stands. Its distribution in Saudi Arabia might have given young Saudi subjects military knowledge that they could put to use in places other than Afghanistan's cities.

Given our current lack of information, it is difficult to reconstitute with any certainty the history of Islamism in Peshawar, from its birth in 1984 to its fragmentation in the early 1990s. Still, it is plausible that relations between Azzam and the Saudis began to grow tense, if not sour, in 1986. The Saudis gradually lost confidence in Abdallah Azzam, perhaps because of the increasingly anti-American tone of his harangues, as the struggle against the Soviets came to an end. By contrast, in the salafist *madafat*—including Bin Laden's—no one criticized the United States. The Service Bureau was also the only *madafa* where young Saudi volunteers, most of whom were from the region of Dammam, in the east of the country, could denounce the behavior of the royal family as they pleased. Furthermore, Azzam's initial hostility toward Wahhabi salafism was well known. In 1982, under the pseudonym Sadiq Amin, he had published a work titled "Islamic Preaching," in which he criticized the salafists for "spending so much time on side issues to which Islamic preachers would do better not to devote themselves at a time when Islam is facing a pitiless war that seeks to tear it out by its roots."[8] Still, he was ready to admit that salafists had "given young people the motivation necessary to look for convincing arguments, and thereby encouraged them to take interest in the texts, especially the prophet's *hadiths,* for which they deserve credit."

Finally, Azzam carried out a symbolic operation that must not have gone unnoticed in Wahhabi Saudi circles. In line with the policy of the Saudi state, the ulema of Saudi Arabia pronounced the Afghan conflict a religious jihad against infidel communism, a development that was crucial to creating the reality of armed jihad, which did not exist at the outset, since Soviet intervention was initially intended to put an end to a civil war between two factions of the Afghan Communist Party. But assigning such significance to the conflict was not the same thing as giving the militants carte blanche for the future. The Saudi ulema never intended permanently to give up their considerable symbolic power to determine which situations could justifiably require a declaration of jihad. As for Abdallah Azzam, he believed that if the Saudi grand ulema had determined that the Afghan conjuncture filled the conditions for jihad, then, by extension, such a battle could be declared "each time infidels trod the land of Islam." If that was the case, jihad would be destined to multiply, since the entire *umma,* according to Azzam, was already in a state of legitimate defense against the forces of non-belief:

> Jihad in Afghanistan is an individual duty, to be carried out through will power and financial means, and requires no one's authorization.

This is the consensus of specialists in *tafsir (mufassirin)*, in *hadith (muhaddithin)*, and in *fiqh* . . . In the "Great Fatwas" (607/4), Ibn Taymiyya wrote: "When the enemy attacks, and no caliphate remains, it is a collective duty *(wajib ijma'an)* to defend religion, the self *(al-nafs)*, and what is sacred *(hurma)*. Therefore, there is no need for authorization from the Prince of the Believers *(amir al-mu'minin)*, even if he is present." Ibn Rushd said: "To obey the imam is necessary, even if he is not just, as long as he has not commanded the sin of sins by forbidding jihad."[9]

Abdallah Azzam's jihad was not burdened by moral considerations—at the time he was writing Soviet bombs were leaving survivors horribly mutilated—and *al-Jihad* (the paper published by the Service Bureau) was no different from any other publication in that it did not refrain from exploiting the victims' misfortunes for political purposes. Its Muslims readers in different parts of the world were shown heart-wrenching photographs of children with amputated limbs and infants with faces disfigured by defoliant burns. This display of violence was intended to justify counter-violence, and implicitly marked a first move toward the legitimation of terrorism. The shift was evident in arguments concerning the murder of "communist women," an act that was considered lawful from a religious point of view regardless of the extent of their participation in the conflict. Women's blood could be spilled, collectively or individually, according to *al-Jihad*, because "their ideological convictions are directed against Islam and are harmful to Islam and Muslims." In support of this position, the paper cited a particularly explicit *hadith*: when two slave women of Abd al-Muttalib's tribe mocked the prophet, his family, and Islam, Muhammad, referring to the women and the men accompanying them, is said to have ordered that they be killed even if they were found hiding behind the curtains of the Ka'ba.[10]

Volunteers at the Service Bureau were of Palestinian, Jordanian, or Syrian origin, and were far more politicized than the recruits of the salafist *madafat,* who came from the Gulf. Guests at Abdallah Azzam's bureau spent time at the Afghan jihad camps in order to acquire crucial military experience for the pursuit of their respective political struggles, once they had returned to their countries of origin. A veteran of the Service Bureau underscored the difference between his colleagues and the salafist *madafat* recruits:

> I didn't come to fight in Afghanistan. I spent a year and a half in Peshawar, and I never went to fight. I was there mainly for the military training . . . Before that, I had gone to sign up with the Palestine Liberation Army in Jordan, but they didn't want me . . . Anyway, I was against the PLO organizations, which were secular . . . We were different from the salafists, who weren't very politically aware. We placed the United States and the USSR on equal footing, but they didn't mention the United States. We considered the United States an enemy power, despite the aid it gave in Afghanistan. We had the experience of Palestine. Without the United States and Great Britain, Israel would not have been created.[11]

Notwithstanding the denials of those who today seek to spare the memory of Abdallah Azzam any link to the al-Qa'ida network, texts written as early as the mid-1980s provide evidence that Azzam did not intend to limit the jihad to Afghanistan, despite Saudi Arabia's insistence that it be confined to the Indian subcontinent. In June 1985, Azzam wrote an op-ed piece in *al-Jihad,* of which he was the editor-in-chief, stating that the continuation of jihad on other fronts was "a responsibility of Arabs before God."[12] For his purpose, he successfully reintroduced a *hadith* about the obligation of believers to expel Jews and Christians from the Arabian Peninsula.[13] According to Azzam, the Prophet Muhammad wanted to "purify" the Arabian Peninsula: "He wanted to make sure that only one religion would exist in Arabia, and that two religions would not mingle there. During the 'Farewell Pilgrimage,' just before his death, he exhorted his nation *(umma)* to that effect once again: 'Satan has lost all hope that worshipers will ever worship (him) in the Arabian Peninsula, but (hopes) to sow the seed of dissension among them' *(hadith* related by Muslim, book 39, 6752)." This interest in expanding jihad also came from the volunteers themselves. For them, Peshawar was not a final destination, but rather one stage in the preparation for a wider war against the Arab regimes.

Using these elements, we may posit that these two groups engaged in an ideological rivalry produced an original synthesis: salafism-jihadism. When they came in contact with the Muslim Brothers, the Wahhabi salafists, who until then had paid exclusive attention to the purity of religious practice and to questions of Islamic morality, willingly leaving the management of worldly affairs to whomever was in power *(waliyy al-amr)*, familiarized themselves with the political questions emphasized by the Brotherhood, whose members rebuked the Wahhabis for their ignorance of the modern world and their religious Pharisaism. For their part, the Brothers may have been influenced not only by the additional legitimacy afforded by mastery of the religious corpus, which the salafists encouraged, but also by the salafists' desire to establish a religious identity free from the corruption of politics. Furthermore, exalting the practice of jihad led almost mechanically to an ever-greater recourse to prophetic traditions in the form of the *hadith* of the first Muslims, the science and study of which constitute salafism's main focus.

The Muslim Brothers in Peshawar, who had experienced armed struggle there, were made up of a majority of Palestinians, Syrians, and Lebanese radicalized by war in their societies of origin. They moved away from the prudent positions taken by the movement's transnational leadership, for whom Middle Eastern issues—first among them the search for a modus operandi with the region's Arab governments—were a priority. During his last trip to Jordan in 1984, Azzam tried unsuccessfully to convince the leadership of the Jordanian Muslim Brothers to send combatants to Afghanistan. He was met with opposition from the supreme authority of the organization's Jordanian branch, the "general supervisor" *(al-muraqib al-aam)*, Muhammad Abd al-Rahman Khalifeh, who preferred to restrict the Jordanian Brotherhood's participation to humanitarian and financial activities. If Azzam's approach had been implemented, it would certainly have tipped the balance within the Brotherhood, strengthening Azzam's position, despite the fact that he had been fired from his teaching position on the order of Amman's military governor, before being pushed into the minority within the Jordanian Brotherhood's leadership. Indeed, soon after the failure of his attempt to secure combatants, Abdallah Azzam's membership in the Jordanian Muslim Brotherhood, of which he had been a key figure before his departure to Saudi Arabia in 1982, was suspended. According to his son Uzaifa, "Azzam was a Muslim Brother, but he had an independent personality. He didn't want the Muslim Brothers to meddle in his affairs."[14]

Two Worlds Meet: The Late 1980s

In the early 1990s, Ain al-Helweh was absorbing the values of a deterritorialized jihad. By that time the camp had long ceased to embody the vanguard of the Palestinian and Arab revolution in Lebanon, and some segments of the Lebanese population, especially among the Shi'ites in the south, had grown strongly anti-Palestinian. In that context, references to the life and work of Shaykh Abdallah Azzam legitimized the movement away from a territorial Palestinian base. Abdallah Azzam was hailed as the architect of global jihad, and struggles that had been confined to a local and regional straitjacket received a universal Islamic dimension.

At the end of the Lebanese war, salafist militants in Ain al-Helweh found themselves in a situation similar to that faced by Abdallah Azzam after Black September, in 1970–1971. Azzam was prevented from acting by the Arab regimes, otherwise known as "Israel's border guards," while the salafists were hampered by a Syrian-Lebanese regional system that frustrated any attempt at Sunni Islamist action against Israel. The "Islamic resistance" that remained in southern Lebanon had become a Shi'ite monopoly, with access to it controlled by Hezbollah, and its capacity for inflicting damage regulated by Syria. Given Israel's military might, furthermore, Syria had nothing to gain by escalating tensions. The salafist militants therefore refused to participate in a conflict controlled by the Syrian regime and Hezbollah, which were pursuing their own objectives, and which, furthermore, lacked religious legitimacy. Thus Abu Mahjin's brother, Abu Tariq, a leader of Usbat al-Ansar, the camp's most violent salafist group, saw no point in participating in armed action against Israel and its Lebanese support troops, since such participation would be tantamount to working for the success of Hezbollah and the Shi'ites, and to encouraging Syria's regional interests:

> I can't take part in Hezbollah's actions in the south for reasons that have to do with faith *(aqida)*. The differences in belief between us and the Shi'ites prevent me from fighting by their side . . . Besides, Nasrallah is a liar. After Qana, he was already making a fuss and Hezbollah didn't do anything. Now that negotiations are ongoing with Syria, they've stopped armed action. Hezbollah has become a Syrian party: it is eating out of Hafiz al-Asad's hand. Everything they said was false.[15]

Given that the Sunnis have not fought on the Lebanese front since 1985, they must find other causes or risk losing their capacity to mobilize. Though Palestine has not been forgotten, it no longer plays a central function in processes of political identification. For a Palestinian dispossessed of his land, to no longer consider Israel a principal enemy marks a symbolic rupture with Palestinian nationalism, including its Islamist version, incarnated by Hamas or Islamic Jihad.

Al-Hidaya, published by the Muslim Student Union, lasted for a year; it ceased publication in November 1991, when the Lebanese state reasserted its military authority in Saida and the surrounding area. During this period, the young Palestinian leaders of the Muslim Student Union made use of all Ain al-Helweh's preachers and religious intellectuals to solidify a jihadist doctrine that had already been tried out in Peshawar. Young Shaykh Abu Dia' took on the role of editor-in-chief; today, he is the imam of Omar Ibn al-Khattab Mosque, one of the camp's largest, which stands next to the office of the popular committee controlled by Sa'iqa, a pro-Syrian organization.

With far more modest financial means, the newspaper followed the editorial policy Shaykh Azzam had laid down in his monthly publication *al-Jihad,* and adapted that line to the dual Palestinian-Lebanese context. But the content—an amalgamation of religious apologetics, prophetic traditions, and geopolitical analyses—had the same goal: to present jihad as a central tenet of religious belief, by giving it a status equivalent to that of the other pillars of the faith, like prayer and fasting during Ramadan.

By studying the texts and information contained in *al-Hidaya,* it is possible to understand how the authors, before the al-Qa'ida network was established, cobbled together a salafist-jihadist ideology, taking as their starting point the interplay between regional upheavals—the 1991 Gulf War—and readings selected within a religious tradition whose interpretation was deprived of any spiritual dimension.

During Ramadan, the Muslim Student Union held "Islamic" contests for young people, in which the questions prefigured the overarching themes of current jihadist preaching. These questions shed light on the kind of education the camps' students received. For instance, students were asked to analyze the meaning of the verse

"Never will the Jews / Or the Christians be satisfied / With thee unless thou follow / Their form of religion" (al-Baqara, verse 120); to reflect upon the influence of the doctrine of allegiance and rupture *(al-wala wal-bara)* on the first generation of Muslims, showing "the reasons for its importance at that time"; to explain the reasons for the destruction of the Islamic caliphate and to propose a means of reconstituting it; to comment on the *hadith* "Behold! God sent me [Muhammad] with a sword, just before the Hour [of Judgment], and placed my daily sustenance beneath the shadow of my spear, and humiliation and contempt on those who oppose me"; or, to write the biographies of Abd al-Qadir al-Husayni (Palestine), Hasan al-Banna (Egypt), or Abdallah Azzam (Afghanistan). The final biographical question followed a dialectical progression, starting with a figure of the Palestinian national struggle, then moving on to the founder of the Muslim Brotherhood, and reaching its apotheosis with the theoretician of globalized jihad.

The first pages of each issue of *al-Hidaya* were devoted to a discussion of religious doctrine that returned repeatedly to the same themes: the opposition between a golden age, that of "first-generation Islam," and the current political and military weakness of the community of believers, which is powerless against the attacks of the hostile West. According to the authors, only two things are real: the Qur'an and the Prophet's deeds and sayings *(sunna)*. Apart from these, humanity must err divided. The first Muslims were able to triumph over their enemies because they were the "generation of the Qur'an":

They had only one slogan at the time: "There is no god but Allah." They had only one program: Islam. They had only one constitution: the Qur'an. The Muslim fighters drew their only satisfaction from the Qur'an. Listen to them in their camps, reciting the Qur'an in a murmur like that of bees. They derived no pleasure from card games, backgammon, wine, or prostitutes.[16]

If Muslims today are divided among multiple political entities ("even inside a single entity, it is impossible to count the number of parties, organizations, and contradictory ideological programs"), if their leaders have never been capable of achieving unity, despite all their speeches on this topic, it is obviously because they have moved away from the Qur'an and the *sunna,* for these represent "the only possible strategic program" for the battle against the enemy. The conflict is not political in nature; in reality, according to *al-Hidaya,* its essence is religious and cultural, even though this phenomenon has been dissimulated by ideologies imported from the West (such as "nationalism or socialism"), which have proliferated in the region and accelerated the dislocation of the Islamic nation (which the paper implicitly associates with the Ottoman Empire). Now that these ideologies no longer produce effects, Islam must reoccupy the place it deserves, and return to jihad so that it can once again become a force to be reckoned with in the conflict. Muslims must mobilize the Islamic world by unveiling the real cultural and religious stakes in the war of civilization against the West. On this basis, the "Islamic movement" will be able to free "the lands of Islam" and set up an "Islamic state." The geographical location of such a state is irrelevant, since the first duty incumbent upon believers is to "establish God's Law on earth."[17]

Some articles in *al-Hidaya* also celebrated Islamic Jihad's military accomplishments and (albeit more discreetly) those of Hamas in Palestine, violently criticized Saudi Arabia's policy during the Gulf War, and readily provided a forum for figures close to Hezbollah (like its former "spiritual guide," Sayyid Muhammad Hussein Fadlallah) or individuals integrated into Iran's networks of influence (this was the case, as we saw in the previous chapter, with Saida's Sunni religious judge, Ahmad al-Zayn). But above all, these articles expressed a tactical concern for maintaining cordial relations with Hezbollah. Other, far more numerous pieces insisted on the need for a return to the sources of Islam, taking as a model the

Muslim warriors during the glorious period of conquest. In articles of this type, no contemporary political experience was taken into account, since none could compare with the utopia of the original period. More to the point, not a single article evoked the Iranian revolution, which was totally ignored. *Al-Hidaya*'s authors preferred to look into the restoration of the Islamic caliphate, "which represents spiritual and temporal power, and which rests on the Qur'an and the *sunna*."[18] In these, the earliest times, we find the Prophet and His Companions, then the three caliphs—Abu Bakr, Umar, and Uthman—who took up the "succession" of Islam after its founder's death in 632. Because of the emphasis they place on Sunni identity, the camp's salafists intentionally omit Ali, the fourth caliph, whose legitimacy Shi'ite Muslims claim today. This omission indicates the salafists' rejection of "impious Islam."

Jihadist Salafism against the Saudi Regime

Abdallah Azzam died less than a year before Saddam Hussein invaded Kuwait, on August 2, 1990, and King Fahd called in American troops, on August 7. No one will ever know for sure how Azzam would have reacted to these events. However, as U.S. aid to the *mujahidin* poured in during the war in Afghanistan, the head of the Service Bureau publicly wondered whether Muslims could legitimately receive aid from a non-Muslim power. He set two conditions. For such recourse to be legitimate, Muslim leaders under threat must have had no other option. Furthermore, they had to be certain that the infidel power whose assistance they were requesting would not seize the opportunity to modify the power balance in its own favor once the enemy was destroyed. Azzam's analysis was also a critical evaluation of the changes jihad had undergone once it had lost its original purity, owing to the corruption brought about by the influx of foreign aid. According to Azzam, the purpose of jihad was not so much to confront the Soviet Union as it was to fight

"Afghan leaders like Muhammad Daud, Hafizullah, and Karmal, who do not govern according to God's Law."[19] Defeating the Soviets would be useless if they and the Americans should agree to set up "a secular figure in Islamic garb." Azzam, who had no illusions regarding the motives for American involvement—"the opportunity for them to take revenge on the Soviets after their defeat in Vietnam"—denounced the possibility of a political process that would put an end to armed conflict: "As the experience of Palestine has shown us, the only valid solution must come from the barrel of a gun. To hand the question over to international authorities is to throw it in the dustbin and guarantee its certain death."[20] Under such conditions, we can logically assume that the break between Azzam and the Saud family would have been complete after King Fahd's call for help on August 7, 1990.

After Shaykh Azzam was assassinated, *al-Jihad* ceased publication, depriving its readers of any chance of knowing how the head of the Service Bureau would have reacted to Saddam Hussein's invasion of Kuwait. From Ain al-Helweh, the Muslim Student Union announced its solidarity with "Iraq's Muslim army and people." In January 1991, the group organized a protest march in Saida, just after Friday prayers. At the time, such demonstrations ran far higher risks in the rest of the country, because Syria, whose troops had not yet reached the Awali River north of Saida, had joined the U.S.–led coalition against Iraq in 1991.

Ain al-Helweh's Islamist intellectuals began to reexamine the religious conditions governing requests for assistance from unbelievers.[21] According to their interpretation of the Prophet's experience, the imam can use weapons manufactured by non-Muslims, as the Prophet did when the Quraysh chief, Safwan Ibn Umayya, who had not yet converted to Islam, lent him his chain mail and weapons before the battle of Hunayn in 630, just after the conquest of Mecca. It is also lawful to fight alongside unbelievers against other unbelievers, as long as the balance of power is favorable to the Muslims, as was the case when Muhammad borrowed Safwan Ibn Umayya's equipment. But if such cooperation threatens to allow non-Muslims to subjugate Muslims, it must be categorically rejected, as ordered in verses taken from Sura 5, The Table Spread: "O ye who believe! / Take not the Jews / And the Christians / For your friends and protectors: / They are but friends and protectors / To each other. And he / Amongst you that turns to them / (For friendship) is of them." According to the authors of *al-Hidaya*, writing at the beginning of the 1991 Gulf War, these verses "perfectly describe the situation in which we find ourselves today." Consequently, recourse to "the new Crusaders—the Americans, the British, the French, and others—with the spiteful Jews fighting in their armies, is strictly forbidden." By seeking protection from "Crusaders and Jews," the Gulf states had placed themselves under the authority of the *umma*'s worst enemies, who sought to destroy Iraq and thereby deprive Muslims of the strength to oppose them. Those who acted in this way were "betraying God and His Prophet."

With the war in Afghanistan, a religious doctrine that legitimized Saudi power evolved into a call for the transformation of all the regimes in the Muslim world. When it moved to Peshawar, salafist doctrine slipped from the control of its guardians—the Saudi kingdom's great ulema—and freed itself from the duty of obeying the Saud family. Borne by warrior communities, this doctrine was enriched by the study of sayings pronounced by the Prophet Muhammad during his wars of conquest. At the same time, its content was politicized by prolonged contact with other radical Islamist groups. The 1991 Gulf War and the invitation King Fahd extended to U.S. troops thus revealed the existence of a new form of Islamism: salafist jihadism. It shared with Saudi Wahhabism a literal reading of religious texts and a rejection of modern politics (elections, parties, and so on), but placed armed jihad at the heart of belief and denounced any sort of subordination to the West.

According to most ulema, only the leaders of a Muslim state can declare a defensive jihad, which corresponds to a state of general military mobilization and is incumbent upon individuals as an absolute obligation *(fard 'ayn)*. For jihadist militants, by contrast, any Muslim can declare obligatory individual jihad, since modern Muslim states are, in their view, the antithesis of a true Islamic state. That being the case, jihad is no longer the dominion of those who hold public authority, and declaring it is no longer the responsibility of those who lead such decrepit states: it is privatized in that it becomes each individual's personal duty.

By identifying themselves with the first Muslim community *(salaf)*, the salafists are trying to build a charismatic community that owes its authority to a direct link with pristine Islam. By retracing the actions of the earliest community of believers, they attempt to free themselves from the weight of the juristic Islamic tradition, which attaches conditions to the controversial questions of jihad and *takfir* (pronouncing "bad Muslims" apostates) to safeguard the Islamic community against heavy-handedness in the matter of religious identity. These legal precautions hinder the salafists' claim to control the boundaries of religious identity by pronouncing definitive judgments against their coreligionists or by excommunicating some of them. Refusing submission to religious tradition and preaching independent interpretation are ways to escape the doctrinal constraints established by the different schools of Sunni jurisprudence throughout history. For the salafists, one's faith *(aqida)* and way of life *(minhaj)* cannot be separated; therefore any kind of participation in a non-religious political organization poses a grave threat to the very content of faith and can be equated with unbelief *(kufr)*. This difference in approach has consequences for mobilization: one of the key features of salafism is that it rests on informal networks and favors mobilization on a small scale, which generally comes about through mosque-based education and private home schooling. The Muslim Brothers, by contrast, resort to more classic methods of participation, such as the creation of political parties, trade union activities, and negotiations with other actors on the political scene.

Al-Nur Mosque and the Combatant Islamic Movement

Today, four religious parties share the camp of Ain al-Helweh: two have already proven themselves on the Lebanese religious and political scene, whereas the other two appeared locally and, while benefiting from informal contacts beyond the geographical limits of the settlement, have no legal existence in the Lebanese political system.

The two parties that are anchored on a national scale and have played an official role in Lebanon's political and religious life since the end of the war are the Jama'a Islamiyya and the Society for Charitable Works, otherwise known as al-Ahbash ("Ethiopians" in Arabic), in reference to the Ethiopian shaykh who started the movement. The Ahbash were set up by Syrian intelligence in the mid-1980s to weaken the appeal of radical Islam in Lebanon after it had been eliminated in Syria, and they have since functioned as a veritable war machine against Sunni Islamism. They established their regional center in the camp (Salah al-Din Mosque) in the early 1990s. These two rival organizations thus entered the camp relatively recently.

The two other movements, more accurately described as networks, formed underground in the mid-1980s: the Combatant Islamic Movement (al-Haraka al-Islamiyya al-Mujahida), led by Shaykh Jamal Sulayman Khattab, currently the preacher at the camp's oldest mosque (al-Nur); and the Partisans' League (Usbat al-Ansar).

Situated on one of the camp's two "avenues" that continues from Ain al-Helweh's main entrance—known as the "lower" road to inhabitants—al-Nur Mosque hosts several hundred faithful of all ages every Friday. On the surface, it is very difficult to tell the members of the al-Nur and Usbat al-Ansar networks apart. Most of the young people who attend the mosque identify with Usbat al-Ansar, an affiliation reflected in their choice of clothing. The Usbat al-Ansar "uniform" is easy to spot: with very few exceptions, the "partisans" do not wear Afghan clothes, but prefer leather jackets and black pants. In winter, almost all the young men wear sailors' caps.

At forty-five, Shaykh Jamal Sulayman Khattab is one of the camp's most important religious figures. He graduated from the prestigious American University of Beirut (AUB) in the early 1980s and holds a degree in management; he was appointed shaykh of al-Nur Mosque by a council *(majlis)* made up of the main leaders of Murshid in the late 1980s. In addition to his religious responsibilities, Jamal Khattab worked as an accountant at UNRWA until he was fired in 1993, after a Saida court convicted him in absentia of inciting sectarian hatred in Lebanon. Since then, he has not left the camp.

Shaykh Jamal gradually gathered a core group of followers who meet every day at the mosque or in the small al-Huda bookstore just next door. The group has realized the ideal of the *umma*'s unity on a microsocial scale, and recruits its supporters from among the camp's original inhabitants, as well as from among all those who have experience on the various fronts of jihad. Abu Muhammad al-Masri, for example, is an Egyptian national who fought in the war in Afghanistan, where he lost three fingers on his right hand while detonating an explosive device. He then carried on the struggle against the Egyptian state as a member of al-Jama'a al-Islamiyya, before escaping from Egypt in 1993. As soon as he arrived in the camp, he was taken under the wing of Shaykh Jamal's group, which gave him housing not far from the mosque as well as work in a small shop.[22] In May 2000, to mark "the first trial of members of a Bin Laden network in Lebanon," the Lebanese daily *al-Safir* published reports from the security services describing the path that had led certain members of the network to the camp. Abu Muhammad al-Masri was cited as one of Bin Laden's local representatives in Ain al-Helweh, right-hand man to all the Afghan veterans in the region, and the crucial intermediary for those seeking access to the head of the clandestine al-Qa'ida network. In March 2004, Abu Muhammad al-Masri was assassinated when a car bomb exploded in front of his restaurant just after he had finished dawn prayers *(fajr)* at al-Nur Mosque.

Twenty-eight-year-old Abu Salim, the son of an Algerian woman and a Palestinian man who worked on a PLA (Palestine Liberation Army) military police task force in Algeria, was born in Algeria and came to Ain al-Helweh, where he has been known since his arrival, in 1996, as "the Algerian" *(al-Jaza'iri)*. He married the sister of a former local leader of Fatah's armed branch in the camp, and lives with his wife (who wears a black *niqab,* veiling her entire body as well as her face) in an apartment near al-Nur Mosque.[23] They do not own a television, because Abu Salim rejects "corruption— *fasad*—from the outside world." What he agreed to reveal about his personal journey follows the geography of radical Islamism's various front lines. He underwent religious training in Saudi Arabia, at the Islamic University of Madina, where he received a degree in religious sciences after a four-year program. Then he spent two years in Sudan, went back to Algeria, and finally headed east again. His religious degrees and knowledge—after he turned fourteen, he decided to memorize the Qur'an, which allowed him to travel free of charge to Saudi Arabia when he was eighteen—prepared him for the position of "second imam" under Shaykh Jamal, whose sermons he records carefully. From his past experience, he has drawn the conviction, which he repeats tirelessly, that "one must know Islam before Muslims," for the latter always tarnish the image of religion. These are not true Muslims, he contends, but merely "Muslims in origin *(bil-hawiyya),* who have forsaken *(kufr)* the true faith."

For Abu Salim, Saudi Arabian society is divided into three categories: men of religion, most of whom are true believers; the rulers, who are "enemies of Islam, slaves to America, and obsessed with sex and alcohol"; and the rest of society, made up of Bedouins still mired in ignorance. His fondest memory of Saudi Arabia is still the Islamic University in Madina, which he describes as an American campus under an Islamic banner, "a city as big as the camp, a real Islamic space, with restaurants, libraries, mosques, free from the influence of Saudi society, where we could live without ever leaving it." Abu Salim's rapid integration into the Ain al-Helweh camp, his popularity among young Islamists, almost all of whom know him, and the prestige his religious education and wide travels in "Islamic states" (like Saudi Arabia and Iran) have earned him all indicate that the terms of struggle in the camp are now perceived differently. The feeling of belonging to the Palestinian revolutionary model as the PLO historically helped define it—in nationalist, patriotic terms—has been weakened.

The camp no longer serves as a "sanctuary" for Palestinian identity, as was the case in the 1960s and 1970s. At least in certain groups, foreigners are no longer considered outsiders; Algerians, Syrians, or Egyptians belonging to militant Islamist networks can put down roots by immersing themselves in an environment that grows increasingly familiar as it becomes more Islamicized. Militants no longer base their solidarity on nationalist claims or demands for freedom, as was the case when Europe's colonies were battling the forces of imperialism. On the contrary, rejection of that very identity justifies the believer's right—and even obligation—to take a position on issues when the future of the Muslim community is at stake, whether in Algeria, Chechnya, Afghanistan, or the former Yugoslavia.

This movement away from nationalism is evident in the works available in the two Islamist bookstores in the camps. The texts offered cover events in the Islamic world and relate the exploits of combatants fighting jihad on various fronts, in Afghanistan, Chechnya, Dagestan, and many other "Islamic" fronts.

A brief description of al-Huda, one of the two bookstores in the Ain al-Helweh camp, can cast light on the ideological orientations of those who gather there every day, for the tiny bookstore is more a place where people meet to chat and socialize than a profit-oriented establishment.

As a bookstore, al-Huda—a Qur'anic term that designates the straight Path, the correct direction toward God—offers its customers school supplies at low cost, as well as a variety of religious products that are in wide circulation on the global Islamist market: panegyrics, anti-Semitic literature, books denouncing the work of Christian missionaries, practical manuals of correct Muslim behavior, traditional and contemporary Islamist literature (Ibn Taymiyya, Sayyid Qutb, Sa'id Hawwa), but alsopublications created and edited in Lebanon, like *al-Wa'i*, the weekly paper put out by the Liberation Party (Hizb al-Tahrir), or—supposedly for a female readership—"Female Preachers' Podium" *(minbar al-da'yyiat)*, by the Lebanese salafist shaykh Hasan al-Qatarji, which is handed out to the faithful every Friday at the door of al-Nur Mosque.[24]

Whereas it is easy to find books about jihad in Algeria (the speeches of Ali Belhadj are prominently displayed), Bosnia, or Afghanistan (all the pamphlets penned by Abdallah Azzam are available), the bookstore sells very few works about the Palestinian struggle. Those who frequent al-Huda describe this struggle as peripheral, almost secondary, owing to doubts about the Islamic legitimacy of individuals and groups involved in the conflict. By distancing themselves from the Palestinian cause, this group differentiates itself from others in the camp: Palestine for them is only one front in the jihad, and does not contribute to the group's identity; or, if it does, it is only in a negative fashion, against the grain, by exploiting the weariness often expressed by Palestinians in the camps toward the slogans and promises of organizations that have embodied the Palestinian struggle since the mid-1960s.

The bookstore also offers an impressive number of cassette tapes, most of which are available in any Islamist bookstore in the world, with the exception of some more subversive examples—like Bin Laden's call for jihad against the United States, which was recorded and distributed as early as the summer of 1997—or tapes directly produced at al-Nur Mosque. The sermons and speeches given by Shaykh Jamal, as he is unceremoniously called, are scrupulously recorded and the tapes then placed on the bookstore's shelves. They are not sold, only lent, and in theory even that privilege is reserved to the members of Shaykh Jamal's group, and to the larger, but still well-known, circle of those who frequent al-Nur Mosque.

The members of the group put together press files when militants accused of belonging to al-Qa'ida are arrested and put on trial anywhere in the world. Emotional identification with the victims of such arrests, "witnesses and martyrs *(shuhada)* of Islam" against the tyranny *(zulm)* of the Arab regimes, is spontaneous and immediate. It helps maintain the conviction that secrecy and violence against the united front of unbelief have become a means of distinguishing true believers from "Muslims in origin." It also gives its adherents the feeling that they belong to an elite army—"we have an army too," Abu Salim affirms—to which God will inevitably grant victory. For the members of this secret army, rejection of all outside influences, opposition to the Arab regimes and any secular body, holy war in the Caucasus, and the assassination of individuals who sell alcoholic beverages in the Saida region are all part of a single cause in the service of Islam.

From a practical point of view, the speed with which outside members of the network find apartments in Ain al-Helweh, in a context where space is at a premium, offers another indication of the local power that Islamists wield in the camp. In the course of my fieldwork, it also became clear that the homes of militants from these networks reflect their privileged position within the local social hierarchy.

Of course, it is extremely difficult to reconstruct the personal histories of these militants in the cause of radical Islamism, since most of them refuse to give biographical information that would make it possible for regional security forces or Western powers to identify them. The fact that they knew about the camp before they had ever set foot in Lebanon, that they chose it as a resting place, and that they were integrated fairly easily shows not only that Ain al-Helweh is the largest Palestinian refugee camp in Lebanon, but also that it plays an important role on the Middle Eastern map of salafist Islamism.

Abu Hamza occupies a special place within the group. He is older than the others—over forty—and originally from Gaza. A former member of the DFLP, and then of Islamic Jihad, he was expelled from Palestine in the early 1980s, after having spent a year in an Israeli military jail. From Egypt, he tried to return to Gaza three times, and each time he found himself incarcerated in Egyptian prisons, where he was treated badly. (Today Abu Hamza says unhesitatingly that the torture inflicted in Egyptian prisons was worse than what he suffered in Israel, and he generalizes this conclusion to all the Arab countries.) He was expelled from Egypt in 1986, and was arrested yet again in Syria, where he spent three months behind bars—long enough, he says, "to convince the Syrian jailers that I wasn't part of Arafat's gang." He arrived in Lebanon the same year, slipping across the Syrian-Lebanese border through the villages in the north. In Lebanon, he spent a few months working at al-Shahid al-Falastini, Islamic Jihad's institution for the families of Palestinian martyrs, which at the time was headed by one of the leaders of Palestinian Islamic Jihad, Shaykh Sa'id Barakat, who was in the group of Palestinians Israel expelled to southern Lebanon in 1991.[25] Abu Hamza then met Shaykh Jamal through Shaykh Barakat. During that meeting, Shaykh Jamal suggested that he take over a small shop in the camp.

As for twenty-year-old Muhammad, another of the network's close acquaintances, he dropped out of an UNRWA school around ninth grade, and began a course of religious study at the age of sixteen at the Murshid center set up in the camp. In 2000, he completed a four-year training program and planned to continue his studies at an Islamic institute in Beirut (either Imam al-Awza'i's Institute or al-Da'wa College, near the Kuwaiti Embassy). Like the network's other members, he took a stand against traditional Palestinian organizations: "I'm against [the idea of] citizenship *(ana didd al-muwatana)*," he noted. "Above all, I'm a Muslim. That's my true identity. As a Muslim, I cannot make peace with Jews, as Arafat did—the traitor. I never go to the national events that are celebrated in the camp."

The ties among the collectivity members are maintained on a daily basis through shared meals, prayers at the mosque, and sessions of *tafsir* (Qur'anic exegesis), generally held in discreet locations: at the home of Shaykh Jamal, or of any one of the militants whose past action or present enthusiasm has won him admission into the group's inner circle. Each of the members is aware of the danger of infiltration by an "agent of the Lebanese state"; hence their suspicion of any unknown observer, or anyone who has not been specifically recommended to them. The nature of the members' relationship to one another brings together the four criteria (time, emotion, intimacy, and exchange) that characterize "strong ties" according to the sociologist Mark Granovetter: in the confined space of the camp, the militants spend time discussing Islamist current events at the local and international level; these exchanges give rise to very intense expressions of emotion; and secrecy facilitates sharing information that must not leave the circle of associates. Finally, on a practical level, the reciprocity of services rendered strengthens the group's cohesion against the outside world. In the universe of the camp's associations, al-Nur Mosque fits into the network of mosques and Qur'anic schools for which al-Murshid, the Islamic association, is responsible. For this reason, Shaykh Jamal is one of the hundred or so religious officials and educators on the association's payroll.

Al-Nur Network's Three Fields of Action

Shaykh Jamal's group has a clear vision of its role in the reduced space of the camp, on the national Lebanese scene, and on the scale—far wider and more conducive to mobilization—of global Islamism, in which it is seeking to inscribe its activities.

Inside the camp, the group has the same goals as Usbat al-Ansar: to provide as much social control as possible, based on strict interpretation of religious norms. Their objective is to transform the Ain al-Helweh camp into an Islamic space on a miniature scale. In 1997, shortly before the renewal of a Fatah military presence in the camp, young salafists boasted of having "given the camp back to the Muslims" by destroying the influence exerted by the *fasa'il*—an expression designating the organizations that make up the PLO—which were seen as "species on the verge of extinction." Islamist pressure can be felt in all areas of life, and increased vigilance has been necessary since satellite dishes appeared, allowing the camp's residents to watch foreign television channels. The small-scale entrepreneur, a Tunisian, who was the first to sell these dishes in the camp was forced to broadcast only Arabic channels to subscribers, so as to block access to pornography. He also launched a pirated channel—HelwehSat—from the camp that broadcasts only advertising and religious songs.

This early experience with broadcast media provided a model for Shaykh Jamal's group, which created a "religious" television station in the summer of 1999: al-Risala ("The Message"), based on the first floor of al-Nur Mosque. Thanks to cable television, the "Islamist forces" now have a new, modern means of expression, accessible to any household with a television and a VCR—in other words, a considerable proportion of the camp's inhabitants. Every morning in December 1999, al-Risala would show the same images of the "holy war" led by the Saudi commander, Khattab, in the Chechen mountains the previous summer. The report, subtitled in Russian and Arabic, showed both how disproportionate the forces were—one could see guerrillas fighting with whatever weapons they had, pitted against Russian war planes—and how successful Islam's warriors were in the field, where they managed to ambush a Russian convoy, borne to victory thanks to their faith. The camera lingered on the broken bodies of enemy soldiers, while martyrs with serene faces were filmed in their green shrouds. At the end of the program, al-Risala carried pirated news bulletins from al-Jazeera, the Qatari station, but a message on the screen told viewers that they were "still with al-Risala." In fact, every time the female anchor appeared on screen, dressed in Western clothes like any of her counterparts at CNN, the censor in al-Nur Mosque would replace the image with the local channel's logo, allowing only the journalist's words to come through. When her male colleague appeared, the image returned. Censorship was also used if, during a report, the images al-Jazeera was broadcasting showed unveiled women onscreen, even if these women were not Muslim, and regardless of the context.[26]

The news was followed by several hours of images from the Intifada, dating back to the late 1980s, while the soundtrack played religious music, produced locally by "Islamist choirs." Sometimes, images of ritual stoning, filmed on pilgrimage in Mecca, were interspersed with pictures of children throwing stones at Israeli soldiers, the physical incarnation of an evil all believers must purge.

These images of the Intifada served a double purpose in the salafists' strategy in the Palestinian camp: immediately received and understood by Ain al-Helweh's population of refugees, they were intended to establish continuity among the different fronts of jihad, and to impose a religious representation of the Arab-Israeli conflict. Al-Risala did not bother with historical coverage of the conflict's causes, or the role of the Palestinian or other Arab political elites; the map of Palestine never appeared on the screen, and no attempt, no matter how partisan, to explain the causes of the conflict was made. On the contrary, history and geography disappeared behind the immediate issue of identity.

These programs also served a tactical purpose. Al-Risala broadcast to the outside world—and thus to the Syrian intelligence services—the image of a militant network that seemed to define itself mainly through its hostility toward Israel and the force associated with it in the camp by Syrian (and therefore Lebanese) security: Yasir Arafat and Fatah. The television channel thereby ensured political safe-conduct for camp Islamists with respect to Damascus.

The question of whether violence may be used is negotiated internally and sometimes gives rise to conflicts among the various salafist groups. In the Usbat al-Ansar network, for instance, members of a "military wing" took the initiative, on June 8, 1999, to machine-gun four judges while they were in session at Saida's Palace of Justice, probably to avenge the execution of four Islamists sentenced in 1997 after the murder of Nizar al-Halabi, the leader of al-Ahbash. The murder of the judges, which Shaykh Jamal publicly denounced in his Friday sermon after the event, does not seem to have been approved by the leaders of the salafist network inside the camp, who were especially concerned with restoring calm after a series of violent acts in Saida and the surrounding area. Less than a month before, the Fatah officer Amin Kayyed and his wife had been killed in Saida.[27] Fatah, which was a victim, like the Lebanese state, of the group's actions, had offered to hand over to the Lebanese government the men responsible for these killings, but the offer, which would have meant a takeover of the camp by "Arafatists," was turned down. Militants inside Fatah said that this refusal was prompted by Syria, which did not want to disturb a status quo it had helped establish during such a sensitive time in the region.[28]

In the Islamic division of labor, Usbat al-Ansar has thus specialized in fighting the Ahbash and agents of the Lebanese state (policemen and magistrates, for instance), which it views as especially guilty of serving the interests of that "heretic" sect, while Ain al-Helweh's salafist networks have taken charge of defending Islamic morality in Saida.

Inside the camp, the al-Nur Mosque group and Usbat al-Ansar thus both play the role of a vice squad or morality police. For members, who are often idle teenagers, this role is not restricted to insulting unveiled women walking alone in Ain al-Helweh's alleyways, or women who dare to speak to visiting strangers (in districts controlled by salafists, most Palestinian women who work for humanitarian associations have been victims of such treatment after conversing with Western experts visiting the camp) but can extend, in certain cases, to meting out punishment that ranges from public humiliation (whipping) to death for those who transgress Islamic morality as they see it. Victims' bodies are usually found in one of the camp's garbage dumps. In June 1992, a DFLP official was assassinated by a bullet to the head on his way home, a bottle of liquor in his hand.

After one young man was whipped for having drunk alcohol, a member of the Usbat al-Ansar leadership declared: "When we have the opportunity to apply Shari'a, we don't hesitate to do so, and we don't seek to hold back in this domain, because it is our legal obligation."[29] This is the case with women accused of adultery, *zina* (sexual relations outside the bounds of marriage), or having undergone or performed abortions. The members of Usbat al-Ansar also execute men suspected of having committed incest (apparently a fairly frequent occurrence in Ain al-Helweh).

According to a study conducted by the Norwegian Institute for Applied Social Sciences (FAFO) that included a sample from all the Palestinian camps, young people show the most conservative attitudes toward women's role in public life: barely more than 20 percent accept the idea of women taking on social and political responsibilities, compared with more than 40 percent of male respondents over forty years of age.[30] It is interesting to observe this generation gap: like all revolutionary movements, the PLO emphasized the role of women in national liberation, and the "Palestinian revolution" witnessed the birth of new role models for women: they were to be emulated not just as mothers but as fighters in khaki military fatigues and kuffiyyehs. This heritage is still visible in the camp, where women play a very important role in all the charitable organizations, including the clinics opened by the Jama'a Islamiyya, which encourages women's involvement in social activism and education. The low levels of support for such involvement among young men under thirty years of age could indicate the success of salafist ideology in this group. In Ain al-Helweh, some preachers are also full-time teachers in UNRWA schools, where they can exert their influence in classes that are gender-segregated for adolescents. According to young Palestinian women who live on the outskirts of Saida but work inside the camp in a humanitarian association, the social control exercised by the Islamists grew considerably stronger in the 1990s. When asked whether they would agree to live in Ain al-Helweh, the women's response was unambiguous: "It's impossible to live in the camp. Here, girls can't go to the beach; they have to wear the veil, avoid saying hello to the boys they meet in the street. It's very tightly controlled."[31]

When Fatah made its comeback, starting in 1998, the Islamists loosened their control, as they no longer enjoyed a monopoly on the use of force within the camp. Their efforts to mete out punishment for religious infractions would have triggered a desire for revenge on the part of the victims' families, and Fatah would have used this opportunity to improve its local recruitment efforts. The presence of Arafat's militia and the interplay of family solidarities progressively dissuaded the zealous guardians of Islamic morality, even though these family ties no longer seem strong enough to maintain a space for intergroup negotiation (see Chapter 4). Walking along the lower road, not far from al-Nur Mosque, one can see signs of popular urban conviviality—backgammon players at the coffee shop and video arcades for teenagers—that testify to the limits of the local strategy of re-Islamicization targeting the camp.

The al-Nur Mosque network, which shares the ideology of the Usbat al-Ansar group and works closely with it, is inscribed at both the local and the transnational levels. Locally, it carried out religious operations similar to those of Usbat al-Ansar: in 1994, a military tribunal condemned three Palestinians for "incitement to confessional hatred, acts of terrorism among the citizenry, and seeking to bring the country back to the time of civil war" after they had attempted to blow up a statue of the Virgin Mary in the Maronite cemetery of al-Namur in Saida, on August 21 of that year.[32] In the years that followed, repeated attacks systematically targeted individuals who sold alcohol, and several stores were blown up near southern Lebanon's capital, a city where liquor is no longer sold.[33] In the country's other "Sunni capital," Tripoli, in the north, similar incidents occurred: bombs were found near the city's nightclubs and cinemas. Shaykh Jamal willingly provides religious justification for such acts (see Chapter 5 on the themes evoked by preachers), and it is plausible to posit a "zone of practical cooperation" between the Usbat al-Ansar circle and the al-Nur Mosque group, with equipment and men being provided by the partisans' "military" wing.

The al-Nur Mosque network, while acting with Usbat al-Ansar on the local level, also seeks to inscribe its actions in the transnational space of global Islamism.[34] Its goal on the international level is to return to action-oriented morality, and not to be satisfied with declarations of intent and hollow speeches. Shaykh Jamal himself explained this conception in a sermon exhorting believers to organize themselves with as much discipline and self-abnegation as their Western enemy—seen as the supreme coordinator of all changes in the Arab and Islamic world—so as to fight back efficiently, or in other words, not only in word but especially in deed:

> These unbelieving nations, my brothers, which fight us ceaselessly and which we claim to confront, these nations work day and night. The lowest employee works sixteen to eighteen hours a day to strengthen his government and defend what his government has acquired, the better to control the nations and peoples to which we belong. Can we fight our enemy when we are in this state of neglect, drowsiness, indifference, when we waste our time, when all the while they are sharpening their swords and slaughtering Muslims in Bosnia-Herzegovina, in Kosovo, in Palestine, and elsewhere? Can we fight them using only words, my brothers, and satisfy ourselves with saying: "Down with America! Down with Israel! Down with the Serbs!" If we continue to say this, what will happen? Nothing. Nothing at all.[35]

On reflection, Shaykh Jamal seemed to have been advocating a form of reverse Orientalism, according to which the first duty of believers is to devote themselves to learning the language and customs of the countries they are combating, so as to understand the secrets of their strength. Perhaps because the shaykh was aware of the contradictions borne by this desire to imitate the West—the image of an Islamist CIA is what emerges, just beneath the surface, from his sermons—he reminded his listeners that the prophet's emissaries never went on a mission without having learned the language of the kings and princes they were going to meet.[36] If Muslims do not try to work "Western-style," with efficiency and discipline, they will be condemned to live under enemy domination, as is the case today:

> War, my brothers, war against the unbelievers: we cannot wage it without determined, serious, and resolute men. Men who don't waste their time, by day or by night. They are always thinking, they are de-

veloping projects, making plans, and setting goals to combat their enemies. This, my friends, is how our enemies act. Look at how they plan everything . . . There are specialists whose only task is to gather everything they find, every piece of information about such and such a country. They plan the way they are going to gain a foothold in a country . . . How they are going to dominate it . . . How they are going to expel the president, and who is going to replace him. These are the things that preoccupy them. They think and act in consequence, and here is where we are today. As for us, we are unable to change a king, a president, or a minister. We don't prepare anything and we don't expel anyone, while they exploit our shortcomings and impose tyranny, dictators, and sin upon us. They are the ones who control us. How can we claim to be masters of our destiny? What must we do to prevent America, or the Jews, from deciding our fate, or the Serbs from deciding that of the Muslims?

This political engagement dates back to the late 1980s, a time when Lebanon was still at war and Shaykh Jamal's mosque emerged as a logistical support center for the Service Bureau for Arab Combatants, created by Abdallah Azzam.

The members of Shaykh Jamal's Jama'a—though they are not the only ones in the camp, or even in Lebanon, to do so—strongly identify with the figure of Osama bin Laden, whom they see as a model to emulate and a jihadist who has terrorized Islam's main enemy worldwide. Unlike political regimes, which ultimately seek to defend their selfish interests, Osama bin Laden to these young men embodies a form of Islamic purity that remains immune to political pressure. The *shabab* (young men) of al-Nur Mosque photocopy his declarations, published in the Arab media, and discreetly swap articles about him, with the feeling of complicity that comes from shared secrets. Some, daydreaming out loud, even joke about "blowing up all the Western embassies in the region." Among the cassette tapes available at the mosque are recordings of Bin Laden's "declaration of jihad against America." Terrorism is unanimously recognized as the only possible solution against an enemy that "only understands violence." The al-Nur Mosque group's participation in a transnational network might also explain the deference the young men show to Shaykh Jamal, who probably owes his appeal as much to the projections of those surrounding him—based on what they know, or think they know, of his international connections—as to his religious knowledge or his skill as a preacher.

Finally, association with the global Islamist movement, in both organization and ideology, could explain why the group's members explicitly reject any "nationalization" of their Muslim identity, which, in their eyes, has become their main source of identification. For example, Shaykh Yasin, the founder of Hamas, who was killed by the Israeli army on March 22, 2004, is never cited in sermons or private conversations, as if his commitment to Islamism is too deeply tainted by Palestinian nationalism and political prudence to mobilize young people who identify first and foremost with the "Islamic nation." To show interest in events taking place in Algeria, Bosnia, or Afghanistan is a mark of commitment to global Islamism. Bomb attacks carried out on American embassies are thus experienced as personal victories reinforcing the group members' impression that, inside the camp, they make up a new fighting elite at the vanguard of Islam.

Terrorism truly fascinates the group's members, especially the younger ones. For instance, those who gather at the al-Huda bookstore think that "religious faith is sufficient to fight the enemy. One just has to be prepared to die for it, even if one has to kill women and children."[37] A few hours after the news that the four judges had been murdered spread inside the camp, young salafists displayed extraordinary excitement. This attitude reflects their hatred of the Lebanese state and their eschatological vision of the region's future.

In the same environment, it is not surprising to find sympathy for the Taliban movement in Afghanistan. An emir from Usbat al-

Ansar expressed this sentiment in the Lebanese press. According to him, the Taliban are

> a movement that works to bring about Islam in conformity with the program laid out by prophecy, and which, for this reason, is exposed to accusations by the enemies of Islam, accusations directed against every sincere Muslim. It is hardly astonishing to see accusations being directed against the Taliban. Before them, the Prophet Muhammad was also accused of lying, witchcraft, and treason. According to what we know, this movement has made no mistakes until now. Essentially, it is a jihadist Islamic movement *(haraka islamiyya jihadiyya)*.[38]

At the time of writing, ten years after the end of the 1991 Gulf War, the salafist dynamic still dominates in Ain al-Helweh. Experts describe the camp today as one of the places in the Middle East where al-Qa'ida's presence seems strongest.[39] After the attacks of September 11, 2001, the media paid special attention to Usbat al-Ansar, the jihadist organization whose emir, Abu Mahjin (Abd al-Karim Sa'di), was sentenced to death in absentia by a Lebanese court for the assassination of Nizar al-Halabi on August 31, 1995. Usbat al-Ansar was described as a small group removed from the rest of Lebanese society, or a circle of disjointed visionaries with grand dreams of global Islamist revolution, whose aspirations belie their inability to exercise a lasting impact on society. The rhetoric and practices of this fundamentalist militia lends credence to such an interpretation. The utopian dimension—the creation, here and now, of a Sunni emirate in a country where Sunni Islam is in the minority—as well as a preference for secrecy and clandestine activity, frequent recourse to violence both inside and outside the camp, the group's spatial location (apparently circumscribed to certain neighborhoods of Ain al-Helweh): all these support the idea of a sectarian splinter group whose members have proven incapable of widening their social base, and who have no political perspective. Swept up in a deadly, and politically unproductive, spiral, they provoke collective reprisals on the part of the Lebanese government that affect all the camp's inhabitants.[40]

The group's leaders, for their part, work to maintain an image of what Michel Wieviorka has called a "social anti-movement," by inverting the three criteria that define social movements in action sociology.[41] They do not claim to protect the interests of a specific, concrete social collectivity—the Sunni Lebanese community, for instance, since they condemn its corrupt elites—but prefer to express themselves through an abstract principle: the defense of Islam. Innumerable enemies, with whom they are engaged in a struggle to the death, populate their environment. Finally, no frame of reference exists that can be shared with the various actors in Lebanese society, since their ultimate goal is not to "lead society now, but to spill over into a realm beyond this one, presented in more or less elaborate terms."[42]

Though not inaccurate, this representation remains incomplete. Usbat al-Ansar is indeed the military manifestation of a more diffuse, profound social phenomenon. It is the product of an environment created in the late 1980s that allowed religious activists to connect with international Islamist networks and thus set up militant sanctuaries. Imaginary migration toward Peshawar reflected a withdrawal into the camps, seen as the sites for a new kind of preaching activity, designed to distance the refugees from "infidel" Palestinian organizations. The excessive attention paid to individual characters (like Abu Mahjin) makes it impossible to understand the social production of jihadist Islamism and its effects, in terms of significance and self-representation, for an unquantifiable proportion of the refugee population. Jihadist Islam thus has an effective social base in the urbanized camps of the Lebanese coast and in the country's Sunni areas. Unlike the Algeria Armed Islamic Group (GIA), Usbat al-Ansar has never given in to indiscriminate violence, since such behavior—which is difficult to contemplate in the context of the camps—would have cut it off from its local support base, to the immediate benefit of competing organizations. Furthermore, groups like Usbat al-Ansar are able (as we saw in the first chapter) to share a frame of reference with far more powerful Islamist organizations, like Hezbollah, in the name of a united front condemning U.S. policy in Iraq, for instance, or supporting the Intifada in the Palestinian territories. Between these two opposite configurations—the tiny group and the social movement—is a conceptual vacuum where these militant Islamists find a place.

CHAPTER 3

The Struggle against al-Ahbash

The Islamic Society for Charitable Works (jam'iyyat al-mashari' al-khayriyya al-islamiyya), known as al-Ahbash, is officially headed by the Ethiopian shaykh Abdallah al-Hirari. According to his official biography, al-Hirari was born in 1920 in Ethiopia, in the village of Hirara, near the Somali border.[1] In 1947 Emperor Haile Selassie expelled him from Ethiopia for unspecified political reasons. At the time, al-Hirari was mufti for the region. He went on to the Hijaz, in Saudi Arabia, and associated with mystical orders during trips to Jerusalem and Damascus. He settled in Beirut in 1950 and emerged from anonymity only in the early 1980s, at a time when the Syrian regime had barely begun to sort out its open conflict with the Muslim Brothers.

In 1983, Shaykh Hirari found himself the nominal head of the Islamic Society for Charitable Works, which had lacked a leader since its founding in Beirut in 1930. In fact, the shaykh served mainly to confer religious legitimacy on a project headed by a graduate of the Dar al-Fatwa teaching center, Shaykh Nizar al-Halabi, who managed the association very efficiently, by retrieving the idle recruits of a neighborhood militia and working closely with a former wrestler, "Doctor" Adnan Tarabulsi. Through militia tactics that blended brutality and intimidation, the Ahbash in the 1980s seized the mosques of Burj Abu Haidar, Zuqqat al-Blat, and Basta Fawqa in the capital's western neighborhoods, imposing their own inter-

113

pretation of the sacred texts and ousting Dar al-Fatwa's legally appointed shaykhs.

Muhammad Nukkari, currently principal private secretary to the mufti of the Lebanese republic, was the preacher at one of the mosques the Ahbash wished to control, as well as a victim of the group's tactics during the "war of the mosques":

> Eleven-year-old children would come and ask questions. If we didn't answer the way they wanted, they would take the responsibility of excommunicating us. That is how they worked, especially after the death of mufti Hasan Khalid . . . In almost all of Beirut's Sunni families, there is a member or a sympathizer of the Ahbash. The leadership is not sincere, and no one knows who they work for. They tell people they can make religious judgments although they have had no training.[2]

Despite the protests emanating from Dar al-Fatwa, which is still seeking to regain control over these places of worship, none of the mosques has been restored to the administration of pious foundations, for any such attempt is vetoed by Syria. The veto will be lifted the day the Ahbash cease to be useful locally or become too burdensome as allies.

Even though the Ahbash claim to belong to the Rifa'iyya Sufi order, they are actually the mirror image of Sunni opposition movements, whose doctrinal references and historical figures they have worked to discredit. The only constant in their cobbled-together religious ideology is their systematic opposition to political Islamism's articles of faith. Far from opening up new intellectual perspectives for a renewal of Islam on the part of Muslim reformers, however, such opposition is expressed essentially through sectarian, threatening behavior that not only targets the figures of contemporary Islam but deliberately situates itself outside the framework of Sunni orthodoxy as it was constructed starting in the tenth and eleventh centuries. The Sunni tradition, imbued as it is with political realism, has always sought consensus and therefore refused to reintroduce arguments regarding legitimacy of succession and the question of the caliphate, which are the source of Islam's main schisms.

By describing Mu'awiyya, the governor of Damascus, as "seditious" and taking the side of Ali, his adversary, Shaykh al-Hirari adopts the Shi'ite tradition of paying special respect to certain members of the Prophet's family—Ali, Fatima, Hasan, and Husayn—while condemning the caliph Mu'awiyya and his son Yazid.[3] The Ahbash thereby reject the dominant values of their religious community; they break with Sunni tradition by granting a symbolic concession to "Alid legitimism" (in the words of Henri Laoust and P. K. Hitti) in the Lebanese context, where tension between Sunnis and Shi'ites is particularly sharp.

To refute Ahbash doctrine, Lebanon's salafist shaykhs place the terms of the debate in the framework of theological differences that cut through classical Islam in the tenth and eleventh centuries. The Ahbash are thus described as new Mu'tazilites who engage in "speculative theology" ('ilm al-kalam) and spend all their time indulging in allegorical exegesis of the divine attributes (al-ta'wil fil-sifat) and in the pleasures of dialectics, all for the purpose of overcoming their opponents.[4] Whereas the greatest traditionalists chose to confirm the existence of divine attributes without attempting to explain their significance or inquire into their modalities (bila kayf), the Ahbash are accused of slipping into anthropomorphism and thereby betraying the teachings of Imam al-Ash'ari, which they exploit nevertheless.[5] This practice is considered contrary to the orientations (minhaj) of the "pious ancestors" (al-salaf), who, while affirming that God does indeed have physical attributes, are careful to defer to Him (tafwid) for their interpretation.[6] Worse still, according to detractors of the Ahbash, their propensity for declaring takfir (an accusation of apostasy) against anyone who does not think like they do puts them on the same level as the kharijites (this comparison is generally made to the detriment of radical Islamism), whose doctrinal exclusivism they share, though they add to it a degree of hypocrisy that did not characterize the kharijites.

By rejecting wholesale an essential part of the Sunni religious heritage, the Ahbash are not engaging in courageous intellectual reform, as some commentators would have it.[7] On the contrary, they are further obscuring the boundaries between Islamism and institutional Islam by offering radical Islamists the possibility of declaring themselves the ultimate defenders—and therefore the representatives—of a tradition richer and more nuanced than the reified vision they derive from it. The salafist Islamists, for their part, accuse the Ahbash of doing nothing to hasten the coming of "God's kingdom on earth," an apocalyptic dimension of their faith that they value as much as the other main tenets of Islam.

In southern Lebanon, the Ahbash set up a "regional center" in the Ain al-Helweh camp and built a monumental mosque (Salah al-Din) in the neighborhood of Hittin in the early 1990s. The site was not chosen randomly: by making it a priority to occupy Sunni areas, as they did in the north and the capital, the Ahbash are opposing their Islamist enemies on their home turf through neighborhood control and social work.

The Ahbash often use the same mobilization methods and target the same individuals as the Muslim Brothers. Unlike their competitors, however, they enjoy close ties with Syrian intelligence in Lebanon. Contrary to the assertions of the sect's supporters, the Islamic Society for Charitable Works would never have been created were it not for the Syrian security services. Prompted by General Ghazi Kan'an, the security forces designed the organization in the mid-1980s as an instrument of police control over religious circles, a tool to divide Sunni Islam, and a war machine against political Islam.[8] Just as they did with other groups in Lebanon, the Syrians created the Ahbash to weaken the Sunni community from the inside—the movement is banned in Syria—and, further upstream, to break any desire for political affirmation. The Ahbash's main opponent, the Jama'a Islamiyya (the Lebanese Muslim Brothers), under Fathi Yakan's leadership, was careful to distinguish its relations with the Syrian regime from the confrontational strategy adopted by the Syrian Muslim Brothers in the 1970s and 1980s. Yet despite its leaders' declarations of allegiance, it cannot claim the same status as the Ahbash in its relations with Syria's ruling elites.

Seen from Damascus, there is a fundamental divide between "organic allies," on the one hand, who make up what could be called the "Syrian party" in Lebanon, and "political allies" on the other. The Ahbash belong to the first category. On the secular scene, their equivalent can be found in groups like the Lebanese Ba'th Party; the Palestinian groups Sa'iqa, PFLP-General Command, and Fatah-Intifada; or the late Antun Sa'deh's Syrian national socialist party. The influence of these groups has been greatly diminished, even if most of them continue to be effective tools in the hands of Syrian security forces in Lebanon. The Ahbash are no exception in this respect; in addition, they had a capacity for popular action among the Lebanese Sunni population in post-war Lebanon that made them far more efficient than a mere pro-Syrian militia. As for Syria's "political allies," their connections outside of Lebanon grant them relative autonomy from the Syrian authorities. This autonomy is directly dependent on the importance that Damascus gives these external forces, and the ability of the latter to exert a moderating influence on Syria's Lebanese policy. The Jama'a Islamiyya, for instance, receives Saudi assistance, which Syria must consider when dealing with the Lebanese Muslim Brothers.[9] Organic allies owe their very existence to the Syrian state; political allies, by contrast, are conditional allies whose allegiance can never be taken for granted. Thus, in the framework of its regional policy, Damascus has used the Ahbash to counter Saudi influence among Lebanese Sunnis, in the hope of fostering religious divisions.

Before the political revolution that resulted in the Syrian military withdrawal from Lebanon in April 2005, the Ahbash openly declared their allegiance to former Syrian president Hafiz al-Asad and organized regular demonstrations in support of the Syrian regime, evoking the "shared destiny of Syria and Lebanon" *(wahdat al-masarayn bayna Lubnan wa Suriya)*. On August 1 every year, celebrations were held to mark "Lebanese and Syrian Armed Forces Day," with the participation of Syria's closest Lebanese allies. The Ahbash also invited the representatives of Lebanon's "Syrian party" to attend events commemorating the "corrective movement" *(al-haraka al-tas'hihiyya)* in Syria, the occasion of Hafiz al-Asad's accession to power.[10]

Syria's goal in creating the Ahbash was to protect itself against direct challenges and delegate control over Islamist circles to a seemingly autonomous organization. Syrian ambitions, like those of the British administration in Egypt during Lord Cromer's time, were to remain more or less hidden; Damascus would pull the strings without ever giving the impression of direct intervention.[11] This strategy, however, was not entirely risk-free; it caused frustrations to build and occasionally led to the impression that the Ahbash and Damascus were one and the same.[12] In Ain al-Helweh, the most acerbic comments directed against Syria mention the Ahbash, who are (justly) accused of reporting to the Syrian *mukhabarat:* "They spend their time watching and denouncing us," complained one Palestinian student, a member of the Jama'a who studied at the Lebanese University and lives in Ain al-Helweh. In Wadi Zayneh, a neighborhood with a high concentration of Palestinians, a dozen kilometers north of Saida, a Palestinian preacher blamed the Ahbash and their repeated accusations for numerous summonses that residents received to appear before Syrian intelligence officers:

As soon as we finished building our center, they denounced us to the Syrians, saying that we wanted to encourage seditious activities against the Syrian authorities among the neighborhood residents. We had to explain to the intelligence officer that we sought only the neighborhood's welfare and that we didn't want to cause any problems. Another time, after a sermon on the threat represented by the spread of Christian missions in Saida, the Ahbash accused us of spreading sectarian strife. We were summoned again. The Syrian services have us under very tight control. Here, people can't get involved in politics or carry weapons. It's not the way it is in the camps.[13]

Every year on Syrian Armed Forces Day, the Ahbash chartered buses and offered the refugees of Ain al-Helweh a free trip to the capital, in a bid to increase the crowds at Beirut's municipal stadium. The Ahbash were also the most ardent promoters of the personality cult surrounding the late Syrian president.[14]

In fact, Sunni Islamists resented the Ahbash less for their close relations with Damascus than for their refusal to allow the rest of the community to benefit from the advantages they had gained through their good relations with the Syrian security apparatus. The Ahbash were thereby breaking the implicit rules governing patron-client relationships in the region: the benefits of protection conferred by the patron, in this case, Syria, must be shared with other members of the client's group.

The Ahbash in fact exploit their status as clients to the detriment of the Sunni Muslim community to which they belong. Indeed, their power ultimately rests on their ability to divide, and therefore to weaken, a Sunni community they will never be able to conquer, both because of their methods and because of the content of their doctrine. Far from valuing Islamic moderation and tolerance, they do not hesitate to use violence and provocation, not against the ruling authorities but to their benefit, and to the detriment of the many Sunni Muslims who do not think as they do. They thereby run the risk of inciting some of the Sunnis to take refuge with Islamist groups and seek their protection.

Shaykh Halabi's Assassination and the Logic of Sectarianism

The Lebanese public first heard Abu Mahjin's name at the end of 1995, several months after Shaykh Nizar al-Halabi was assassinated on August 31. The security forces arrested five young men, three Lebanese nationals and two Palestinians. Before taking violent action, these men had been harassed by the Ahbash in the mosque of Beirut's Arab University, in the heart of the popular Sunni neighborhood of Tariq al-Jidaydeh, where Islamist groups usually control street politics. In prison, they "confessed" to having undergone military training with the head of Usbat al-Ansar in the Ain al-Helweh camp. From then on, the Lebanese judiciary—in this case, the Council of Justice, a special court authorized to handle any breach of "national security"—considered Abu Mahjin the "brains" behind the operation, and condemned him to death in absentia on January 17, 1997. The tribunal also issued death sentences for three of the five men arrested. The sentence was carried out on March 24, 1997: the three Islamists—a Palestinian, Munir Abbud, and two Lebanese men, Ahmad al-Qassam and Khalid Hamid—were hanged at dawn in the courtyard of Rumiyyeh Prison. To prevent possible disturbances, domestic security forces and the Lebanese army were put on alert in the capital and in Saida.

Everything about this affair was exceptional: the speed with which the authorities expedited the whole process (investigation, arrests, legal proceedings, execution), the political character of the institution responsible for judging the guilty parties, and the brutality of the final punishment. These factors provoked an emotional response in Sunni religious circles, whose proposals during the trial for a theological explanation of the motives had been rebuffed by the tribunal. Several ulemas from Dar al-Fatwa officially declared their solidarity with the condemned men and attempted to have their sentences commuted. The mufti of the republic, for his part, maintained an embarrassed silence.

These ulemas faced two proverbial lines in the sand during the crisis. They had no qualms about crossing the first—the code regulating relations among elites of the different religious communities—but prudently stopped at the second, which concerns Syria's role in the country, and the memory of the conflict between Damascus and the Islamists. The first line was crossed when several ulemas from Dar al-Fatwa directly challenged the (Maronite) head of state to explain the failure of their intercessions on behalf of the condemned men. As head of a delegation made up of several clerics, the mufti of Mount Lebanon, Shaykh Muhammad Ali al-Juzu, was not received by President Elias Hrawi, and ultimately held the president responsible for the execution of the three men.

By insisting that the president was solely responsible for the executions, and thereby running the risk of inciting sectarianism, Shaykh al-Juzu was conveniently able to avoid naming the people who had actually inspired the judiciary's decision. This kind of scapegoating was used throughout the war, has reappeared since then, and is certainly one of the most serious side effects of the Syrian presence in Lebanon, undermining the credibility of declarations regarding the positive role Damascus has played in national reconciliation since the end of the Lebanese conflict. This strategy can be summed up as follows: when, in a given situation, the balance of power is so unfavorable that it would be dangerous to point out the actual decision makers behind a particular action, yet at the same time the community and religious elites cannot remain indifferent to an event perceived as a challenge to their authority and an attack on the interests of the group they represent, it becomes politically useful for them to direct their community's anger against the representatives of another, politically weaker group. In other words, "if you can't strike who you want, strike who you can." By turning their anger against the weakest party, the disaffected group can consolidate its internal solidarity in the short term and reestablish its integrity, to the detriment of any hope for a peaceful coexistence. The ulemas who were most involved in the struggle against the Ahbash thus chose to challenge the personal attitude of the president of the republic—which, according to them, was motivated purely by Maronite resentment of Muslims—rather than naming the Syrian sponsors of the rival organization.

The close ties between the Syrian authorities and al-Ahbash are behind the diligence shown by Lebanon's judiciary, which, for once, fulfilled its role. This time, Syrian reprisals for Islamist violence were carried out through the Lebanese state apparatus in the form of the courts. Everyone in Lebanon realized that this was the case, but of course it was impossible to say so in public. Outside the country, by contrast, things were stated much more directly. In an article titled "The Execution of the Martyrs: A New Chapter of Oppression in Lebanon," *Nida'ul Islam,* a jihadist magazine published in Australia, described the "heretical sect of the Habashies" as an invention consistent with plans for a "new world order" destined to strike against the "Islamic awakening" in Lebanon and all of Greater Syria.[15] The sect, which had at its disposal "considerable funds of unknown provenance," used violence and assassinations during the war of the mosques, and was now seeking to "seize the resources" of Dar al-Fatwa, the better to "spread its ideology" and arouse hatred among Muslims. The assassination of Shaykh Nizar al-Halabi, "a beautifully executed mission," was carried out in this climate. The trial was described as a parody of justice: contrary to what took place in Egypt, the ulemas were not allowed to provide religious expertise in defining the organization Halabi headed, which would allegedly have legitimized his execution and made it possible to emphasize the apostasy of al-Ahbash.

The most interesting part of the article dealt with the regional situation. As the author stated, it was impossible to isolate this political ruling from the local and regional climate. The new Lebanese regime, seen as no different from other apostate regimes in its struggle against Islam, was merely obeying orders from Damascus "to the letter," since it was considered impossible for the Lebanese regime to carry out this punishment without its leaders' consent. During the civil war, the article continued, Muslims' rights had been shamelessly attacked, especially after the strikes carried out by Syrian forces in Tripoli, Beirut, and other cities. By making a martyr of the Islamic movement in Lebanon, the Lebanese regime was thus conforming to the wishes expressed by Damascus, which sought to neutralize any opposition to the peace plans being hatched for the region—plans to which, the article argued, the Islamic movement posed the only obstacle.

Usbat al-Ansar and the Defense of Lebanese Sunnism

Ain al-Helweh's Islamist jihadists experienced the struggle against the Ahbash brotherhood first and foremost as the confirmation of a break between their own group, on the one hand, and Hezbollah and Iran, on the other, after Shaykh Sharaydi's assassination. It was becoming more obviously contradictory to polarize forces around the defense of Sunnism while maintaining visible ties with the political representatives of Shi'ite Islam in Lebanon. By placing themselves on the front lines of the anti-Ahbash struggle, and by transforming what had initially been merely one of Hezbollah's military arms in Ain al-Helweh into a religious militia serving radical Sunni Islam, Usbat al-Ansar's militants moved from the space of the Palestinian revolution to that of a wider struggle. Nizar al-Halabi's assassination had international repercussions in the Islamic world, making Usbat al-Ansar known beyond Lebanon's borders. With this success, the Ansar acquired the financial means to free themselves from their former Iranian sponsor, to acquire social visibility inside Ain al-Helweh, and to attract some of the camp's young people, who had become socially disaffected since the end of the Lebanese war and politically disoriented by the signing of the Oslo Accords and the complex labyrinth of Palestinian-Israeli negotiations. The struggle against the Ahbash therefore prompted an intensification of Sunni identity and gave rise to militant solidarities with new political affiliations. A division specific to radical Lebanese Islamism (the "Brothers" versus the "Ethiopians") made its way into the camps and was felt very strongly by the inhabitants: at least for some of the refugees, this development in itself indicates a decrease in the intensity of Palestinian identity (in the sense that it no longer screens the entry of external conflicts); a "Lebanization" of religious life in the camps, which have integrated the divisions of Lebanese Islam; and involvement in causes that have little to do with the Palestinian struggle.[16]

Faced with the Ahbash's militant offensive, Abu Mahjin exploited Dar al-Fatwa's powerlessness and the frustration experienced by certain segments of the Sunni community to invest his group with a grandiose mission: the defense of Sunnism in Lebanon. Shaykh Halabi's assassination was thus an "ideological victory" for Usbat al-Ansar in the mid-1990s. On this particular question the group managed to put its specific objective—fighting the Ahbash—on the agenda of a far wider religious community.[17]

In their attempt to defend Sunnism, the new salafist militants in Ain al-Helweh sought to re-create a form of action morality in the vacuum that had ensued when, in the 1980s, the ideal of armed struggle was gradually abandoned under local and international pressure. In the past, armed struggle in the Palestinian movement represented an outlet: its purpose was not so much to contribute concretely to the reconquest of Palestine as to affirm a shared Palestinian identity and attachment to a certain territory, beyond the contingencies of dispersion throughout the various Arab countries in the region. In the 1990s, on the local level of the camp, jihadist militants subverted that link between action and identity. They no longer preached armed struggle to "liberate" Palestine, a task impossible to implement from Lebanon once Hezbollah had built its monopoly in the south of the country; instead, by insisting that true believers take immediate action, they were exhorting the faithful to commit acts of violence disconnected from any territorial struggle.

Before taking violent action against the Ahbash leader, the members of the salafist network attended sessions aimed at explaining the doctrine of Shaykh Halabi's organization and its deviant character in relation to Sunni orthodoxy. Trained shaykhs in Ain al-Helweh's mosques provided a public that did not master the corpus of Islamic texts with the intellectual instruments necessary to upend the Ahbash's religious posturing and contest the organization's dialectics.

Thus, in the early 1990s, young Palestinians from the Muslim Student Union had already invited Hasan al-Qatarji, a Lebanese shaykh who taught *hadith* sciences at Dar al-Fatwa's Faculty of Islamic Law in Lebanon, to lecture at al-Nur Mosque on the dangers inherent in rashly using *takfir* and about the conditions for its valid use, as established by Muslim theologians and jurists *(fuqaha)* in Islamic history.[18] The theme of Hasan al-Qatarji's lecture was not chosen randomly, for the Ahbash were notorious for their propensity to brand as apostates all those who rejected their interpretation of the religious texts. In the introduction they wrote to the lecture, the editors of *al-Hidaya* recapped their guest's academic career, noting that he had "received lessons from the very best shaykhs." After an early education at Dar al-Fatwa's al-Azhar Faculty in Beirut, Hasan al-Qatarji attended the Islamic Faculty in Damascus for two years, and then went to Saudi Arabia, where he studied at the Faculty of Theological Sciences in Riyadh. There, he "learned from the great ulemas of the Hijaz region and took lessons in jurisprudence *(fiqh)* and its principles, as well as *hadith* and *sunna* sciences."

In his talk, delivered as he sat between Shaykh Ghunaym and Shaykh Jamal Khattab, Shaykh al-Qatarji denounced the "grave threats" posed to religion by all those who rush to pronounce *takfir* against their coreligionists: as long as it is not justified by irrevocable arguments, he explained, the accusation of *kufr* will turn against the person who makes it, and who is thereby guilty of having sown discord in the community. He emphasized the gravity of such action, not only in religious terms (it becomes acceptable to kill a Muslim who has been found guilty of apostasy; and that person, if he does not repent before he dies, is condemned to eternal hellfire) but also socially, since *takfir* tears Muslim society apart from within, dramatically inverting the image of a community united against its enemies: when Muslims are divided they conclude alliances with non-Muslims. As Shaykh al-Qatarji saw it, the gravest threat posed by the manipulation of *takfir*—here the audience understood that the salafist shaykh was referring indirectly to the Ahbash's behavior—is that it saps Muslim energies:

> The outcome of this serious issue is that Muslims are currently turning away from the path traced out for them by our Lord, the Almighty. Our Lord has commanded us to combat God's enemies and to participate like the soldiers of Islam in the struggle against ignorance *(al-jahiliyya)*. Otherwise, the fight will no longer pit Muslims against *kuffar* but will be among Muslims: between factions, communities, confessions . . . This is the gravest threat whose effects we can see today.[19]

By recalling the reservations of traditional Muslim theologians toward the issue of *takfir,* and by emphasizing that these theologians were fully aware of the serious consequences that such a decision could entail, both for the guilty party and for the community of believers as a whole, Shaykh Hasan al-Qatarji, in turn, was indirectly accusing those who would make unconsidered use of such a weapon. In that regard, whoever misused *takfir* placed himself at the margins of a religious tradition that has worked to circumscribe the practice and limit the dangers it poses. Shaykh al-Qatarji could cite Islam's greatest jurists in his denunciation of the hasty use of *takfir;* for example, he could turn the teachings of al-Ash'ari, an eminent theologian, against those who, like the Ahbash, called themselves Ash'arites, and back up his argument with a citation from an Ash'arite ulema, Taqiyy al-Din al-Subki (d. 1355), who, when questioned about *takfir,* replied that it was "better to spare a hundred unbelievers than to spill one drop of a Muslim's blood."[20]

Shaykh Hasan al-Qatarji also heads the Association of Islamic Unity (Jam'iyyat al-Ittihad al-Islami), which has its headquarters in the Beirut neighborhood of Basta, and which established a center less than six miles from Saida in 2005. Shaykh al-Qatarji does not just hold conferences in Ain al-Helweh; thanks to the contributions he collects on his frequent trips to the Arabian Peninsula, he is also one of the main donors of the *zakat* committee at al-Nur Mosque. His view of the refugees is purely sectarian; he sees them as a population persecuted because of their adherence to Sunni Islam. This vision allows him to gather money in Saudi Arabia in the name of defending Sunni Islam; it also influences the way the refugees perceive their own identity. The struggle against the Ahbash, which receives widespread support in Saudi Arabia, allows him to request funds from very diverse circles. But beyond the battle against a religious sect that is, after all, marginal, his goal is to reinforce the demographic weight of Sunnis in Lebanon, in order to prepare them for a possible clash with Shi'ite Muslims.

Dar al-Fatwa in Disrepute

The vast majority of spontaneous reactions that followed the sentences passed against Nizar al-Halabi's alleged assassins illustrated Dar al-Fatwa's virtual lack of legitimacy in the eyes of many Lebanese Sunni Muslims.

Dar al-Fatwa suffers from an original sin dating back to the historical conditions of its creation. During the Ottoman period, the mufti of Beirut was an employee of the imperial state attached to Istanbul's religious administration: his role was to diffuse fatwas, control the local ulemas, and administer religious schools and the assets of pious foundations. As an official body representing Sunni Islam, Dar al-Fatwa was created in 1922 by the French government, which was a mandatory power at the time, to oversee the management of pious foundations in Lebanon and Syria. The context was one of hostility on the part of Sunni Muslims in the region, most of whom opposed the dismantling of Greater Syria (Bilad al-Sham) by a foreign power. The French high commissioner in the Levant, General Gouraud, sought to use the creation of Dar al-Fatwa to readjust the status of the Sunni Muslim majority, by aligning its administration with that of the other religious communities, a move that provoked outspoken reactions from the religious establishment.[21] The institutionalization of Sunni Islam by the mandatory power may have reduced the corruption that had become endemic in the last years of the Ottoman Empire, but it also led to the imposition of French control over pious foundations.

In a bid to complete the nationalization of Sunni Islam, the high commissioner created the office of mufti of the republic in 1932. This post should have gone to the mufti of Beirut, Shaykh Mustafa Naji, but he turned it down in protest over the creation of Greater Lebanon. As a result, an electoral college made up of thirty-six ulemas chose a new mufti, Muhammad Tawfiq Khalid, the same year. Khalid was keen to restore legitimacy to an institution whose future was now linked to Lebanon's national existence, and to that end he allied with a *za'im* (political notable) from Beirut, Riyadh al-Sulh, in opposing the mandate authorities. Religious circles publicly denounced "the involvement of a non-Muslim authority in Muslim affairs" within the framework of the struggle for national independence. When Riyadh al-Sulh became prime minister in 1943, the mufti was rewarded for his political support: he received financing for the construction of Dar al-Fatwa's compound in the heart of Beirut, in the A'isha Bakkar neighborhood.

The nationalist struggle, however, concealed another question: that of Dar al-Fatwa's independence as a religious institution in relation to the state. Until 1955, the Lebanese government had refrained from modifying the arrangements it inherited from the mandatory power. After Muhammad Tawfiq Khalid died in 1951, Maronite president Camille Chamoun allied himself with the new mufti, Muhammad Alaya, thereby reviving the question of Dar al-Fatwa's autonomy from political power. Some suggested that the president institute a total separation between religious institutions and the state on both the financial and the political levels. On January 13, 1955, the Lebanese government headed by Prime Minister Sami al-Sulh ratified legislative Decree 18, which became the reference text for the organization of the Sunni community in Lebanon. This legislative decree *(marsum ishtira'i)* sought to bestow "total independence" on the Sunni community by officially recognizing the existence of a Supreme Islamic Council (al-Majlis al-Shar'i al-Islami al-'A'la) that benefited from the delegation of legislative powers and elaborated laws regarding the community's internal affairs, without intervention on the part of the National Assembly.[22]

From that point on, the status of the Sunni community was similar to that of the other Lebanese communities, which administer their religious assets autonomously. Although the council remained independent in principle, links were maintained between the (Sunni) council's presidency and Dar al-Fatwa, especially concerning the appointment of the religious institution's administrators.[23] The process whereby the mufti is appointed, and the make-up of the Islamic electoral college (al-Majlis al-Intikhabi al-Islami), as provided for in the decree, gave effective preeminence to the Sunni political notables and to the civilian members of the community rather than to high-ranking clerics, who were now in the minority. Subsequently, a continual intermingling of the secular and the religious took place despite the 1955 reform, and sometimes originated from authorities outside the framework of the Sunni community, as had been the case in 1952. Shaykh Hasan Khalid, who was elected in 1966, thus benefited from the support of (Maronite) President Fuad Shihab, whose goal was to weaken the political influence exercised by Beiruti *za'im* Sa'ib Salam, president of the powerful Maqasid Society.[24]

Lebanon's Islamists opposed the mufti nomination process and demanded that the electoral college be expanded in favor of the most active religious figures within its ranks. Their goal was to "guarantee wider Islamic participation in the mufti's election, and to endow him with the Muslim vote of confidence, to back up Dar al-Fatwa and its institutions."[25] They sought especially to strengthen the militant base of the electoral college to include "a representative of every Islamic association," as well as "representatives from the mosque committees" and "influential figures in Islamic charity work." By imbuing the mufti's election with a religious hue and giving a voice to the "living forces" of Sunni Islam, the Islamists wanted to open up the institution to different trends of Lebanese Islamism whose adherents challenged the mufti's representativeness as well as his institutional ties to the state. The Islamists therefore sought a mufti who would be subject to their influence, and who could be removed at any time if he did not meet their expectations. According to this model, the mufti would be powerless and answerable to the most radical segments of the Sunni population in Lebanon.

Contrary to these expectations, the institutional reform devised by advisers close to Rafiq al-Hariri, like Radwan al-Sayyid and Muhammad al-Samak, and carried out on December 28, 1996, reduced the mufti's electoral base by a considerable margin, further increasing his dependence on the political authorities. The Supreme Islamic Council modified the legislative decree of January 13, 1955, organizing the election process for the post of mufti of the republic, so that the Islamic electoral council was thereafter composed of the current prime minister, former prime ministers, current Sunni ministers and deputies, members of the Supreme Islamic Council, regional muftis, retired religious judges, Dar al-Fatwa's secretaries from Beirut and Tripoli, and, finally, the general administrative director of pious foundations. On the very day the reform was carried out, Shaykh Muhammad Rashid Qabbani, who had been interim mufti since May 18, 1989, when his predecessor, Hasan Khalid, was assassinated, was unanimously elected by the eighty-six members present. Rafiq al-Hariri publicly endorsed the mufti and, as an ex officio member of the Supreme Islamic Council, officially presented Shaykh Qabbani's candidacy, with the unanimous approval of all the council's members as well as all the former ministers who were still alive at the time. Two days before he was elected, the mufti had been received in Damascus by President Hafiz al-Asad, which deterred any dissident candidates, and immediately put an end to the increasing mobilization of Lebanon's ulemas, who had been excluded from the vote.[26]

Before the reform, in fact, the electoral body had represented approximately 2,700 people; the December 1996 decree brought it down to a limit of 100 people and excluded most current Sunni religious officials. According to the Islamist sectors of Lebanese society, the reform was designed to keep Sunni Islam out and neutralize its opposition potential. In their view, the Shi'ites represent the countermodel, for they benefit from powerful, independent community institutions that draw their legitimacy from very broad popular representation, while the mufti electoral base keeps shrinking away.[27] After the 1996 reform, Rafiq al-Hariri was seen as the "supreme voter" for the mufti of the republic. In a Friday sermon, the secretary-general of the Jama'a Islamiyya, Shaykh Faysal al-Mawlawi, surmised that the Hariri government took this step to rein in all criticism and make religion a policy instrument.[28] From his mosque in Saida, Shaykh Maher Hammud lambasted the renewal of the mufti's mandate as a "tragi-comedy" and a "humiliation (ihana) for all Muslim men and women." The only person responsible for this situation was "Rafiq al-Hariri, who wants to impose total control over all public and private institutions." According to Maher Hammud, the question was not merely the personal fate of Shaykh Muhammad Rashid Qabbani, since Dar al-Fatwa had lost its representative capacity and "become an annex of the Lebanese government."[29]

When the mufti's opponents denounce his "weakness," they are referring not only to the officeholder's lack of charisma but especially to his submission to the prime minister and his inability to resist political orders, for want of a militant base like those supporting the religious leaders of Lebanon's other communities. Though they denounce the mufti's personality and actions, however, opponents have also benefited from his inability—or refusal—to exercise his authority. As a result of his ineffectual leadership, they have gained freedom of speech and great autonomy from an institution that is normally responsible for controlling both their religious management, at the organizational level, and their interpretation of Islam, at the doctrinal level.

On paper, the mufti, as "religious leader of Muslims," is responsible for all Dar al-Fatwa's offices. As such, he controls the administration of pious foundation assets and heads the only institution equipped to manage the interests of Sunni Islam: the Supreme Islamic Council. He appoints civil servants and religious leaders—imam, *khatib*, teacher, Qur'an reader, and *muezzin*—supervises their promotion, controls their deontology, and can remove them from office at his discretion. He monitors the conditions affecting Muslims and makes sure that their religious and social interests are respected throughout Lebanon; he exercises authority over the regional muftis, who take their orders directly from him. He is supposed to oversee the sermons and Islamic awareness programs that are submitted for his approval once every three months. The mufti's wide-ranging power over Sunni Islam in Lebanon provides further fuel to the arguments of all those who wish to subject the institution to the supervision of the community base it is supposed to represent.

Paradoxically, though, if the mufti did actually exercise the authority delegated to him, his critics inside and outside the institution would soon be the first victims of this reestablishment of central control. Indeed, they have benefited from his impotence by creating niches for themselves within the institution and enjoying de facto independence on the local level.[30] The protests voiced in December 1996 must therefore be read as a warning to the mufti not to change the status quo. According to the dean of al-Da'wa College, Shaykh Abd al-Nasir Jibri, for instance, Dar al-Fatwa's strength is its weakness: the mufti's lack of willpower provokes more intense mobilization among believers and, ultimately, is an asset for those who seek to preach independently ("because the top is weak, the bottom must be strong").[31]

Control over assets belonging to pious foundations is one of the issues liable to crystallize tensions between the mufti and his opponents. Currently the system is completely decentralized: an asset is declared to be in mortmain by the religious tribunal of the *muhafaza* (an administrative division) at the simple request of the concerned parties, for the courts register the requests presented to them more or less automatically. For the past several years, the administration of Dar al-Fatwa has been alluding to a reform that would entail prior approval from the general administration of pious foundation assets, but such a project was most likely conceived mainly in response to external pressure. The directors of Dar al-Fatwa are aware of the opposition such a modification would generate, and they have not been in any hurry to change the current registration procedure, for fear of triggering another crisis at a time when Dar al-Fatwa needs the Islamists to resist the pressure exerted by the Ahbash.

Five days after the three Usba militants were executed, a religious radio station devoted a program to the Ahbash, taking calls from listeners who were thus able freely to express their anger at the Lebanese state and their frustration with the community institution that is supposed to represent Sunni Muslims in Lebanon.[32] The show's content is an exceptional oral document of discursive violence as practiced by some Sunni Muslims against the Lebanese state and their own community organization. Their reactions are all the more surprising given that Rafiq al-Hariri, who enjoyed relative autonomy and a popular support base, was still prime minister when the program aired. The "presidentialization" of the Lebanese regime that followed Emile Lahoud's election—as well as Hariri's subsequent ousting—buttressed these attitudes, for the state sectors singled out for criticism by the Islamists (the judiciary, the police, interior, and defense) became more important when the army and security services became major actors in the Lebanese political system, at least until the assassination of Prime Minister Rafiq al-Hariri.

Most of the listeners' comments concerned the same observation: unlike the other Lebanese communities, the Sunnis have no real religious leadership to defend their interests. If they had had such leadership, the Ahbash could not have become as large as it did nor extend its activities with utter impunity throughout all the country's Sunni regions, to the point where it became a factor of discord *(fitna)* within the community, endangering its unity and, according to some, its very existence. This development showed that the mufti's negotiating power vis-à-vis the state was nonexistent; through the mufti, Sunni Muslims felt humiliated by their official institutions. At the end of the day, the young men who were executed (and who, according to the listeners who called in, were martyrs—*shuhada*—of Sunni Islam) died because the mufti, Muhammad Rashid Qabbani, was unable to carry out his mission as the guardian of Islam. Had he fulfilled his religious responsibilities, he would have led the struggle against heresy. His passivity toward the Ahbash forced young men from the Sunni community to carry out in his stead the religious obligation to "enjoin good and forbid evil." Such an event could not have occurred in any of Lebanon's other communities, all of which, according to these critics, were fortunate enough to have real religious dignitaries to defend their vital interests.

The sister of one of the condemned men called in to the radio program, adding a dramatic note, and her account of the course of action taken with Dar al-Fatwa revealed the mufti's spinelessness and desire to avoid his responsibilities. The mufti had gone so far as to free himself from the traditional rules governing honor and hospitality by refusing to receive a delegation made up solely of women related to the accused:

> We went to see him several times, but he refused to meet us. We believed that those who defend the Sunnis *(ahl al-sunna)* are their leaders (literally, their "heads"). But unfortunately, the community has no leader in this country. We went to see him . . . We had no men and no weapons with us . . . First, he refused to see us at Dar al-Fatwa. He avoided us. Then he refused to see us in his home. Even on the telephone, he refused to talk to us . . . I feel that we have no leader in this country, and that we have no mufti. We are not only asking him to resign, we are asking him to disappear from our lives. No one can stand him anymore. He doesn't represent us. We want men to represent us, like Shaykh Mahir, like Shaykh Sa'id. We want to bring up real men. Our children will be heroes: thanks to them, there will no longer be errors on the face of the earth.

The terms the young woman used reclaimed the values of traditional Arab culture: these were Muslim women, determined to defend their sons or brothers; they were deprived of the attributes of virility (in that they carried no weapons, for instance), but, in the tragic circumstances befalling the Sunni community, only they embodied the values of struggle and courage. In this way they may be contrasted with the mufti, whose passivity and weakness reflected the humility and submissiveness traditionally associated with a fundamentally feminine nature.

The callers' comments betray a deep suspicion of Lebanese state institutions. Judicial institutions are suspected of bias: in this view, such institutions favor only the Ahbash, as one caller, "Sister" Amina, noted:

Many people have filed complaints against the Charitable Works Society, and have seen lawyers about attacks on shaykhs or ordinary people, or about accusations of unbelief . . . These complaints have been shelved. Is this the state's doing? Is this what the state wants? Why are the only grievances dealt with those that target the Sunni community *(ahl al-ta'ifa al-sunniya)* and not the others?

Shaykh Maher Hammud was at the radio station for the broadcast and argued that, in fact, the state was responsible for the assassination of Shaykh al-Halabi. By refusing to take any action against the Ahbash, and by acting only against the Ahbash's enemies, it was exercising tyrannical injustice *(zulm)*:

> We have warned the state, and we will continue to do so, so long as it pursues its unjust policy, sparing some people legal action and taking illegal action against others . . . It lets some crimes lie, yet investigates others according to criteria unrelated to the law, crimes that are not in the interest of the Lebanese people or their country . . . And so many parties commit the same errors repeatedly. Why? We must put the question to the authorities. We know that the government is making an error. Why is it doing so? We don't know.

The emotion triggered by the execution of the "three martyrs" exacerbated the feeling of confessional identity that has been one of the major phenomena of post-war Lebanon in every religious community. Among Sunnis, this intensification of religious identity reveals alienation from the Lebanese state, which is deemed guilty of serving the interests of other communities while neglecting those of the Sunnis. Sunni Islamists experience their Lebanese identity as perpetual oppression, and the details provided by the sister of one of the condemned men regarding the conditions in which the three were detained corroborate this view of things in dramatic terms:

> I would like Shaykh Mahir not to worry about the mufti too much. I want to say something else. Our *shabab* were treated unjustly from

the moment they were caught. At the ministry of defense, they were treated unjustly: they were beaten, tortured . . . They weren't allowed to shower without their clothes . . . Anyone at the ministry of defense could kick and insult them. They had only God as their sole source of support. If they are really guilty, God will do justice. They weren't allowed to speak in court. . . It should be called not the "Council of Justice" (Majlis al-Adl) but rather the "Council of Injustice" (Majlis al-Zulm). It should be called anything but a council of justice.

As the Lebanese analyst Joseph Maila emphasizes, "the more closely a community is inserted in the political system, the more it tends to see this system as the guarantor of its survival and the defender of its interests. Conversely, the less integrated a community is within the political system, the more it tends to see that system as an alienating straitjacket, contrary to its aspirations."[33] The listeners' comments reflected the image of a Muslim minority oppressed by a state that refuses to take their demands into account.

According to a shaykh from Saida, an employee of Dar al-Fatwa who is close to Maher Hammud, Lebanese Sunnis, in terms of influence and decision-making capabilities, "come last among Lebanon's communities":

The Lebanese state is dominated by Shi'ites. They are the ones running the country. Hariri doesn't represent the Sunnis. In his charitable institutions, there are members of all the communities: Christians, Sunnis, Shi'ites . . . But he doesn't devote himself to the interests of the Sunni community as such. On al-Manar television, for example, the Hezbollah channel, there are only Shi'ites. In what institution can one say the same of Sunnis?

Interestingly, such accusations often emerge from circles that were once very close to Hezbollah and Iran; in fact, such ties are still maintained. But the enthusiasm demonstrated in the past has given way to bitterness linked to the evolution, considered excessively confessional, that Hezbollah has undergone. More prosaically, it is probably linked to a decrease in the financial aid that Iran used to provide in a bid to rally Sunni Islamists to the Iranian revolutionary cause. As one Sunni noted, "I preferred them when they were dispossessed *(mustad'afin)*, in the 1980s. At the time, saying that one belonged to Hezbollah was an act of bravery. Today, power has changed them."

In addition to the confessional divide between Sunnis and Shi'ites, which has grown wider since the end of the civil war, the Sunni community in Lebanon is undergoing an internal crisis, even though the Taif Accords theoretically widened the (Sunni) prime minister's prerogatives at the expense of the (Maronite) president. This crisis is due primarily to the disappearance of the urban elites who traditionally led the community. Until the civil war broke out in 1975, the Sunni community was headed by political leaders who knew how to use their resources to maintain strict control over their coreligionists, while sharing political power with the Christian elites.[34] The role of these Sunni notables *(zu'ama)* was therefore essential in preserving the Lebanese political order. As ministers or deputies, they had access to public resources that allowed them to finance their networks of clients and to channel any excesses to the "Sunni street" thanks to mediation by *abadays* (neighborhood strongmen) who acted as control and communications structures between leaders and their community bases.

By propelling the Palestinians into the position of "armed wing" of Lebanon's Sunnis, the 1975 war undermined the state foundations of Sunni patron-client relationships. The Sunni elites were forced to rally the Palestinian resistance, which was freeing the abadays from their tutelage, making the *abadays* obsolete and thereby weakening their negotiating abilities with their Christian political partners. Incapable of taking the slightest initiative during the war years, they found themselves reduced to pressuring their allies of circumstance to take more moderate stances, in the hope of neutralizing the radical ambitions of the charismatic head of the National Movement, Druze leader Kamal Jumblatt. When the Israeli invasion of 1982 took place, the Sunni *zu'ama,* like Sa'ib Salam, were forced to negotiate the evacuation of the weakened Palestinian resistance fighters, and left their community defenseless against the emergence of Shi'ite and Druze armed militias. Having lost control of the street, they were unable to rejoin the power game, for the "presidentialization" of the regime under the authority of Amin Jumayyil made their participation in politics difficult. In 1986, the country's last major Sunni city—Beirut—fell to the Shi'ite and Druze militias. Tripoli had fallen shortly before to Alawite militia assaults, and in both cases Syria had lent military and political support to the Sunnis' opponents.

At the end of the war, the Taif Accords revitalized the prime minister's office, and in less than a decade a dynamic businessman—Rafiq al-Hariri—put an end to the political pluralism that had been a traditional characteristic of the Sunni leadership since independence. Hariri was able to impose himself as the community strongman, but despite—or perhaps because of—this one-man hegemony, Lebanon's Sunnis came across as a deeply divided community. They were weakened by many religious currents—almost all of which were hostile to the prime minister and reluctant to accept the values expressed in the national pact—and marginalized by the strategic alliance made up of Hezbollah, the Lebanese army, and Syria. After the last generation of Sunni *zu'ama* had been eliminated, whether as victims of the war or because they had been methodically obliterated in the post-war legislative elections in all the country's major Sunni cities, Islamism became the only popular opposition force to Prime Minister Hariri.

The various representatives of Lebanese Islamism, like Shaykh Maher Hammud, who is very close to Hezbollah, knew that the Syrians were not unfavorable to the existence of a faction weakening

Rafiq al-Hariri's national influence on the Sunni street. They had carte blanche to criticize the prime minister's actions, often in very violent terms. Despite this opposition, these two political forces (Hariri's partisans and Islamist opponents) each managed to exploit, in its own way, the bases of "community patriotism" by maintaining Sunni *ihbat* (frustration), which echoed that experienced by Lebanon's Christians since the end of the civil war.[35]

Hariri's partisans attributed this feeling of exclusion to their boss's dismissal from his position as prime minister after Bashar al-Asad chose to support army commander Emile Lahoud in the 1998 presidential elections. The feeling was destined to disappear with Hariri's return to the helm in the summer 2000 elections. For the Islamists as a whole, the lack of support for Hariri expressed a lasting reality linked to the structural exclusion of Sunnis from the state apparatus, as a consequence of the political ascent of the rival Shi'ite community, Hezbollah's military and political success, and the continued presence of Christians in many leading positions despite their demographic inferiority.

As elements marginal to Lebanese society sought to establish their control over the defense of Islamic orthodoxy, Islamism in Lebanon underwent a metamorphosis. In its Sunni dimension, it ceased to be a strictly Lebanese form of Islamism and gradually became more diverse and widespread, bringing together not only Lebanese actors but also Palestinians, Syrians, and Kurds. This change was evidence of the difficulty encountered by traditional Islamist formations (like the Jama'a and, in Tripoli, the Islamic Unification Movement) in perpetuating their existence on the national political scene. The situation is very dangerous, for it opens up space for religious entrepreneurs who condemn any kind of political participation and whose lessons and sermons resonate among all the groups excluded from Lebanese society, whether in the Palestinian camps or in the working-class neighborhoods of the coastal cities.

PART II

CIVIL WAR IDEOLOGY

CHAPTER 4

The Struggle to Control the Camp

In the Ain al-Helweh camp, control of physical space is at stake in power struggles between the salafists and the nationalists. At the northern entrance to the camp, just after the Lebanese army checkpoint, a portrait of the "martyr" Fathi Shiqaqi, secretary-general of Islamic Jihad until he was assassinated by the Mossad in 1995, once hung from a mosque-shaped portico, while a gigantic portrait of Yasir Arafat presided over a boundary stone bearing the name "Palestine Liberation Organization." Amid the tight web of alleyways *(zawarib)*, two main roads cross the camp (the "upper road" and the "lower road"): these are also the only two throughways linking the northern entrance, less than two kilometers from the center of Saida, to the southern one, on the way to Darb al-Sim, near the Christian village that perches on the peaks of Maghdousheh. In that space, Usbat al-Ansar controls two mosques, while the Combatant Islamic Movement, which shares the same ideological orientations, has two others, each of which holds a central position on the two main roads, near the vegetable market. In contrast to this religious demarcation of space, the military sentry posts belonging to Fatah, the PLO's main organization, control only the northern and southern entrances, at opposite ends of the camp. The PLO has abandoned the heart of the city to other groups.

Space is also taken up vertically. If the height of religious edifices

143

serves to tell the camp inhabitants where the real hierarchies can be found, it becomes easier to understand why mosques and their minarets are not only expanded but also raised on a regular basis. Several examples serve to illustrate this strategy, which places bricks and mortar in the service of Islam. A year after having added on an extra floor in 1998, al-Nur Mosque expanded its prayer hall. The "Islamist engineers" used a giant crane to speed up work, despite restrictions that officially limit the movement of construction equipment into and out of the camp. Renovation work on Shaykh Hisham's mosque, begun in summer 1999, linked the mosque's upper floor to the first floor of the building across the way, so that now a covered passageway spans the upper road, overlooking the cars and pedestrians moving about below. These projects were financed by a "mosque committee" that brings all the camp's mosques together and helps reinforce solidarity among all the Islamic forces, from the salafists to the Lebanese Muslim Brothers. Such architectural overhauls also have a strong symbolic value, given the context in which they are undertaken: in June 1999, Fatah attempted to renew its military control over the camp at a time when a clash seemed imminent between Yasir Arafat's organization and the Islamist groups. The Islamists, from a position of relative military inferiority, have sought to assert themselves on the level of spiritual conquest and a territorial domination. To that end, they have increased as much as possible the physical dimensions of the mosques they control. They have crisscrossed the camp with places of worship controlled by preachers who remain determinedly hostile to any form of religious or political expression other than their own.

Contrary to their representation in both the local and the international Arabic-language press, Ain al-Helweh's salafist jihadists are present in every one of the camp's neighborhoods, and their networks go beyond a single solidarity group based on shared village or clan origins. Because Abu Mahjin's family was from Titba', a town near Safsaf, in the *caza* (administrative division) of Nazareth, the articles written about Usbat al-Ansar in the local press have assumed that the rest of the group is of the same origin, and that its presence is restricted to the only neighborhood that bears the village's name. Yet Abu Ubayda, who heads the "military wing" of Usbat al-Ansar, comes from Jaffa, today part of the Tel Aviv agglomeration, while Shaykh Jamal's family is from Safuriyya, in the *caza* of Nazareth; the same is true of Usbat al-Ansar's spokesman, Shaykh Abu Sharif. The salafists have supporters throughout the camp, and their four mosques, spread out at Ain al-Helweh's four corners, contribute to their influence. Walls near the mosques are covered with Qur'anic verses, while the few portraits of Yasir Arafat are torn to shreds. On the military level, the salafist jihadists control al-Zib neighborhood (named after a village on the coast, near Acre) in the alleyways facing al-Nur Mosque, in the southern sector of the camp, as well as that of Safuriyya, in the heart of the camp, and Safsaf, further north. Fatah's only loyalist base is found in the Baraksat zone (from the French "baraques" or huts, a name reminiscent of the camp built in the 1930s for Armenian refugees), at the camp's northern entrance, just past the government hospital.[1]

Ideological divisions cut through all the clans—a reality that is hardly unusual in an Arab society—but in this case family ties no longer seem able to neutralize or attenuate violent conflicts. Far from playing a moderating role, neighborhood committee gatherings, which are supposed to bring representatives of notable families together, had little influence during the series of crises between Fatah and Usbat al-Ansar. According to the pessimistic prediction of a member of the Safuriyya families' neighborhood committee:

> When regional circumstances are ripe, Ain al-Helweh will commit collective suicide. If there are clashes, the Lebanese army will exert even more pressure; it will allow civilians to be evacuated to preserve its own image, and there will be clashes between the Baraksat area,

which is the military base of the Fatah loyalists, on one hand, and the Safuriyya and al-Zib areas, controlled by Usbat al-Ansar, on the other. None of the forces is capable of triumphing over the other in a definitive way.[2]

The Seeds of Palestinian Civil War

After Fatah made its comeback in Lebanon in the late 1990s, the camp at Ain al-Helweh was the setting for several armed clashes between religious groups and Arafatist militants. In May 2003, machine gun and mortar attacks killed seven Fatah combatants who were defending their post in Baraksat as the salafist militias deployed more than two hundred armed men in Ain al-Helweh's two main arteries. Previously, in July 2002, a dissident Usbat al-Ansar faction led by Abdallah Sharaydi, the young son of the late Hisham Sharaydi, had attacked this same post to avenge the assassination of a man who had survived the Diniyeh clashes and taken refuge in the camp.[3] These events must be seen, not as a result of external influences, as regional political culture would have it, but as a consequence of salafist religious groups and networks establishing themselves inside the Palestinian camps.

The ideology of civil war spread by the camp's preachers has transformed the figure of the enemy, who is not only an Israeli settler or soldier, or one of the Arab regimes that persecute "true believers," or even the "hateful Lebanese communities" (the Shi'ites and Maronites): in the camp, that enemy can also be a supporter of Yasir Arafat and a member of Fatah, the organization that played a key role in constructing a nationalist frame of reference in the 1960s. The enemy has become internal as the camp has been transformed into the site of a struggle over the definition of identity.

The battle against Fatah initially took on a symbolic dimension manifest in the salafists' systematic effort to destroy the values and beliefs crystallized in the political definition of Palestinian identity.

The nationalist vision valued, even idealized, territorial identity. A refugee who was asked about the post-1969 period testified that, when Lebanese control over the camps was lifted, for the first time religious activists could freely speak of their homeland in the mosques, without having to justify themselves to the Lebanese police. Twenty-five years later, preachers still evoked Palestine in the pulpits of refugee camps, but the national struggle had been fused with other causes, countries, and representations; the Palestinian reference had been so normalized as to dilute the meaning of national belonging. Religious activists worked to channel the refugees' expectations into a new ideological project, devoid of any nationalist dimension. Their main purpose was to give a new significance to the memories of the individuals and groups they address in order to mobilize them. At worst, the Palestinian past is abolished; at best, it is reinterpreted, but it is no longer considered an experience of national dispossession. By cutting the link between the refugees and their past, salafist activists have chosen another future for them, precisely because they see themselves as part of a larger militant universe. Their hatred for the Palestinian political leadership has led them to withdraw their solidarity from the weight of its history and symbols, and to free the refugees from any political loyalty toward the Palestinian national movement. As Abu Tariq, Abu Mahjin's brother and a leader of Usbat al-Ansar, explains it, "1924 is a more important date than 1948. That date—the destruction of the Islamic empire—put an end to over 1,300 years of Islamic rule . . . The war for Islam is a world war, taking place everywhere: here, Chechnya, Kosovo . . ."[4]

This sort of statement is a declaration of war against a political culture built around the memory of the 1948 catastrophe *(nakba)*, the martyrs' fifty-year litany, and the celebration of defining moments in the history of the Palestinian people, in Lebanon and in Palestine. According to the French philosopher Paul Ricoeur, "through commemorations, an ordinary community reactualizes

the events that it believes founded its identity. The symbolic structure of social memory is at stake. No one knows if there have ever
been societies that had no relation to inaugural events—events that
appear, afterward, to be the origin of the community itself."⁵ The
salafists' symbolic takeover has reclassified the components of identity by relegating the traumatic 1948 exodus to the status of a secondary event in relation to the original fall: Mustafa Kemal's aboli-
tion of the Islamic caliphate in 1924. That decision, in retrospect, is
seen as the main cause of political decline for Muslims from the Balkans to the Middle East.

It is as if, for the first time in the Palestinian people's Lebanese
history, their national bond no longer protected them from the dangers of internal division. The sense of solidarity that had always
played in Yasir Arafat's favor at the popular level, during the different phases of the Lebanese civil war—in 1983, in Tripoli, when
Fatah dissidents rebelled, or during the war of the camps in Beirut,
between 1985 and 1988—will probably no longer work to prevent
a Palestinian civil war if a grave crisis occurs.

Since the civil war ended, we can no longer speak of "Palestinian
society" in Lebanon, so deep are the rifts at both the national level
and the local level of families and clans. Today, the camp poses no
obstacles to the spread of conflicts and contradictions external to
the Palestinian political universe. The recent memory of the suffering that the Palestinians have endured collectively in their Lebanese
odyssey can no longer guard against the threat of violence among
individuals who have different interpretations of their common history. The refusal to address the Other even has practical consequences: Ain al-Helweh's Islamists have dug their own well in the
camp to avoid depending on a water-pumping company financed
by the PLO for their water supply.

Further evidence of the extent to which Palestinian society is divided in Lebanon can be found in the willingness of the various
groups to conclude alliances with outside forces in order to obtain

advantages over their local enemies. The salafist networks, several of whose leaders were sentenced to death by the Lebanese judiciary, see this as a survival strategy of sorts. In the 1990s, denouncing the peace process and producing a discourse of hatred against the head of the Palestinian Authority allowed them to negotiate the equivalent of safe-conduct, albeit temporary and fragile, with Syrian intelligence in Lebanon. Their political practices have thus been part of a strategy, called *istiqwa'*, that has become commonplace on the Lebanese political scene. For vulnerable groups—and not even Hezbollah, in Lebanon, fails to realize how vulnerable it is—this consists of anticipating the ruling power's wishes in order to preserve and strengthen their own position in the local political game. At the micro-political level, this strategy echoes a familiar pattern in Middle Eastern societies, in which each party readily allies with an outsider, the better to fight an immediate neighbor or even a brother.

Every time tension arose between Usbat al-Ansar and Fatah in the camp, prominent Islamists attempted to get Lebanese and Syrian officials to lift the sentences passed against certain salafists. In exchange, they offered to help intensify the struggle against Yasir Arafat's supporters on the ground. The deliberate preservation of internal divisions thus became the radical networks' only guarantee of survival. During the crisis between Usbat al-Ansar and Fatah, in spring 1999, a representative of the Lebanese Jama'a Islamiyya mediated between Usbat al-Ansar and the Lebanese security services. One of the more noteworthy offers he made to Lebanese officials at the time, in exchange for their overturning the sentences passed against some salafist leaders, was cooperation against Fatah in Ain al-Helweh, "since everybody was aware of how useful Usbat al-Ansar were in fighting against Fatah." For their part, Fatah's leaders also said they were ready to cooperate with the army in handing perpetrators of sectarian attacks over to the Lebanese authorities, in the hope that in exchange for contributing to security efforts inside and outside the camp they would receive political recognition.

For example, Fatah's newspaper in Lebanon, published from the pro-Arafat camp of Rashidiyyeh, cited the way the PLO and Fatah had condemned threats to security: "Fatah even placed its resources in the service of the government and the law to block the way to troublemakers."[6] In fact, one of the aims behind the death sentence passed by the Judicial Council in December 1999 against Yasir Arafat's representative in Lebanon, Sultan Abul-Aynayn, was to put an end to collaboration between some Lebanese army officers and Fatah members. The Islamists responded to this judicial decision with a sigh of relief, since it forestalled the possibility of co-ordinated action being carried out against them. By condemning the Palestinian Authority's representative in Lebanon, the Judicial Council was establishing an equivalence between Usbat al-Ansar and Fatah: the same judiciary body had sentenced Abd al-Karim al-Sa'di, also known as Abu Mahjin, to death a few years earlier. Once political enemies have been made into criminals, they become guilty parties with whom no relationship is authorized.

The members of the salafist militia exploited a political opportunity provided by the conflict of legitimacy between Syria and the PLO, and by the accusations of treason directed against Yasir Arafat after the Oslo Accords were signed in 1993. They were thereby fulfilling a function within the regional system, by acting against Fatah's networks and limiting the Palestinian Authority's influence in the refugee camps of the south. Similarly, by encouraging the conflation of Palestinian camps and sectarian tension, they were offering arguments useful to all those who warned of the dangers inherent in allowing the Palestinians to settle in Lebanon. As for the Syrian regime, by instrumentalizing religious networks, it was benefiting from the same method Yasir Arafat had used against Syria in Tripoli in the 1980s, when the PLO provided financial and logistical support to Islamist groups hostile to Damascus.

Violence in the camps is not merely symbolic, as is clear from the retaliatory attacks that have grown increasingly frequent in the past ten years or so between salafist militants and Arafat supporters. After Shaykh Shukri Sabri, a cleric close to Yasir Arafat's movement, was assassinated in May 2001, a Fatah leader, speaking on condition of anonymity, accused Usbat al-Ansar militants of the crime:

> Only they can act this way and kill people in the camp. He was assassinated around midnight, in front of his house, in the Ra's al-Ahmar neighborhood, which is controlled by the Usbat al-Ansar. They kill inside the camp and they do nothing against the Israelis. They never carry out operations in Palestine. They cry about the "Muslim people" in Chechnya; they don't cry about the members of Force 17 killed in Palestine. They're ignorant; they know nothing about the world. Before he became a shaykh, Hisham Sharaydi was a butcher in the camp.[7]

After the second Intifada broke out in September 2000, those who attended al-Nur Mosque organized their own solidarity demonstration in the camp, refusing to join the demonstrations organized by PLO adherents—a principle on which Shaykh Jamal has been unyielding since he became leader of the group. The shaykh of al-Nur Mosque did not feel that the second Intifada renewed the Palestinian leadership's legitimacy in any way. Despite the clashes between Fatah and the Israeli army that marked the first months of the al-Aqsa Intifada, he maintained his view that the Palestinian Authority was ready to make every possible concession and compromise with the Israelis. Nor was Yasir Arafat's refusal of Israeli and American demands at the Camp David Summit held in summer 2000 to the credit of the Palestinian leadership: if it avoided giving in, according to the shaykh, it is only because of "the pressure that the Arab and Muslim states placed on the question of Jerusalem and sovereignty over the Muslim holy sites there." The group's members remain hostile to any idea of a union with the Palestinian organizations. A few days after the second Intifada began, they reaffirmed in their own way the fundamental divisions between the

PLO and their own group: by leading a donkey that bore a sign reading "I believe in peace with Israel" through the camp's lower road.[8]

The Badih Hamadeh Affair

When three military intelligence officers came to his home in Saida on July 11, 2002, to interrogate him on his alleged involvement in the clashes that pitted jihadist Islamists against the army in the Diniyeh region of northern Lebanon (see Chapter 7), Badih Hamadeh killed them and went to hide in Ain al-Helweh. In the camp, he joined the group of Lebanese militants—the "Diniyeh group"—that had settled in the Tawari' neighborhood, at the northern end of the camp, with Usbat al-Ansar's support.

The incident reopened the question of the Palestinian camps' status in Lebanese society; but, in contrast to the assassination of the four judges at the Saida court in June 1999, the death of the three military men came after the events of September 11, 2001. The "Hamadeh affair" thus posed an apparently insurmountable problem to the Lebanese and Syrian authorities: arresting the fugitive implied bringing in the army, a solution the Syrians were reluctant to choose as long as negotiations with Israel remained frozen. Waiting for the PLO police force (al-Kifah al-Musallah) to turn him over was equally unacceptable because to do so would be to endorse Fatah and Yasir Arafat as the representatives of Palestinian refugees. Furthermore, such a choice would have triggered a confrontation between salafists and Fatah combatants, which would have caused a bloodbath in the camp's alleyways that might have required military intervention. The regime was thus faced with an impossible task. The affair brought together issues that were international (effective Lebanese and Syrian participation in the fight against Islamist terrorism), regional (the refugees' future after the collapse of the Oslo process), national (the opposition-led demand for Lebanese state sovereignty over all its territory), and local (maintaining the status quo in Ain al-Helweh, so that neither the salafists nor the nationalists would be able to assert their control definitively over the camp), all in the same space.

These constraints notwithstanding, it was impossible to avoid doing anything at all, because of the outrage aroused by the murder of the three military men, and especially because of the blow that had been dealt to the army, which had been called on to play a role in the country's political reconstruction when General Emile Lahoud was elected head of state in 1998. The solution, then, had to be found by involving various local figures who were accustomed to mediating between Ain al-Helweh's most radical circles and the hallways of power. This task fell essentially to Shaykh Maher Hammud. The scion of a prestigious family from Saida and the grandson of the city's mufti, he had graduated from Damascus University's faculty of religious law and served as the shaykh of al-Quds (Jerusalem) Mosque in Saida. Maher Hammud was one of Hezbollah's first Sunni supporters, from the early 1980s. He cofounded the Congregation of Muslim Ulema—established, as mentioned in Chapter 1, to rally Sunni clerics around Khomeini's revolution—and served as an intermediary among the Syrian security apparatus in southern Lebanon, Hezbollah, and the radical groups in Ain al-Helweh.

Usbat al-Ansar leaders, aware that their survival was at stake, showed an astonishing degree of political flexibility. They held a series of meetings with all the PLO's "atheist" factions, with the notable exception of Fatah. In a detailed narrative of events, communicated to the salafist publication *Nida'ul-Islam,* Usbat al-Ansar members showed a need to explain their attitude during this crisis to their sympathizers via the Internet.[9] Their primary concern had been to gain time by offering Badih Hamadeh money and false identity papers that would have allowed him to depart discreetly. He turned down the offer, claiming that "Ain al-Helweh, which

[was] worth no more than Afghanistan, [could] be destroyed just like Afghanistan." The salafist militias then subdued Hamadeh as he was preparing to attack an army checkpoint in the Tawari' neighborhood, which, according to the Usbat al-Ansar version of events, was "under siege by all the nationalist factions, and especially Arafat's Fatah, in cooperation with the Lebanese state and with Syria's consent."

Thanks to the mediation of Saida's religious leaders, and despite the resistance shown by an indomitable minority that later swore to turn Ain al-Helweh, and all Lebanon, "into a pool of blood," Badih Hamadeh was then smuggled out of the camp in Shaykh Hammud's car and turned over to the Lebanese army. The salafist leaders justified their actions by referring to the treaty of Hudaybiyya, concluded between the Prophet Muhammad and the Meccans in 628—a reference generally cited by the "regime ulema" to justify peace treaties with Israel. According to the terms of the treaty, Muhammad was to turn over to the Meccans any convert who had left Mecca and sought refuge with the Muslims in Madina. According to the Islamists, the case of Badih Hamadeh could be compared to that of Abu Basir, a Meccan convert who had escaped his fellow tribesmen twice to join his coreligionists in Madina, and whom the prophet had turned over to his Quraysh enemies twice, in the name of Islam's higher interest. Even though Muhammad found it difficult to secure obedience because his companions found his decision so shocking, Islam's later victory showed decisively that he had been right to temporarily break the bond of solidarity among believers. Confronted with an enemy, Fatah, "which hates Muslims even more than do the Jews who entered Jenin, since it obeys their instructions," members of Usbat al-Ansar were obligated to protect the future of Islamic preaching in the camp by avoiding a clash. Before making their decision, and to avoid giving "the *umma*'s enemies" an opportunity to break its ranks from within, the group requested a legal opinion *(fatwa)* from Muslim jurists "in several countries, which it is pointless to mention here." After reflection, these jurists *(fuqaha)* presented fatwas in favor of handing Badih Hamadeh over to the Lebanese authorities.

Notable Islamist members of Hamas, gathered around Khalid Ibn al-Walid Mosque, also played a part in resolving the crisis. Indeed, the realism of the Usbat al-Ansar leaders was due in part to their awareness of the threat posed to them by the new camp presence of Hamas, an Islamist group with two advantages: access to the Syrian regime, and popularity within the camps, thanks to the operations it carried out in the Palestinian occupied territories.

Hamas and the Salafist Networks

In late 1999, Damascus authorized Hamas's political bureau, represented by Musa Abu Marzuq and Khalid Mish'al, to take over the religious networks that the Lebanese Muslim Brotherhood had set up in Lebanon's Palestinian camps. Shaykh Yasin was not involved in this decision, which not only had strategic motives—to maintain a high level of regional tension by delegating the right to speak in the refugees' name to the Islamist-Palestinian configuration—but also was a means for the Syrian leadership to promote Islamist figures who identified themselves first and foremost with the Israeli-Palestinian struggle, and who made opposition to the Oslo process (and any other, subsequent formula for cooperation) their main raison d'etre among local forces.[10] In response to the second Intifada, then, posters signed by Hamas appeared on the walls of the Ain al-Helweh camp, proclaiming in large letters: "Safad, Haifa, Gaza, Jerusalem, freedom for all Palestine!"

The introduction of a group like Hamas in the Palestinian camps, which was widely publicized in the Lebanese press, fulfilled an internal function that was not directly linked to regional balances of power: that of hampering the progress of the salafist jihadists and, if necessary, justifying their elimination at the hands of figures whose religious and nationalist legitimacy was irreproachable. Syria's role in this operation did not go unnoticed by the Palestinian refugees. One of Hamas's principal leaders in the Nahr al-Barid camp admitted as much: "Sometimes people tell us . . . we have to say it frankly . . . people tell us: You're the Syrian Hamas, not the Palestinian Hamas . . . That's how some people see us. Politically, our instructions come from Hamas's representative in Lebanon, Usama Hamdan."[11]

Palestinian salafists and nationalists drew totally divergent conclusions from their shared adherence to political Islam. From the outset, Shaykh Yasin, Hamas's founder, focused on the Palestinian territorial framework in the Islamist movement's strategy. Hamas's founding charter, written in 1988, proclaimed unambiguously that nationalism was "an integral part of religious faith." For the jihadists, by contrast, nationalism is a poison introduced by the West to divide the Islamic *umma*—an idea that is echoed among certain Palestinian refugees, who would like to destroy the administrative and territorial frameworks—the modern nation-state systems—that lie at the origin of their exclusion. This contradiction was powerfully obvious in an interview with Shaykh Yasin, published in *Nida'ul-Islam*. Asked about his organization's ties to "the apostate regimes in the Arab world," which were established only "to defend the Zionist entity" and which "openly adopted the alternative of surrender" by recognizing Israel's existence at the Beirut summit in March 2003, the shaykh reaffirmed that the struggle was in Palestine, and that widening it was out of the question.[12] Shaykh Yasin's refusal to proclaim solidarity with Islamist movements in the region is linked to the priority Hamas gives to the national struggle, as well as to the need to obtain external support. Hamas's local representatives would have liked to find a modus operandi with Syria comparable to that which Hezbollah managed to negotiate in the early 1990s. For the salafist-jihadists, by contrast, the idea that an Islamist group might be integrated within a regional and national system—as is the case for Hezbollah in relation to Syria and the Lebanese state—is enough to raise suspicion that it is guilty of compromising with infidel regimes.

While Palestinian Islamism founded its legitimacy on the principle of the struggle for the liberation of Palestine, salafist-jihadist groups have rejected the nationalist dimension of Hamas's orientation. Nevertheless, because Hamas is so popular with the refugees, the salafists have sought to link their vision with that of Hamas, by claiming to achieve for the *umma* what Palestinian Islamism is achieving for Palestine. The shaykh of al-Nur Mosque, who saw the second Intifada as no more than the localized manifestation of a jihad being waged on a global scale, might agree, therefore, with the leaders of Israel's Likud party, who see Bin Laden–style terrorism as no different from the activities of Hamas or Islamic Jihad:

> Jihad or Hamas in Palestine, Islamic Jihad in Egypt: they are all the same, with the same program. The difference is only one of tactics. In Palestine, they have the choice of fighting the Authority or fighting the Jews. They fight the Jews so as not to give them the satisfaction of a Palestinian civil war. But if the Jews weren't there, they would fight in the same way against the Palestinian Authority. In Egypt, they are waging their jihad against the regime, because they know that the Egyptian regime, like the other Arab regimes, serves and protects Israel's interests. When Egyptian Jihad attacks an American ship in Aden, it is fighting against the power that supports Israel. It's the same struggle as that being waged by Hamas.[13]

This perception is shared by al-Qa'ida ideologues. In the permanent taxonomical struggle between "resistance" and "terrorism," they have been preoccupied mainly with inscribing their action in the framework of a defensive jihad. Al-Qa'ida operatives have recycled the ulema's argument regarding the legitimacy of suicide attacks in Israel so as to justify the indiscriminate use of violence against the United States. Taking advantage of the collapse of the peace process, they have sought to take over the Palestinian question by placing its specific stakes on a religious continuum. Resistance by "al-Qa'ida *mujahidin*" is thus made to appear as the extension, at the level of the Islamic nation, of resistance by "Palestinian *mujahidin*" to the Israeli army of occupation. In the same vein, the U.S. military elimination of some of the jihadist network's cadres is compared to the Israeli army's targeted assassinations of Palestinian leaders. The methods used on both sides suggest that their struggles are identical. This point is made clearly by Ayman al-Zawahiri, the main ideologue of al-Qa'ida:

> We don't want to pretend that we live on another planet, by behaving as if the threat were a thousand years away. Every morning, we open our eyes and see Jewish tanks destroying houses in Gaza and Jenin, before surrounding our houses. The campaign against Iraq, with all its consequences, the murder of Abu Ali al-Harithi by American missiles in Yemen, as far as we are concerned, are all signs that the method used by the Israelis to assassinate *mujahidin* in Palestine has been extended to the Arab world as a whole. Any of us could be the next target of American missiles. America's accusatory finger will not spare a single sincere preacher.[14]

To secure the support of Lebanese society, Hamas militants have deliberately focused most of their criticism on the PLO's leaders, targeting both their previous actions in Lebanon and the strategic choices they have made since Oslo. Hamas representatives in Lebanon accuse the Palestinian Authority of encouraging refugees to settle permanently in the country and give up the right of return. Hamas has sought to establish itself as heir to the Palestinian central decision-making body, without committing the same errors in relations with the region's host states. As early as 1998, the militants in the movement had created a "Palestinian Ulema League," whose goal was to federate the various Palestinian Islamic figures.

Advocates of this initiative believed the time was ripe to replace the PLO's discredited elites with new religious leaders, and to provide a disoriented, vulnerable population with an "Islamic" framework for guidance. Thus, during the Camp David negotiations of July 2000, the league published fatwas forbidding Palestinians to leave Lebanese territory if a regional settlement was reached that called for the refugees' emigration to Europe, Canada, or Australia. During the crucial period of fall 2000, the league's directors issued multiple warnings "against any attempt seeking to abort the Jerusalem revolution *(thawrat al-Quds)* or to exploit it for insignificant political gains."[15] In another tract, they condemned "the Palestinian Authority's position on 'heroic martyrdom' operations, the condolences it extended to the families of Jewish victims, and its commitment to impeding jihad combatants." They also called on the PA "to free all the combatants and put an end to its humiliating coordination of security activities with the usurpers."[16] The movement's representatives in Lebanon, in permanent liaison with members of the Hamas politburo in Damascus, preach the continuation of an armed uprising in the occupied territories, and do not hesitate to cite the Hezbollah model of Islamic resistance in southern Lebanon as the sole liberation strategy for the Palestinian territories.

The Ulema League has also pursued a more discreet, but no less important, goal: that of imposing its hegemony on the camps' religious space by gradually absorbing salafist preachers, who for their part have greeted the initiative with suspicion. The fairly lax conditions for adherence to the league were set so that preachers of the Usbat al-Ansar persuasion could join the group. Candidates thus had to hold a degree in religious sciences or to have served as imams of the same mosque for several years running. The desire to counter the influence of the salafist networks by retrieving their main figures was intended to translate into the creation of an "Islamic university" that would train—and therefore control—religious personnel, by ending the anarchy bred by self-proclaimed imams and by depriving the Islamic institutes of a considerable proportion of their clientele (see Chapter 6).

Not surprisingly, the Ulema League did not manage to rally all the Palestinian camps' religious personnel around its initiative. The salafist preachers have been increasingly introverted in the past decade or so, preferring electronic contact with the shaykhs of Britain's "Londonistan" to the launching of an open negotiation process with Islamists who do not share their ideological orientations. For this reason, they refused to join a project that was conceived, ultimately, to strip them of their jihadist character. Differences with Hamas and the Jama'a Islamiyya, organizations perceived as Saudi Arabia's local allies, were overwhelming to preachers who have felt nothing but contempt for the Saudi royal family and its compromises with the United States since the Gulf War. In the July 2000 elections, the majority of seats (seven out of eleven) on the league's consultation council (Majlis al-Shura) went to Muslim Brotherhood / Hamas. To maintain surface unity, a seat was attributed by cooptation to a salafist who was very close to Usbat al-Ansar: Shaykh Yusuf Tuhaybash, Abu Mahjin's brother-in-law. Shaykh Ali, former secretary to the Ulema League, recalls that the salafists would have run, "but on condition that they receive the majority among the council's eleven members! Anyway, we don't want people like Abu Mahjin in our organization. They live in another world."[17]

Differences between the two groups in terms of how they relate to their environment are not only strategic but also social. Individuals who identify with Palestinian Hamas belong to a Palestinian middle class made up of merchants, entrepreneurs, engineers, and journalists, all largely assimilated to Lebanese Muslim society (several of its leaders have even received citizenship). The most integrated fringe maintains an image of reformist Islam and rejects the thought of theoreticians who have advocated violent action against the state, like Sayyid Qutb in Egypt or Sa'id Hawwa in Syria, whom they consider relics of the past. Hamas's liaisons inside the camps are of the same social strata and live much better than the mass of refugees. The emphasis they place on Palestinian identity goes hand in hand with a concern for economic and social integration. By contrast, militants who belong to Ain al-Helweh's salafist networks, and who leave the camp infrequently or not at all, tend to underemphasize Palestine and focus on Islam's victory on geographically dispersed fronts: Afghanistan, Kashmir, Bosnia, and, since the end of the 1990s, Chechnya. The first group follows the latest news from the Palestinian territories closely, and identifies with the Palestinian scene, albeit from a distance, while the second prefers to project itself into a more distant geographical space, extending from the Balkans to Central Asia.

Before the second Intifada, the salafist jihadists ostensibly displayed their indifference toward "Islamic-nationalist" demonstrations organized by the Muslim Brothers in the Palestinian camps. In Ain al-Helweh, none of the members was present at a protest meeting organized by the Jama'a Islamiyya against the signing of the Wye Accords.[18]

Despite these clear differences on matters of principle, things are certainly more complex at the local level. Inside the camp, Shaykh Abbas of Hamas-controlled Khalid Ibn al-Walid Mosque is the Lebanese representative of Human Appeal International, an organization based in the United Arab Republic. He distributes part of the aid he receives from that organization to all the religious groups of Ain al-Helweh, except the Ahbash. Shaykh Abbas is linked to networks that have good relations with the Saudi regime. Furthermore, the royal family is not subject to criticism by leading Jama'a elites, while the salafist religious networks are openly hostile to it. On the ground, however, this gap is minimized in the name of "solidarity among the camp's Islamic forces," so that groups that con-

demn the Saudis for the compromises they have made internation-
ally and their alliance with the United States also benefit indirectly
from financial aid disbursed by the kingdom.

The Salafist Jihadists and the Syrian Regime

At the ideological level, all the Sunni Islamist groups—with the exception of the Ahbash—feel profound aversion toward the Syrian
regime owing to its Ba'thist ideology, its leaders' religious identity,
and the repressive policy line taken by Hafiz al-Asad against the
Islamists in the late 1970s. Sunni Islamists see the regime as inherently illegitimate, since its leadership, which revolves around the
Asad family dynasty, belongs to the Alawite sect, a branch of Shi'ite
Islam. From his Peshawar *madafa,* where many Muslim Brothers
resided after having fled Syria, Abdallah Azzam denounced the role
played in Lebanon by the "Nusayri Phalangists," who had relent-
lessly "hunted down Palestinian Muslims, committing massacres
and exterminations."[19]

The term "Nusayri" refers to the founder of Alawite beliefs, Ibn
Nusayr, who lived in the ninth century C.E. The word, then, renews
medieval categories of Sunni writings on heresy, in which the sect
represented absolute deviation, the most complete expression of ex-
tremism *(ghuluw)* that led its adherents to attribute supernatural
qualities to Ali, the Prophet Muhammad's cousin and son-in-law, or
to one of his companions, Salman, whose very existence is uncertain. One of the major references of the contemporary Islamist
movement, Ibn Taymiyya (1268–1323), personally participated in
a military expedition in 1305 against Nusayri peasants in Lebanon's Kasrawan region. He described the Nusayris as "heretics,
more heretical yet than Jews and Christians."[20] In French Mandate
Syria, this heterodox community benefited from the high commissioner's policy on minorities, which gave them not only privileged
access to the army but also recognition of their religious rights, es-

pecially the right to be called Alawites, which located them more accurately in the Shi'ite tradition with which they identify.

Since an "Alawite regime" came to power with Hafiz al-Asad in 1970, the theological threat has been a strategic one as well. In texts published from clandestine locations or written outside Bilad al-Sham (Greater Syria), the Islamists have denounced the formation of a Shi'ite regional axis that passes through Iran, Syria, and Lebanon, and whose role, they argue, is to stifle any expression of Sunni political Islam. Syria's support for Hezbollah, in their view, was intended to prevent Sunnis from participating in the struggle against Israel, which was monopolized by Hezbollah's "Islamic resistance"—by definition, a Shi'ite resistance.

Such hostility, however, is repressed and expressed only privately. Like other Lebanese groups, the salafist Islamists internalized Syrian constraints and believed that Lebanon had become a "Syrian province *(muhafaza)*, with a governor in Saida, another in Beirut, and a third in Tripoli." From their pulpits, the preachers who criticized the Lebanese state and its institutions the most vehemently avoided uttering the slightest word against Syrian policy. Abstract condemnations of the Arab regimes applied primarily to those governments that had concluded peace deals with Israel, like Egypt and Jordan.

For all these groups, even those with a clandestine or semi-clandestine existence (like Usbat al-Ansar and the Combatant Islamic Movement, respectively), the rule was exactly the same as that applying to other groups in Lebanese political society: they enjoyed relative freedom of speech, provided they refrained from crossing any red lines and criticizing the Syrian regime or its symbols in Lebanon. In return, they could revile the West and the Arab regimes in general as much as they liked.

On the other hand, these groups were quite capable of defending Syria when its role in Lebanon was attacked. In summer 2002, demands formulated by the Christian opposition in Kurnat Shahwan triggered counter-demonstrations at which Sunni religious figures were called on to denounce the opposition, which was accused of seeking U.S. protection against Syria, a few months before the anticipated invasion of Iraq.[21]

In all their Friday sermons, Islamic preachers denounced the political decisions of Arab or, more generally, Muslim leaders, whom they accused of having led the Muslim community down the "path of error and deviation" *(inhiraf)* because they had been blinded by the Zionist entity's "diabolical nature." They also blamed Syria's expulsion from Lebanon on Lebanese "isolationists" who sought Western support. In the short term, the preachers mobilized believers so as to legitimize the Syrian regime, whose Arab nationalist credentials had run out in the 1990s.

Until an eschatological outcome—the overthrow of all the region's regimes—is fulfilled, the failure of the Palestinian-Israeli peace process has made a "new regional order" unlikely. The Islamist networks, which would be excluded from such an order through long prison terms or physical elimination, in some cases, have continuously denounced it. Furthermore, the absence of any settlement has enabled the Islamists to consolidate local power and, with the approval of Syria's representatives, discredit the Palestinian Authority's attempts to gain sway over the refugee population, to keep the camps outside state control, and, finally, to enroll new recruits. By adding a religious interpretation of the conflict to the essentially political and historical interpretations of the Syrian leadership, the various Islamist movements have sought to give an exclusively cultural dimension to the Israeli-Arab conflict in Muslim public opinion. In this way, they hope to impose their veto on regional peace projects. Thus did the Syrian regime become the target of Islamist opportunism; it received nominal legitimacy, though the very same individuals who praise its actions in public privately detest the regime and its leaders.

In the salafist view of regional space, Lebanon under Syrian domination was a sanctuary, in contrast with countries like Egypt or Jordan, which entered the "domain of war" (Dar al-Harb) through the mistakes their leaders made when they signed peace treaties with Israel. The imbalance of power, the requirements of physical and political survival, Lebanese society's fragmented nature, and, finally, the identification of shared interests, at least in the short term, are all reasons for the truce that prevailed among Islamist groups in Syria.

Those who have a place in Islamism-jihadism's international networks, for their part, know that if a regional peace does come about, they will be the first victims of security cooperation arrangements between the United States and the Syrian political leadership, since the latter is particularly keen to avoid being grouped with the "rogue states" that disturb the international order.[22] When negotiations were officially reopened between Syria and Israel in mid-December 1999, before collapsing a few months later, some militants in the camp reacted violently, revealing accumulated hatred against the Syrian regime that had been more or less disguised until that occasion. Involved parties immediately made the link between the negotiations and information circulating on salafist websites that was not addressed in the Lebanese media. According to those sites, several hundred Syrian Islamist militants, members of the Liberation Party, were arrested on the night of December 13, 1999, in Homs, Aleppo, Hama, and Damascus. The event loosened the tongues of some activists, as indicated by the spontaneous remarks of a Partisans' League leader:

Now, they are all unbelievers. Hafiz al-Asad, the Lebanese state, Arafat . . . I was with the Syrians! . . . I was with the Syrians before Barak and Faruq al-Shar' met! But now, this is a regime hostile to Islam. We are against the Lebanese state, the Syrian state, Iran . . .

We're like the first Muslims, at Badr, and all the others are Quraysh. In Badr, the Muslims were unarmed. They triumphed thanks to God's help. [23]

Many people admit that Lebanese society's sectarian structure poses an obstacle to the success of preaching campaigns, and so religious leaders have integrated the regional Syrian dimension in their political calculations. As a salafist leader put it: "In Lebanon, a community can never dominate the others completely and take exclusive power. Each must constantly negotiate and compromise. If we want to think about change, we must think on the regional scale, at the level of geographical Greater Syria. Change is only possible at that level."

This comment echoes a remark made by Shaykh Kan'an Naji, the former leader of the Islamist organization Jund Allah ("God's Soldiers"), created in Tripoli at the beginning of the civil war: "We don't see any future for Islamic mobilization in Lebanon. Lebanon exists thanks to outside support. It's the result of a sectarian, political, geographical, and demographical reality. The Muslims are incapable of setting up their project in Lebanon. We are with those Muslims who are determined to carry out their project in the region as a whole."[24] Still, the salafist networks of Ain al-Helweh, Beirut, and Tripoli have no contacts in Syria that might make them threatening to the regime. Roundups of Liberation Party militants in Homs and Aleppo were exposed via the party's website—al-Nur Mosque's computer system is sophisticated enough—and not through direct contacts in those places. This lack of a presence on the ground makes it extremely easy for the region's various intelligence services to manipulate these groups. In the absence of regional peace, the benefits that Damascus derives from such a situation seem far greater than the costs, which in any case are borne not by the Syrians themselves but by Lebanese society.

Regional Crises and the Ability to Adapt

After discovering that the U.S. State Department had classified them as members of a terrorist organization linked to Osama bin Laden, Ain al-Helweh's jihadist militants immediately organized a demonstration in support of the Palestinian Intifada, although it had played a very minor role in their own movement. For the occasion, they reappropriated the discourse of ruling elites in Damascus and Beirut regarding the need to differentiate between terrorism and resistance. The demonstration echoed the retrieval of the Palestinian cause that Bin Laden had sketched out in his message broadcast on October 7, 2001. Popular mobilization in solidarity with "the Muslim Afghan people," triggered by American strikes on Afghanistan, gave the salafist networks an opportunity to voice their hatred of America alongside the other Islamist groups. A crisis of this sort represented an ideological victory for the Islamist networks, since the feeling of exclusion was symbolically extended to all Muslim societies.

The agents of mobilization never stood a chance, whether in Lebanon or elsewhere, of taking power, but they did prove capable of moving the public debate in a direction that conformed to their interests. The theme of "the war on terror," which became the principal axis of U.S. foreign policy after 9/11, renewed the need in religious and nationalist circles for an objective definition of the concept, which was to apply to Israeli government policy as well as to the actions of al-Qa'ida members. It was impossible for the activists to become recognized players within the Lebanese political community, but they compensated by intensely exploiting international current events. The desire of the United States to include Hezbollah or Hamas on the list of terrorist organizations, and the deterioration of the situation in the occupied Palestinian territories, supported the dominant vision in Lebanon, according to which the term "terrorism" exists in the U.S. lexicon only to be applied to organizations that resist Israeli occupation.

In a society inflamed by daily images of the Intifada, transmitted to Lebanon via al-Manar ("The Lighthouse"), Hezbollah's television station, and by the other Arab satellite channels, Islamist organizations could call on Muslims to defend the *umma,* given the cowardice and impotence of which they accused the Arab regimes. The crisis, then, allowed religious groups in the camps to change their relationship to those sectors of the Lebanese system that had been most hostile to them in the past. Evidence of this change can be found in the declaration made by general prosecutor Adam Addoum, shortly after the State Department published its new definition of terrorism. Addoum, one of the most eminent representatives of Lebanon's apparatus of repression, noted that "Usbat al-Ansar, as such, does not belong to the category of terrorist organizations." The Bush Administration's insistence that al-Qa'ida and organizations like Hezbollah, Islamic Jihad, Hamas, or the al-Aqsa Martyrs' Brigades be grouped under the same rubric provided a tactical opportunity for Islamists in Lebanon, who exploited it fully.

These salafist groups enjoyed relative immunity, which depended directly on the rhythm of negotiations with Israel, the Syrian regime's propensity to give in to American pressure in the war on terrorism, and the likelihood of regional peace. Until such time as peace is achieved, the salafist networks are useful to the Syrians. Inside the camps, their mere presence poses an obstacle to Fatah's political and military influence. Outside, their murderous "Islamic purification" operations—from the execution of shopowners who sell alcohol to the assassination of policemen or magistrates—help maintain a negative image of the Palestinian camps in Lebanese society, and thus create a climate of insecurity that precludes normalization of this issue. Furthermore, such actions feed sectarian tension in the country, thereby legitimizing Syria's role as the ultimate reference for settling religious conflicts, and the only power capable of preserving civil peace. Incidentally, the masterminds behind these attacks, whether in Saida or in Tripoli, have always been careful not to attack Syrian targets, soldiers, or symbols in Lebanon, despite the hostility they feel toward Ba'thist ideology and the ruling dynasty in Damascus. Given the many advantages Syria derives from these groups and their actions on the ground, Damascus has never considered the salafist networks a real threat to its interests in Lebanon. If clashes take place, the regime can call on its many allies in Lebanese society or within the state apparatus, starting with the army and the judiciary, without having to dirty its own hands by engaging in repression directly.

CHAPTER 5

Preaching Topics

At a conference held at al-Nur Mosque shortly before Lebanon's first post-war legislative elections in 1992, Shaykh Jamal told the faithful who had assembled to listen to him—all of them Palestinian refugees, and therefore legally deprived of the right to vote, since they were considered foreigners residing in Lebanon—why believers should stay away from the ballot boxes and refrain from electing representatives. In essence, his argument illustrated the idea that voting in a *jahili* state was tantamount to a declaration of apostasy.

Shaykh Jamal is an intermediary: his role in the camp is to circulate religious principles and interpretations of Islamic and secular history conceived in Islamist salafist circles. The Palestinian shaykh is also greatly influenced by the ideas of the Egyptian Sayyid Qutb, whose work has been seminal in the intellectual dynamics of salafism-jihadism. His main contribution is thus to explain and adapt these concepts to a Palestinian audience in a refugee camp, where such discourse has had real success among certain groups, showing the readiness of many refugees to reclaim it for themselves.

In the history of the Palestinian movement, discourse has played a crucial role in constructing a collective national imagination and in making Palestine "a nation of words," as the poet Mahmud Darwish put it. Though the preachers in the camps come from a tradition of militant discourse, this continuity is one of form, not content, for the preachers' sermons have been designed to subvert the terms of the Palestinian national lexicon, to undermine its foundations, and to modify its grammar radically. Palestinian nationalists have realized the threats inherent in this linguistic politics: in Mash'uq camp (which UNRWA has not ratified), near Tyre in southern Lebanon, Fatah engaged in a "war of mosques," financing the construction of Khalil al-Wazir Mosque in 1998, in a bid to limit the influence of a Palestinian shaykh with ties to Hezbollah. This reaction came too late, however, for in Ain al-Helweh and Nahr al-Barid alike, religious space had already slipped beyond the control of the nationalist movements in the late 1980s.

Speaking from his own mosque, Shaykh Jamal was in a safe place, addressing a congregation he knew personally, and who listened to his sermons every Friday. This was no *mahrajan*—the public gatherings that are a routine exercise in the Palestinian camps, with carefully regulated rituals, predictable speeches, and a virtual audience that is almost always larger than those listeners who are physically present. On the contrary, it was far closer to a religious sermon, given the framework and the target audience. This chapter will explicate the "text" uttered at Shaykh Jamal's conference by adding extracts of sermons he gave in the 1990s. The themes he chose were diverse—ranging from the situation of Muslims in Bosnia to the reasons for the decline of the Ottoman Empire. He also discussed civil marriage, UNRWA, and repression in the Arab countries. This diversity illustrates Shaykh Jamal's ability to use a wide variety of topics in emphasizing a salafist-jihadist religious identity as the only possible response to Muslim decline in the world today.

Like many radical Islamist militants, Shaykh Jamal received no formal religious education. He graduated from the American University of Beirut (AUB) with a degree in business administration, which helps explain his lack of linguistic skill: his literary Arabic is conventional and uninspired; he occasionally makes grammatical mistakes and often slips into Palestinian dialect when the importance of his argument requires it, addressing his listeners directly and citing examples from daily life. Shaykh Jamal opened the conference with the following introduction:

> The subject today is a very important one. It's the topic of the day; of course, I mean the matter of the elections. We who are gathered here can wonder why this topic concerns us, since none of us votes or participates in the elections. What's it got to do with us? Why should we talk about it? Before continuing, it is necessary to remove this objection immediately, so that we can understand the importance of God's Law in relation to this grave question, and update the Truth that we must know, teach, follow, and apply.

This comment is one of the very few concessions Shaykh Jamal made to the concrete situation in which the Palestinians in Lebanon find themselves. It is a minor concession, however, for everything relative to the Palestinians' experience in Lebanon is implied but not actually stated. The objection to the legislative elections that the shaykh evokes as a rhetorical device at the outset of the conference relates to Western legal and political categories; for Shaykh Jamal, these have no Islamic meaning and therefore no validity in terms of religious law: "If it is true that the Muslims make up a single community of believers *(umma)*, then borders, national sentiments *(qawmiyya)*, and regional identification *(iqlimiyya)* cannot divide them. This means that all Islamic questions concern them."

As a Muslim, Shaykh Jamal feels entitled to express his views on a topic—the Lebanese legislative elections—that should not concern him as a Palestinian. The shaykh removes this initial obstacle to discussing a Lebanese issue by stating that any Muslim living on Muslim territory is universally qualified to express himself on Islamic matters. This change in perspective implies a redefinition of identity: Shaykh Jamal is speaking not as a Palestinian—and indeed would not be authorized, as such, to discuss this subject—but as a

Muslim who can legitimately have an opinion on questions relative to the community of believers, wherever they may happen to be. Intervening during the first legislative elections to be held since the end of the war in order to enlighten Lebanese Muslims about the risks that such an event entails for their faith is not only the right of every Muslim, but a duty incumbent on any believer worthy of the name.

Shaykh Jamal's position marks a complete break with the official PLO line; at a time when it was completely immersed in the Lebanese civil war, in 1976, the PLO never publicly renounced the official principle guiding its diplomacy: non-intervention in the domestic affairs of Arab states. Even more revealing is the fact that Shaykh Jamal's speech stood apart from the grievances expressed in numerous memos, which the various Palestinian organizations addressed to the Lebanese authorities at the end of the war, and in which the authors, careful not to rouse the demons of civil war, evoked only social rights. Shaykh Jamal, who belongs to several Islamist networks, none of which occupies the same ground as the Palestinian organizations established in the camps, can freely violate a long-standing taboo under the pretext of carrying out his religious duties and remaining faithful to the Prophet's message:

First of all, everyone knows that our religious Law touches on everything. God (the Almighty, may He be praised) described His holy Book by saying: "We have sent down / To thee the Book explaining / All things, a Guide, a Mercy" (16, 89). God (the Almighty, may He be praised) has said: "This day have I / Perfected your religion / For you, completed / My favor upon you, / And have chosen for you / Islam as your religion" (Qur'an, V, 3). Therefore, my brothers, our religion is complete; it has left nothing in shadow, neither the smallest thing nor the greatest: each of us is capable of recognizing the Truth in these things and of causing it to be recognized . . . Believers have no choice, once they are acquainted with God's Judgment, but to follow it and say: "We have heard and obeyed Your Mercy; You are the Way." This is the aim of faith and of Islam. When you submit to God Almighty, you bow to His orders and submit completely to His judgment . . . Knowledge is a deposit and a responsibility, and this is why we must take responsibility by showing people the Truth, rather than remaining silent about God Almighty's orders (may He be praised), which must be revealed . . . To be a Muslim means to submit to God Almighty's Law.[1]

For Shaykh Jamal, Islam is a system of orders, prescriptions, and prohibitions that legislate on the most diverse aspects of social life and deprive humans of the slightest autonomy. He chooses Qur'anic citations on the basis of this essentialist strategy; their accumulation produces the image of Islam as a legalistic religion in which absolute respect for divine injunctions becomes the only criterion for selecting "true Muslims."

Shaykh Jamal emphasizes the perfection of divine laws only to deduce an immediate morality of action and to link indissolubly the ethics of conviction with the ethics of responsibility. In this part of his sermon, he repeatedly uses a syntactical form known as the cognate object *(maf'ul mutlaq)* in order to highlight the importance of submission and the impossibility of avoiding it without becoming an apostate. All Muslims must act in accordance with God's Law, and faith is a permanent commitment; each Muslim's task, therefore, is to spread knowledge of the divine regulations so that everyone may submit to them in every area of social life. Once the superiority of religious over secular norms has been established as a fundamental element of religious belief, each individual's duty is to act through example and preaching, in order to impart this superiority. The demonstration is based on a syllogism that brings together a major element ("God has taken everything into account for Muslims"), a minor element ("by definition, to be Muslim means to submit to divine orders"), and a conclusion ("if I follow another system of authority, I am no longer submitting to God, and I am therefore in a situation of apostasy").

The enemy—or, in other words, the secular system of law that exists alongside the divine system—is represented as the Lebanese political system, which draws legitimacy from the principle of popular sovereignty, expressed through the election process. Being characterized as Muslim or, on the contrary, passing into the damning state of *kufr* thus depends on how close one is to the Lebanese state. The two poles, institutional and religious, are mutually exclusive: to draw closer to the first by voting implies that one has renounced one's Muslim faith, while a religious attitude, should it be consistent with the Islamic ideal as conceived by Shaykh Jamal, must necessarily lead to rejection of all the demands made by the profane political system. The relationship to political institutions is consequently a main feature in the definition of a "true Muslim." Sayyid Qutb's influence, while not cited explicitly, appears clearly in the shaykh's words; Shaykh Jamal was providing his own response to a question the martyred ideologue had left open when the Nasser regime executed him in 1966: What are the implications of the concept of pre-Islamic ignorance *(jahiliyya)*? Must accusations of "ignorance," which justify a declaration of apostasy, be limited to leaders of infidel states, or must they be extended, rather, to all those in society who accept a system that draws its authority from human, not divine, laws?

Shaykh Jamal clarifies his response gradually throughout his sermon, leaving no doubt as to his position on the question: beyond the matter of participating in the elections, what was really at stake was the total incompatibility between one's identity as a Lebanese citizen and one's identity as a Muslim who respects the divine injunctions.

Jamal Khattab's sermon, then, is an expression of radical Islamism that the camp's borders protect from action by the Lebanese state; as such, it echoes similar ideas advocated by Lebanese imams who do not enjoy the same freedom of speech, but who agree with what Shaykh Jamal has been declaring in public since he took over as head of the mosque in the early 1990s.

Shaykh Jamal's Palestinian audience heard him suggest a new definition of its social situation. By reversing the perspective, the pariahs of Lebanese society are transformed into a small Muslim elite, in a position that allows them to expel from the *umma* any Lebanese Muslims guilty of exercising their citizenship rights, since such rights violate their duty of obedience to God. The camp is no longer a peripheral place where the descendants of a Palestinian community excluded from reconstruction in post-war Lebanon still eke out a living; instead, it is a sanctuary of Islamic purity, separated from a political order hostile to Islam. The political categories of legality and illegality are replaced by religious categories of legitimacy and illegitimacy. Shaykh Jamal, who was on the run from the Lebanese authorities after a liquor store was blown up on the outskirts of Saida, is no longer an outlaw but rather a Muslim unfairly persecuted for defending Islam.

By giving a fastidious lecture in constitutional law on the way the Lebanese regime functions, detailing the precise dates of the different amendments made to the Lebanese constitution from the time of the French mandate until the Taif Accords of 1989, Shaykh Jamal was also showing his listeners that he mastered both semantic systems. His expertise gave additional authority to his efforts to point out the systems' contradictions. It also contributed to his social prestige before an audience that, for the most part, had not reached high school, whereas he had graduated from the American University of Beirut.

In Shaykh Jamal's view the Lebanese system is an anomaly, since it functions on the basis of a consensus among sectarian political elites and not according to a majority principle. Here Shaykh Jamal reiterates the argument, developed earlier by the *qadi* of Saida, Shaykh

Ahmad al-Zayn, that political change is impossible in Lebanese society:

> We have to start out by explaining that in Lebanon, elections are very different from those held in other countries. There might be ambiguity about how useful it is to hold elections in other countries, but there is no such ambiguity in Lebanon's case, because political change in Lebanon is impossible *(amr ghayr mumkin)*. As everyone knows, the president, in Lebanon, is a Maronite. Until now, this is something that the Nazarenes [that is, Christians] will not give up (indeed, they have made it a condition of their national pact). In the same way, the number of seats is fixed by law and cannot be increased.[2] All this exists only in Lebanon: a number of seats for the Sunnis, the Shi'ites, etc. Elections cannot change the regime's nature. It is even impossible to modify the constitution. Everything is predetermined, and different people occupy niches created for them, contrary to what happens in other countries, like Algeria, for example, where a majority in parliament can modify the constitution (that is what the Islamic Salvation Front wanted to do).

The Lebanese state comes across as an incongruity planted in the heart of the *umma:* it is sectarian, which prevents the Muslim majority from changing the regime's nature; it was invented by a Christian power (France), which reinforces its alien character; and it is based on principles of legitimacy totally foreign to those of Islam. The rupture between "us" and "them," "friends" and "enemies," is no longer between Palestinians and Israelis, or even between Palestinians and Lebanese, but between Muslims and all others. The latter make up a heterogeneous category that includes Christians as well as Lebanese Muslims who have supposedly broken with their religion, since they have agreed to participate in elections, and thus to sanction principles of legitimacy that disregard divine supremacy and are therefore hostile to Muslims. Non-religious institutions, according to Shaykh Jamal's logic, are necessarily anti-religious. The Lebanese state, and all those in the Muslim population who make themselves its accomplices by voting (an act of collaboration), therefore represent the enemy.

For the purpose of his argument, Shaykh Jamal took official texts literally. His critique was not based on a comparison or opposition of abstract principles and political practice, as was the case in the Marxist and progressive analyses of the Lebanese system fashionable in the pre-war intellectual milieu; nor was it a resumption of the conservative Muslim elites' call during the war for greater Muslim participation *(musharaka)* in political institutions. Rather, he undertook a comparison / opposition of two systems, one of human origin and the other of divine origin. Although he denounced the Lebanese situation specifically, he concentrated his attack not on such anomalies, more or less exceptional in relation to classical political theory, but rather on an affirmation that the speaker judged as scandalous: to wit, that "the people are the source of all authority."

Sermons also signify by their silences. Shaykh Jamal was careful not to allude in any way to Syria's leading role in post-war Lebanon, though he could condemn the legitimacy of the Lebanese state publicly, insult its leaders, and brand as unbelievers the Muslims who support it, even minimally, by going to the polls. This voluntary omission of the Syrian regime, which was the patron of Lebanese politics until April 2005 (and which never renounced its influence on Lebanese politics), says a lot about the extent to which local groups have internalized the control exercised by Syrian surveillance over all modes of political expression, even in a camp where Syria's presence is indirect (there is one Sa'iqa position in Ain al-Helweh, but other groups have regular contact with Syrian security services). When a preacher criticizes Damascus—which remains an extremely rare occurrence—he generally receives a warning in the form of a visit that dissuades him from repeating the offense.[3]

The Syrian security services, of course, knew everything that was said in the sermons delivered at the camp's mosques, just as they knew the main preachers who have led the camp's religious life with remarkable continuity in the past several years. An inhabitant of the camp summed up the situation by joking about the suicidal tendencies of anyone reckless enough to utter anti-Syrian sentiments in public. Ain al-Helweh did not enjoy total political impunity any more than did the other camps, and its extraterritoriality was relative: rhetorical red lines that cannot be crossed without incurring arrest or assassination were crude translations of the power relations prevailing in Lebanon, outside the legal forms that covered up this situation, more or less skillfully, in the rest of Lebanese society.

When the council of ministers approved civil marriage as a matter of principle in March 1998, at the initiative of Elias Hrawi, the president of the republic at the time, al-Nur Mosque sponsored another conference to deal with the question. At that time Shaykh Jamal repeated his earlier arguments, explaining the council's decision by reference to Lebanese politicians' murderous and corrupt nature:

> They're hashish traffickers, starting with the head of state, or traffickers in public funds, who steal this money from the people. They're murderers, like the head of the Lebanese parliament, or gang leaders, whose followers are thieves, killers, or thugs . . . They've set themselves up as leaders in this country, and unfortunately, for the most part, the people have put them in the places they currently occupy! Through elections, they have enthroned many killers, militia leaders, and instigators of massacres like the ones at Sabra and Shatila, Rashidiyyeh, and so many others.[4]

Although he claims to take a strictly religious perspective, Shaykh Jamal must make concessions to his audience by invoking the most violent episodes of Palestinian history in Lebanon, as Shaykh Abdallah Hallaq also did in a similar context, in order to give his argument more force. The strategy of "de-Palestinianization" has limits, and these are situated in memories of the Palestinian experience—even though Shaykh Jamal seeks to change its perception and meaning.

The Anti-Christian Theme

Anti-Christian arguments are another common theme in Shaykh Khattab's sermons. At one conference, he recycled all the stale lines in Muslim apologetics, evoking the way the earliest Christians altered Scripture and invented the crucifixion episode in order to hide the message that Muhammad, the last prophet, had been heralding. Christians are seen essentially as agents of Western corruption in society. This theme recurs in most of the sermons I have examined. It reappeared in the conference held on civil marriage, which gave Shaykh Jamal the opportunity to divide Lebanese society into a politically submissive Muslim majority and a Christian minority with undue power over Muslims. Such a scandal gave him an additional pretext to blast Lebanese Muslims for their lukewarm religiosity and their acceptance of a political regime that contradicts every one of Islam's prescriptions:

> An unbeliever like Hrawi tells us that forbidding a man to marry his wet nurse or his nursing sister is nonsense. He says that it's licit for someone to marry his wet nurse and that a man can marry his nursing sister. This is what civil law has to say on the matter.[5] He dares to tell us: "Muslims, put your Qur'an aside!" . . . Where is the Muslims' zeal? There are many more Muslims than Christians in this country. If many Muslims are silent and do not remove so-called members of parliament or ministers from power, this is clear proof of the subordination in which they have been placed, and the neglect of the religion they received. They are indifferent to the fact that the Qur'anic texts are not applied, and that God's Shari'a is suspended. An impure unbeliever—since, as God says, polytheists are impure—an impure man tells Muslims: "Leave your Qur'an; leave your reli-

gion; here, civil law can regulate your lives. You would do better to follow it!"

On this point and others, the group from al-Nur Mosque does not follow classical doctrine regarding the "people of the Book" (that is, scriptural religions) in Muslim lands. In Shaykh Jamal's speech, the assertion of Christians' legal inferiority is not accompanied by relative tolerance. The violent words and polemical expressions ("polytheists") that he uses to designate Christians illustrate this extreme position. In Lebanon, such rhetorical violence was seen only at the peak of the civil war. For the camp's religious figures, it is as if the war never ended and so Muslims should see themselves as permanently under attack by their political and social environment. These preachers make no effort to attenuate religious differences when addressing their audience, whereas Lebanese preachers consider the contraints of inter-communal life when speaking in public, at least before a religiously mixed audience.

In a 1997 sermon that touched on the cult of personality as a main reason for the fall of the Islamic caliphate, Shaykh Jamal blamed Christians for the phenomenon, since they were the ones who "allowed themselves what God has forbidden" and thereby paved the way for a cult of the individual, which undermined devotion to God. Christians, according to Shaykh Jamal, are therefore associated with religious transgression and disregard for religious prohibitions:

They strayed from the straight path. They allowed that which God had forbidden, and they prohibited that which pleased God. Despite this, you will find those who trust them and give themselves over to them. Almighty God has said: "They take their priests / And their anchorites to be / Their lords in derogation of God, / And (they take as their Lord) / Christ the son of Mary" (Qur'an, IX, 31). They worship their Doctors, their patriarchs, and their vicars; they associate them with Almighty God. They have begun to allow themselves that which God has forbidden, and to forbid that which God has allowed. They make drinking wine and eating pork licit . . . This is a warning for us, so that we may not be led astray as they have been, because Muslims, my brothers, obey essential things: not blindly, but clairvoyantly, as a result of the orders of God and His Prophet.

In more traditional terms, Shaykh Jamal draws on the argument that it is impossible to obey a non-Muslim. He makes extensive use of the concept of "associationism" or polytheism, which is extended, for the occasion, to all the Muslim deputies who participate in electing the (Christian) president of the republic, and to all Muslims who take part in the electoral process. Shaykh Jamal is playing on the Arabic root sh-r-k, found in both "polytheist" *(mushrik)* and "participation" *(musharaka),* to make his flock believe that participating in the elections would be tantamount to associating human values with God. The anti-Christian theme thus serves as a pretext for an intellectual construct designed to dissuade Muslims from voting:

> You also know that the chamber of deputies elects the president of the republic. The brothers who argue in favor of taking part in the elections leave out this sensitive issue. They never bring up the fact that one of the chamber's tasks is to elect the president of the republic. Maybe they're embarrassed, and that's why they don't want to bring this matter up. So, the chamber of deputies elects the president of the republic. According to the still current Lebanese practice, the president is a Maronite Nazarene. As you know, it is forbidden for a Muslim to give *(tawliya)* an unbeliever *(kafir)* authority [to govern] Muslims. Even if we presume that those present in the assembly don't elect the president, their mere presence nevertheless makes them polytheists *(mushrikin).*

In this light, the national pact of 1943, which was based on a compromise between Muslim and Christian elites, who commit-

ted themselves to sharing power in exchange for renouncing recourse to foreign powers, appears as a second-best option, granted
to Christians to appease the fear caused by their minority status.
The preacher, sentenced and isolated in his Ain al-Helweh mosque,
was willing to grant those Christians *dhimmi* (protected people)
status if they agreed to live in an Islamic state:

> Do you know, my brothers, why the head of state is a Maronite? Be-
> cause of the fear complex. Why is the commander in chief of the
> army a Maronite? Because of the fear complex. When Riyadh al-
> Sulh and Bishara Khuri met, they agreed on this point and developed
> the national pact formula: "You Maronites, as long as you are afraid
> of the Muslims, it's better that you avoid merging with them *(ahsan
> ma tadhub fihim)*, so you can head the state. You're afraid that the
> Muslims will destroy you, so you can lead the army." What are the
> Nazarenes so afraid of? The Nazarenes don't want to submit to Al-
> mighty God's Law. God Almighty commanded us, saying: "And
> fight them on / Until there is no more / Tumult or oppression, / And
> there prevail / Justice and faith in God" (Qur'an, II, 193). So they
> must submit to God's Law, so that the state may be ruled by Islam's
> law. They can stay in our state, and we won't force them to become
> Muslims, but Muslim Law must be dominant and hegemonic.

Fighting Reformist Islam

The Islamist parties that run in the elections muddy the waters and
confuse Muslim ranks. Whether they like it or not, according to
Shaykh Jamal, they are paying allegiance to a Christian president,
giving their approval to an impious constitution, and altering the
value of religious teachings. "Ideological citizenship" of the sort
Shaykh Jamal defends is opposed to any concession to the political
order so long as it does not coincide perfectly with the religious
order.

Shaykh Jamal is thereby reaffirming a central aspect of salafist Islamism, of the jihadist and quietist varieties alike, in its relationship with political institutions: for those who accept that belief *(aqida)* and way of life *(minhaj)* cannot be separated, any form of participation in a political sphere that bears a religious legitimacy has a retroactive effect on the content of faith, where it sows the seeds of unbelief. The salafists' logic makes no distinction between religious and political orders; participatory democracy, then, is likened to a form of associationism *(shirk)* that leads to polytheism and idol worship, since Muslim deputies legislate in the name of values different from those of the Shari'a.[6]

The same argument applies to the administration of justice that is not carried out in the name of divine commandments. To have recourse to such a form of justice implies that one recognizes its legitimacy and therefore poses a challenge to the fundamental elements of faith. Shaykh Jamal later attacked the position adopted by the Jama'a Islamiyya to justify their participation in the elections. Jama'a leaders admit that the full implementation of the Shari'a is impossible in Lebanon, owing to the confessional nature of the political system and the country's division into eighteen religious communities. Political realism therefore dictates a gradual solution. According to the Jama'a, once Islamist deputies have been elected, they must seek to promote only those values, among those the Shari'a contains, that are compatible with the beliefs of Lebanon's other communities.[7] Shaykh Jamal finds this selective application of divine law, based on a realist political reading of local constraints and the balance of power on the regional scene, unacceptable; he sees in it nothing less than religious treason:

> I would surprise you if I told you that some shaykhs, when people go and ask them if it is allowed for a Muslim to elect a Nazarene deputy, answer: "Yes!" You can hear such things in Saida's mosques these days [repeated] . . . "Yes, you are allowed to elect a Nazarene,

choose the least bad of them! If one is an extremist and another is not, choose the one who is not." The Congregation of Northern Ulama even made a statement to that effect. What sin is greater than this, what catastrophe is more awful? We know that giving an unbeliever authority is forbidden. To elect a deputy is a serious matter: he is the one who represents you and makes laws for you. He is the one who sanctions the government that is going to apply these laws and this legislation . . . How can a Muslim give a mandate to a Nazarene to represent him and make laws that violate the Law set down by the Lord of the universe? All this, my brothers, only leads to one thing: it opens the way to sinners and causes us to associate with them in the places they prefer.

When parliament usurps divine functions, the effects are visible in daily life: this transition allows Shaykh Jamal to leave aside his commentary on institutions and describe Lebanese society and its moral collapse. He thereby creates a link between a constitution that most of his listeners have never read, on the one hand, and a society where anyone can easily see how religious morality is neglected, on the other. The freedoms guaranteed by the constitution are not merely an incitement to debauchery; indeed, they are blasphemous in that they place humans at the same level as God, seen as the absolute legislator, to Whom true believers must submit without seeking to improvise new rules of conduct outside the field of divine competence. Shaykh Jamal refers to debauchery not only to prove the regime's illegitimacy by the standards of religious law; he also makes debauchery the immediate consequence of the principle of liberty contained in the preamble to the Lebanese national pact—as if such abstract principles could condition social behavior directly:

> They also say that one of the first tasks incumbent upon us is the "safeguarding of public freedoms, which [represents] a primary goal." Public freedoms mean that you don't have the right to intervene in a

person's life . . . Women can go out wearing shorts. If they want to, they can wear a bathing suit to the beach and go swimming. Anyone can drink wine . . . That's public freedom, and you don't have the right to intervene. Is protecting public freedoms a priority for us? Well, is it?

Social freedoms in Lebanon in particular were debated in the aftermath of the war, when Muslim religious authorities requested—and obtained—the reinstatement of cinema and television censorship.[8] During the conflict, the Lebanese Broadcasting Corporation (LBC), which was established and controlled by the Lebanese Forces, a right-wing Christian militia, abandoned censorship of that particular sphere in an effort to show the West that "Christian Lebanon" was more modern than, and therefore superior to, the country's other regions. In spite of this, Lebanon is still an exception in a far more conservative Arab environment, owing to its (relative) freedom with regard to images on billboards and in advertising, symbols of consumption (alcohol and fashion), and sexual license (prostitution concentrated in certain nightspots, especially on the highway linking Beirut to Juniyeh).[9] Denouncing the permissiveness of Lebanese society allows Shaykh Jamal to link the different generations that gather at al-Nur Mosque every Friday. For the older people, preserving traditional values is a way of remaining loyal to the memory of pre-1948 Palestine, while for younger people—who cannot afford the hedonistic lifestyle or the upscale restaurants and nightclubs frequented by the loud, party-going minority—such denunciations provide assurances of moral superiority:

In Lebanon, it is legal to sell alcoholic beverages, for instance, as long as the seller has a license. Any shopowner can get such a license. Anyone can sell wine, in any place and to anyone he likes. This constitution also allows fornication *(zina)*, as well as prostitution. It allows any man who wants a woman to go into a brothel and fornicate there. He doesn't risk being punished for this, and the women are not punished either. They're only punished if they don't have a license allowing them to practice their trade. Such laws are clear denials *(takdhib wadih)* of God Almighty's Laws. He prohibited wine and they allow it; God, Who is Exalted, praise to Him, prohibited fornication and they allow it; God Almighty, praise to Him, prohibited usury and they allow it; and so on in all their affairs. God says: "This is forbidden! Don't do it!" And they say: "You're allowed to do this, so go ahead!" Where can there be greater impiety than in he who contradicts God Almighty's Word? The truth is that the Lebanese regime and its legislative institutions radically contradict Islamic law: this [regime] fights one of the most sacred attributes of Almighty God—sovereignty *(hakimiyya)*, the ability to make licit *(tahlil)* and the ability to make forbidden *(tahrim)*. God says: "the Command / Is for none but God: He / Hath commanded that ye worship / None but Him: that is / The right religion" (Qur'an, XII, 40). Any regime that is un-Islamic is a *jahili* regime *(nizam jahili)*.

These statements are not merely rhetorical, just as their violence is not simply symbolic: Shaykh Jamal was providing religious justification for a series of murderous acts targeting alcohol sellers in Saida and the surrounding area in the mid-1990s, and carried out by people said to be Usbat al-Ansar members from Ain al-Helweh.

The point is not to establish Shaykh Jamal's material responsibility for the assassination of alcohol sellers and the bombing of their shops, but it would be difficult to deny his moral responsibility. From his pulpit, Jamal Khattab spread a "discourse of depreciation" that helped create "a mechanism for the direct or indirect justification of physical violence, carried out in the name of the group that seeks to establish its dominance, by invoking the defense of its values."[10] True, such rhetoric is a response to what large segments of the Lebanese population say about the Palestinians. It is also likely that this type of discourse would be less popular if the state were to recognize the Palestinians officially, instead of relegating them to the physical, social, and legal margins of Lebanese society. But it is important to point out that Shaykh Jamal is not speaking on behalf of a national minority—Palestinians in Lebanon. Instead, he devotes himself to producing new representations among Palestinians, in order to link their exclusion to a hidden rationale: the fact that they are Sunni Muslims.

Shaykh Jamal's speeches gave meaning to the refugees' social frustrations through a shift in significance that served three purposes: to restore self-esteem; to allow a simplified reading of the current situation; and to channel social hatred against those who attack the group's collective identity, which is now defined exclusively in religious terms, even though the victims of such aggression—shopowners on Saida's outskirts or policemen directing traffic—are hardly responsible for the refugees' misery. By modifying the terms of the Palestinian question through religious categories that are originally foreign to it, the camp's preachers—the trend that Jamal Khattab represents dominates religious expression in Ain al-Helweh—contribute to dissolving the Palestinian cause and creating militant groups made up of Palestinians as well as Lebanese citizens. As the Palestinian cause dissolves, links with new groups grow stronger. These groups, for their part, seek to extend their intellectual influence and recruit young urban poor with nothing to lose.

By rejecting any participation in the election process, Shaykh Jamal shared the same options as the Algerian salafist-jihadists in the early 1990s, when they returned from Afghanistan convinced that jihad was the only means of setting up an Islamic state. They unwillingly accepted the decision of the Islamic Salvation Front (FIS) to participate in the Algerian legislative elections of 1991 and were among the first recruits of the Armed Islamic Group that appeared in Algeria in 1992 and 1993. In another sermon delivered in 1997, Shaykh Jamal also attacked the Arab countries' interior ministries, which opted to use repressive tactics against "a shaykh, an ulama, a preacher," rather than to act against the Zionist enemies. As for international jihadists, Shaykh Jamal compared them to the Prophet's companions, who, in the fifth year after Revelation, fled Mecca for Abyssinia to escape persecution at the hands of Quraysh: "If someone who went into exile to defend his religion escaped death while he was on jihad in Bosnia, Afghanistan, or Kosovo, if he escaped death at the hands of unbelievers, he will not escape the death he receives upon returning home, death at the hands of the Arab interior ministries."[11]

The Language of Permanent Crisis

Shaykh Jamal's argument had much in common with a presentation by Dar al-Fatwa's director-general, Husayn al-Quwatli, published in the daily paper *al-Safir* on August 18, 1976. According to al-Quwatli, Lebanese Muslims were experiencing a conflict in loyalty between their religious identity and their citizenship, since the creation of the Lebanese entity in 1920 replaced "Islam's authority" with "Maronite power." Muslims, who had "given up on the idea of building an Islamic political order since Lebanon achieved its independence," thereby made "a major concession" that posed a grave threat to their religious integrity, for "true Islam cannot be indifferent with regard to the state." Al-Quwatli concluded by emphasizing that this last point, far from "expressing fanaticism," was merely "the manifestation of authentic Islam." Even though he kept to a negotiator's mindset—given such a concession on the Muslims' part, so the argument went, Christians should give up their preeminence in the state apparatus, in order to allow a "middle ground" to emerge—al-Quwatli maintained a position on principle for the future, since, to him, "the essential solution for Muslims is still the creation of an Islamic state."

The article sparked much debate at the time. It served mainly as a political justification for the Christian militias, which thus received—far more clearly than anything internal propaganda could have provided—confirmation from their very adversaries of the significance of their struggle. Situated in its original framework, however, the argument was less a "Sunni ultimatum" than a further example of dialectical exaggeration, in a climate of ideological civil war fueled by intellectuals and religious figures of every stripe.[12] Before commenting on the article's content, which he discussed along with an analysis of "Maronite intellectuals from the Holy Spirit University of Kaslik" in a book published in 1986, the late Lebanese professor of constitutional law Edmond Rabbath warned that such satires—"whose interminable course the war unfolds ceaselessly, *ad nauseam*"—should be read as the expression of a crisis, in a context where "opinions on both sides of the front take inspiration . . . not from real history but from a vividly fevered imagination."[13]

Twenty years later, the preachers of Ain al-Helweh picked up where the most radical figures of the Lebanese civil war had left off, and fed this "vividly fevered imagination" in their sermons. By taking up the thesis of the ideal, abstract, and extemporal Islamic city, as the theologians might have imagined and developed it in the darkest moments of Islamic history, Shaykh Jamal was giving a religious lesson to Lebanon's Sunnis. He believed they had forgotten the bases of their own religion by accepting integration into a political order from which true Muslims should instead seek exclusion. By placing himself in a religious utopia, he transformed collective marginalization into a religious virtue. Like the other preachers at the mosques in Ain al-Helweh, he projected himself into a time of perpetual civil war, defining a reality where it was necessary to fight and confront a hostile environment.

These sermons are not just meaningful to a few individuals on the run from the Lebanese judiciary; they also appeal to large segments of the population who are excluded from the labor market and for whom the camp is the only available space for socializing. Relations with the outside world, mediated by the press and television—especially al-Jazeera—are decoded and explained by the mosque imams, who "regulate meaning" at a time when the PLO's institutions of socialization and control can no longer fulfill the function of explaining the social and political world.

Sultan Abdul-Hamid and Modern Arab Political Regimes

In another sermon, Shaykh Jamal launched into a vibrant defense of the last Ottoman caliph, Sultan Abdul-Hamid, whom he compared with contemporary Arab leaders, the better to condemn them. Of course, Shaykh Jamal was describing not the historical sultan but rather the idealized image of a pan-Islamic symbol who pitted heroic resistance against the ambitions of the West and the international Zionist movement. For Shaykh Jamal, the fact that Western opinion has cast Abdul-Hamid in a bad light merely serves as a further guarantee of his political and religious sincerity with regard to the Muslim masses. The sultan appears as a scarecrow that the shaykh shakes at the West, and especially at the Arab regimes that obey Western orders. This apologetic story of the sultan contains another historical omission: the fact that, in the late nineteenth century, the Muslim reformist trend, with which Shaykh Jamal happens to identify today, considered Hamidian despotism a betrayal of Islam's true values and decided for this reason to effect a major leap from Islamism to Arabism. According to Shaykh Jamal, "Secularists accuse [the sultan] of having been a bloodthirsty tyrant, a despot, etc. For us, no man can be perfect or flawless, but if we compare what that sultan did with the achievements of his successors, we can only speak highly of him, because, my brothers, at least he stood up to the corrupting insinuations of Herzl and the international Zionist movement."[14]

In fact, the "red sultan" mainly serves as a means of denouncing the Arab leaders, whom Shaykh Jamal accuses of weak morals and of being corrupt agents in the service of the United States:

> Today, my brothers, there are very many heads of state who are on the payroll of U.S. intelligence, according to congressional reports. In these reports, one can find information on the lifestyle of presidents of developing countries. A young man who saw this happen told me about the way these presidents visit the United States. He said, "They stay in the best places; they receive beautiful gifts." All this, of course, is paid for by U.S. intelligence, my brothers: all these bribes, so that these leaders carry out their wishes and help execute the projects of these unbelievers. A pretentious woman came to Lebanon to discuss security, the Marines, the explosion at the embassy, Subhi Tufayli, [and] Resolution 425, which she says "you must apply, even if it harms you, since you are taking orders here."[15] If there were leaders worthy of the name, they would not take orders from these unbelievers who have no right . . . If they are not true Muslims, how then can they be leaders in the name of Muslims? This is the great catastrophe we have to bear.

Unlike current leaders, the shaykh argued, Sultan Abdul-Hamid had been able to resist international pressure, and turned down the money Herzl offered him to replenish the empire's coffers in exchange for the creation of a Jewish national home. This is historically accurate, but Shaykh Jamal does not mention the fact that this policy failed: in 1908, according to historian François Georgeon, 80,000 Jews lived in Palestine, which means that in thirty years, the proportion of Jews increased from 5 to 10 percent of the total population.[16] Nothing can change the image of the last Muslim empire, given that the other target of Jamal Khattab's sermon, besides the corrupt Arab leaders, is nationalism, which divided the land of Islam into a multitude of statelets.[17] Among those guilty of introducing the virus of ethnic nationalism into the heart of the Ottoman

Empire, Shaykh Jamal refers directly to the principal ideologue of the Young Turk movement: Ziya Gokalp, the essayist who called for the unification of all Turkish-speaking peoples, from central Asia to the Balkans, in a single political entity. According to Gokalp, the Turks, who had always placed their political and military genius in the service of other dynasties, should "return to their ancient glory," represented by conquerors like Genghis Khan and Tamerlane, and privilege the Turkish element in the empire so as to pave the way for the coming of a new nation. In one of his nationalist poems, he wrote: "The land of the Turks is not Turkey, nor even Turkistan. Their country is the eternal land of Turan."[18]

"When Ataturk came," Shaykh Jamal continued,

> he gave Palestine away. For nothing! For two piastres, under the pretext that . . . "Palestine isn't ours, Lebanon isn't ours. We're the nation of Turan!" These nationalist ideas, which imperialism created and spread, had no other goal than to destroy the Islamic *umma*. Instead of saying "we are the Islamic *umma,*" we started to say: "We are one Arab nation (and we must do everything to make it that way!)." The Kurds say: "One Kurdish nation (and we must do everything to make it that way!)." The Berbers: "One nation (and we must do everything to make it that way!)." And you can see them for yourselves, inventing new nationalisms every day within their single nations!

The Legitimacy of the Palestinian Presence in Lebanon

In his discussions of UNRWA, Jamal Khattab repeats some of the accusations traditionally directed against the international agency. As soon as it was created in 1951, UNRWA was seen as the weapon of all those who wanted to liquidate a Palestinian state in the region. As a creation of the United Nations, which recognized Israel's existence in 1948, it therefore suffers, according to Shaykh Jamal, from an original sin that determines its functions and true nature, beyond the humanitarian tasks it has taken on:

> My brothers, let us turn to the past and remember that UNRWA is an agency that the United Nations created just as it was officially recognizing the Zionist entity, a predator on Palestinian land. What can be the aim of this decision, my brothers? Is the aim to bring us back to Palestine? If that were the case, they wouldn't have recognized the Jewish state and granted it international recognition . . . International legitimacy, as they say . . . So that's not the situation. That agency was founded to end the Palestinian cause, and to put an end to what they call the refugee question.[19]

Relations between UNRWA and the Palestinian refugees have always been ambiguous. Since its creation, the agency has periodically been contested. It was immediately seen as the symbol of the international community's inability to resolve the refugee question by imposing the implementation of Resolution 194, regarding the Palestinians' right of return. Moreover, UNRWA has been accused of serving Israeli interests by gradually eliminating the very existence of a refugee problem. The refugees saw the cutback in aid, which dwindled dramatically in Lebanon after the signing of the Oslo Accords, as the sign that the Western states which finance the agency were no longer interested in dealing with the problem. Shaykh Jamal expressed a sentiment that prevailed inside the camp:

> The stated goal was to assist and work for the people of Palestine. Assistance where the Palestinians are in the Diaspora, and services where they are dispersed. During this period, what happened, my brothers? Permanent pressure, uninterrupted massacres, the door of emigration opened before our people in Denmark, Germany, Canada, where they will melt into Western society, losing their faith and becoming apprehensive like Westerners themselves *(haythu*

yudawwab fi bilad al-gharb wa yusbih mithlahum fil-kufr wal-khajal) . . . As we know, we are currently in the worst possible economic situation. There is no more aid. The Gulf states are no longer willing to give money to the Palestinian people . . . You might be surprised to learn that UNRWA doesn't help a sick, elderly person, someone who is over sixty and has heart problems. Because he's over sixty, he can just die! He's not allowed to live until the age of seventy or ninety. That's forbidden. We all know that school supplies have been suspended. There's nothing left for the students. For the past ten years, they paid school fees until middle school . . . But our people don't have the right to be educated beyond eighth grade. Any further education is forbidden.[20]

This account, however, does not lead Shaykh Jamal to exalt the unique destiny of the Palestinian people, or to reaffirm the uninterrupted and unchanging organic relationship among the people, its land, and its history, as Yasir Arafat did before the United Nations in 1974. The Palestinian Authority, furthermore, is explicitly singled out for playing a role in the planned annihilation of the refugees' cause: its budget is "greater than UNRWA's," and "the Jews give most of it to the PA." These comments are allusions to the mechanisms restoring the Palestinian Authority's control over tariffs and taxes on Palestinian goods. According to Shaykh Jamal, this injustice is mainly due to the refugees being Sunni Muslims: for this reason, they are martyrs in Lebanese society. This is probably the most important part of his sermon, since it defines a new causality with far more dangerous consequences for the Lebanese balance of power. After denouncing the "international community" in terms on which everyone ultimately agrees, Shaykh Jamal launched a violent attack on those "who belong to this *umma*" within Lebanese society, and who nevertheless act in conformity with the international community's alleged wishes. He thus unveiled to the refugees the real significance of their suffering by pointing out the guilty parties, who were no longer abstract entities—the U.N., the international community—but rather communities that are present on Lebanese soil and occupy leading positions within the state apparatus:

> We don't need to settle in one country or another . . . God gave us Islam first, and then he gave us membership in this *umma*. Some of those who belong to this *umma* [involve themselves] in local conflicts, [show] a *jahili* sense of solidarity, and are trying to exclude us from among this nation's peoples, under the pretext that we are strangers "to whom we have offered hospitality" and other ridiculous, meaningless formulas. When the *ansar* [the "Helpers" who received and assisted the Prophet Muhammad and his companions, the "Emigrants," after their migration or *hijra* to Madina] welcomed the *muhajirin,* no one said a word in this vein; they didn't bother with all this publicity! . . . If the majority of our people were Christian—and thankfully, this is not the case—there would have been no problems. They would have received the nationality, and there would have been no more Palestinian problem. They bring in Armenians, settle them here, give them a passport, the nationality, and the problem is solved. The problem exists, my brothers, because we're Muslims, that's it. Apart from that, there is no problem. Unfortunately, some people who are considered Muslim in this country are participating in this conspiracy, with the United Nations, the state, and all the regional forces that are hostile to Islam and the Muslims.

The reference to the Armenians highlights a significant contrast: that between, on one hand, a culturally and religiously distinct community that is not Muslim and does not claim Arabic as its native tongue but is successfully integrated, at the political level, within the Lebanese entity after having experienced massacres and expulsion at the hands of a Muslim power—the Ottoman Empire—in 1916; and, on the other, a community whose culture is Arab and whose religion is Islam, expelled by a non-Muslim military and political power in 1948, and still excluded from integration into Lebanon despite geographical, cultural, and religious proximity. Shaykh Jamal's analysis is not isolated: more generally, religious Sunni society manifests an "Armenian complex."

During a celebration organized by Dar al-Fatwa at Anjar, a village of the Beqaa region, against a background of conflict over property between the *waqf* administration and the local Armenian community, the mufti of Mount Lebanon, Shaykh Muhammad Ali al-Juzu, clearly compared the two communities, the better to juxtapose the injustice done to one with the privileges granted to the other:

We won't tell the Armenians in Anjar: "Go back to your country!" But they have no right to seize our property, whatever the circumstances. We tell our guests *(duyuf)*, the Armenians, there is a category of people who speak Arabic and who are living in a dramatic, dangerous situation. This category of people lives in the camps; it owns nothing and cannot live in dignity. In the name of the right of return, it has been dispossessed of the right to live in society. We are one Islamic nation *(umma wahida)*; we do not recognize the borders laid down by French imperialism . . . We will not beg the state for this right; we are asking for such rights to be protected under the law. We turn to the Maronite patriarch, Cardinal Mar Nasrallah Butrus Sfayr, to ask him to encourage dialogue among all citizens, and not to act only in favor of one party, which resorted to Israeli assistance during a certain period, and in fact did not hesitate for even a single second to use that assistance. Let us start by being fair ourselves, and let us learn the rules of life in common *(al-'ish al-mushtarak)*, by eliminating political sectarianism first and foremost, and by ensuring equality among all citizens. All citizens must receive the same treatment: agents who betrayed their country cannot return to a hero's welcome while Muslims who are merely related to those who participated in the Diniyeh events are persecuted for that reason alone.[21]

By alluding to the Palestinian Christians who were naturalized as Lebanese citizens under the presidency of Camille Chamoun in the 1950s, Shaykh Jamal reaffirmed the strictly sectarian, domestic dimension of the problem, to the detriment of its regional dimension: the refugees, according to him, are excluded not because they are Palestinians but because they are Sunni Muslims. He did not evoke the goals of Syria's regional policy, and thereby attributed responsibility for the Palestinians' exclusion to the Lebanese state alone—in other words, to the Christians, the Shi'ites, and the Sunni political elites who betrayed their duty of religious solidarity.

Jamal Khattab's version of Islamism thus comes across as absolute, anti-reform, anti-Palestinian ("Palestinianism" as a form of nationalism), revolutionary, and conflictual in essence, since the Lebanese state's otherness represents the negation of its own mode of existence. Replaced in its context, this Islamism illustrates the totalitarian propensity that dominated groups can nurture and develop after several decades of social and political frustration and discrimination. Shaykh Jamal owes his position to the system of exclusion that weighs on the Palestinian population in Lebanon and has become an indispensable element of his work in building a radical, closed identity. If this system were to disappear, Shaykh Jamal's "situational charisma" would no doubt find fewer takers within the camp. [22]

This chapter has shown that Lebanon as described by Shaykh Jamal was an abstract, mythical entity, essentially defined by its 1943 pact and its constitutional values: a Lebanon of public freedoms and peaceful communitarian coexistence. With the exception of a few incursions into more or less current affairs, and allusions to the country's allegedly permissive values, Shaykh Jamal does not mention Lebanon as it really is. It would be impossible to recognize the country's social and political reality—even in mirror reverse—in the portrait painted by the Palestinian preacher.

For Shaykh Jamal, the struggle is no longer geographical but symbolic: it is necessary to take back not only the land of which the Palestinians have been robbed, but their identity as well. Even though the trend he represents does not have a majority of adherents in Ain al-Helweh, the social conditions obtain for a small religious entrepreneur with a place within multiple solidarity networks to satisfy the expectations of an audience deprived of the traditional instruments of socialization.

CHAPTER 6

The Role of Islamic Institutes
in Lebanon

Until the end of the Lebanese war, the Palestinian refugee population placed a high value on education: for an entire generation, investment in schooling constituted capital in the political struggle and a chance for economic survival. Palestinians in Lebanon made up the best-trained community of the diaspora, thanks to UNRWA's scholarship system and, for many young people, admission into prestigious Lebanese universities. Moreover, they benefited from a fund for Palestinian students, financed by Palestinian and other Arab businessmen.[1]

In the mid-1960s, the economy of the Gulf countries opened up professional opportunities for all segments of the population, while the Lebanese labor market was growing increasingly accessible to the Palestinians as the PLO consolidated its presence in the country. Many young Palestinians also went to study in Egypt, as the Nasser regime, eager to spread the country's cultural and political influence, sought to attract Arab youths to its institutions of higher education. Those who were unable to emigrate attended Beirut Arab University (BAU), the Lebanese branch of Alexandria University, while the children of the middle class became militant activists at the prestigious American University of Beirut (AUB), where George Habash went on to found the Arab Nationalist Movement (ANM) and to lead the Popular Front for the Liberation of Palestine

(PFLP). When the PLO set up its offices in Lebanon in 1970, the Palestinian central command was able to diversify its training policy by signing cooperation agreements with "friendly" Eastern bloc countries that financed scholarships for thousands of young Palestinian students.

Today, that curve has been reversed dramatically. Levels of education collapsed as the conditions that underlay the successes of the 1960s and 1970s disappeared. The reversion undergone by the PLO's social institutions, the drop in UNRWA assistance, the closing of the Gulf market, and the collapse of the Eastern bloc together had a negative effect on education. This situation has made the future bleak for young Palestinians and limited their chances of emigrating to Europe or the United States. Compared with Palestinians in other Arab countries, the Palestinian population in Lebanon has become the worst educated: according to a study carried out in 1999 by the Norwegian research institute FAFO, 20 percent of the camp's inhabitants are illiterate, and of these, 8 percent are between the ages of fifteen and thirty-nine. Thirty percent of young people over the age of fifteen have never been to school, while 80 percent of those who began school left before completing their secondary education.[2] UNRWA schools in Lebanon have the worst results in terms of grades repeated, while dropping out is now the rule for teenagers. Among young people age six to seventeen, only 44 percent are enrolled in school—compared with 98 percent of young Palestinians living in Syria.[3]

The first generation of Palestinians in Lebanon participated enthusiastically in the educational revolution, with all age groups entering UNRWA schools en masse. Now, however, more than half of all teenagers are leaving the international agency's schools before the end of ninth grade. They are discouraged by mediocre training, a lack of professional opportunities, teachers who are frequently absent, and overflowing classrooms (with forty to fifty students per class in elementary school). The example of educated, unemployed parents deprived of access to the job market by Lebanese legislation, coupled with the urgent need to bring money into the household, discourages young people from pursuing their studies very far. While in the 1950s parents of peasant origin could nurture hopes of professional success for their children, thanks to the social mobility that UNRWA's education system offered, in the 1990s parents tend to orient their offspring toward the search for paid employment rather than the quest for a diploma. Even more than UNRWA's deficient infrastructure and financial support, sociopolitical changes—foremost among them the lack of opportunities offered by Lebanese society—are behind the magnitude of this crisis.

Lebanon's Palestinian population is probably a unique case of the generation gap in school or university education that has opened up to the detriment of the younger members of society: those born in the 1970s and 1980s are less educated than their elders. This is an exceptional phenomenon. In the Arab world as a whole, the most significant gap pits the generation of 1945 against that of 1975: the latter benefited from lengthier schooling and better access to higher education. In Lebanon, the Palestinian population has escaped this tendency for young people born in 1975 to be more skilled than those born in 1945.[4] Young people today are becoming as uneducated as the exodus generation, and are further deprived of the system of peasant values that their grandparents and great-grandparents enjoyed.

The effects of such regression naturally extend to higher education. Beirut Arab University is a perfect example of this decline. Located in the heart of the Fakahani neighborhood—dubbed "the Republic of Fakahani" in the 1970s because the PLO had clustered most of its activities and offices there—Beirut Arab University had a student body overwhelmingly made up of Palestinians.[5] The relative importance of this Palestinian component diminished gradually throughout the 1990s. For the 1989–90 academic year, at the end of the Lebanese war, there were still 1,771 Palestinian students in a global student body of 15,342.[6] In 2002, more than ten years after the conflict ended, BAU had only 691 Palestinian students, and 4,662 of Lebanese nationality, in an enrolled student body of 7,044.[7]

Because of these structural difficulties, and the bitter observation that "education leads nowhere in Lebanon," the fact that a significant number of young Palestinians have chosen to study at Islamic institutes in Beirut, Tripoli, or Saida deserves closer attention. The fact that the phenomenon has taken on new dimensions since the end of the war seems to be a sign that a process of intellectual resocialization through religion is taking place.

The Lebanese Market in Sunni Religious Education

In Beirut, three institutes share the market in Sunni religious education: Dar al-Fatwa (al-Azhar) College in the Mar Elias neighborhood; Imam al-Awza'i Institute, just next to BAU in the Tariq al-Jadidah neighborhood, opposite Beirut's municipal stadium; and the Islamic Preaching College (Kulliyyat al-Da'wa al-Islamiyya), also known as al-Da'wa Islamic College. On the whole, students tend to prefer either Imam al-Awza'i Institute or the Islamic Preaching College. Unlike the other two institutes, the Islamic Preaching College has the advantage of being free, and does not require its students to have a high school diploma. Situated in the Bir Hasan neighborhood, behind the Kuwaiti Embassy, the college was built in 1989 with Libyan funding. It is a branch of al-Da'wa University in Tripoli, the Libyan capital.

The activities of Imam al-Awza'i Institute are not restricted to teaching: its directors have also set up a media center on Islam and the Muslim world (which publishes from Cyprus *al-Kashshaf al-Islami,* a periodical that aims to provide an exhaustive bibliography of everything written on Islam worldwide). It also provides quality-control certificates for *halal* food products, and in that field cooperates with more than 450 chambers of commerce and industries worldwide.[8] During the war, members of the board published a monthly review, the "Islamic Report" *(al-Taqrir al-Islami),* which expressed the most radical viewpoints of Lebanese Sunni Islam.

To understand the kind of education dispensed at the Imam al-Awza'i Institute, and the reasons it has been so successful among certain segments of the Sunni population in Lebanon, it may be useful to review the careers and positions of the most important figures in the administration and the faculty.[9]

The institute's founder, Tawfiq Huri, belonged to one of Beirut's Sunni families whose relatively recent prominence dates back to the French Mandate period in Lebanon. His father, Rashid, who made his money in trade and real estate and owned extensive properties in the Tariq al-Jadidah neighborhood, was elected to Beirut's city council in 1952. He was also one of the founding members of an Islamic charity *(al-Barr wal-Ihsan)* that sought to distinguish itself by its religious orientation from the network of charity *maqasid,* financed by Beirut's notable Sunni families. Like most of the "Sunni street" in the 1950s, Tawfiq joined the Arab nationalist cause. He provided the land on which BAU, twinned with Alexandria University, was built in 1960 with Egyptian government funding.

Tawfiq Huri's drift toward radical Islam dates back to the late 1960s, when he joined an organization called Ibad al-Rahman, one of the nuclei of the Jama'a Islamiyya. Two members of his family were also among the founders of the Jama'a brotherhood in 1964.[10] From the start, he openly supported the Palestinian cause, which he saw as the natural extension of his Islamist leanings. He made contact with Abu Jihad, one of Fatah's most prominent early leaders. While he was still a member of the Muslim Brothers, Abu Jihad appointed him editor-in-chief of "Our Palestine" *(Falastinuna),* Fatah's first newspaper, published in Beirut starting in October 1959, less than a year after the Palestinian organization had been established in Kuwait. In 1974, Tawfiq Huri also participated in the creation of the "Movement for the Support of Fatah" (Harakat al-

Musanada li-Harakat Fatah), to which many Sunni religious figures belonged. In the meantime, the Palestinian leadership had concluded from its failure in Jordan that it must act at a deeper level on
the Lebanese social and political situation in order to protect itself
against the possibility of another conflict with local society, even if
it meant becoming involved in Lebanon's contradictions. Tawfiq
Huri's activism, then, was inscribed in the solidarity networks set
up and maintained by Abu Jihad, who based his political strategy
on a quest for the greatest number of possible allies in Lebanon's
Muslim circles, Shi'ite as well as Sunni.[11]

Against the wishes of family members who were also on the university's board of directors, Tawfiq Huri wanted to develop the curriculum's inadequate religious studies component. For that reason,
he set up Imam al-Awza'i Institute—the first Sunni institution of
higher education in Lebanon—in 1979. At the time, he made no secret of his ambition to become mufti of the republic one day, and to
remedy the Sunni community's organizational weakness from the
top down.[12]

During the war, Tawfiq Huri also headed the institute's publication, al-Taqrir al-Islami ("The Islamic Report"), which advocated
the implementation of Shari'a on Lebanese society as a whole, and
specialized in denouncing the "cowardice" and "complacency" of
Lebanon's Muslim elites. The journal accused these religious leaders of being more concerned with the codes of confessional coexistence than with the defense of their faith, as al-Taqrir al-Islami's
writers conceived it. For instance, these elites had not raised a finger
to oppose the 1977 beatification of Sherbel Makhluf, "whom the
Maronites declare to be the patron saint of Lebanon." In the same
vein, the publication lambasted the leaders of Islamic associations
who allowed their employees to participate in funeral services held
in churches.[13]

These articles, which showed indirectly that civility persisted in
everyday life and that the values of religious coexistence were reaf-

firmed despite the war, also expressed frustration with Lebanon's Sunni elites, whose social power the Islamists sought to destroy. The journal's writers compared Lebanon's Islamic associations and ulema to deserters of the faith who defended Islam in the manner of "a fighter who has withdrawn from the battlefield, or suffered defeat there." The Sunni elites felt a bond with the Christian elites whose social values and material interests they shared; for this reason, they were accused of having chosen to maintain their status at the expense of their religion. If Muslims in Lebanese territory— "Lebanese, Syrians, Palestinians"—overcame their national divisions and broke their political loyalties, the authors of the "Islamic Report" argued, they could place themselves in the service of the Shari'a.[14] Nor did they spare the official Sunni establishment: there would not have been so many "boutiques" funded by foreign powers and sowing discord within Lebanese Muslim society if Dar al-Fatwa had been able to provide the Sunni community with the financial means to obtain its independence.[15]

Although these articles were written in a context of crisis, the institute maintained its protest-oriented Islamism after the end of the conflict. This goes some way toward explaining its success among students who have been excluded from the country's networks of political and economic reconstruction.

According to Tawfiq Huri, the institute is different from other centers of religious education because of its academic eclecticism. Though religious knowledge makes up most of the subject matter taught, it still leaves a place for secular learning. "The courses taught relate to the study of dogma *(aqida),* jurisprudence *(fiqh),* and religious law *(shari'a),*" he explained, "but do not neglect positive law, history, politics, or the study of civilization and psychology."[16] A glance at the course catalog for the 1999–2000 academic year provides some context for this statement, however: of the ten courses offered to first-year students at the institute, seven are related to Islam (and the others to Arabic language and literature as well as a foreign language). The same proportions obtain in the second and third years, though classes on "political regimes" and "economic orders" are also included on a menu strongly dominated by religious subjects.

In the fourth year, classes on "Orientalism and evangelism" or "secret and esoteric movements" reflect the founder's ideological intentions: according to Tawfiq Huri, the Sunni religious elites' historic mission is to fight Western influence in Lebanon. He is convinced that Western research and educational institutions in Lebanon are secret corridors to the hidden plans of various Western governments, which may compete with one another but remain united in working against Islam. He sees the institute in the framework of this clash with the West, which he traces back to the nineteenth century, during the Ottoman period, when Beirut was the spearhead of "Islamic popular reaction" to the dual influence of the Syrian Protestant College (today's AUB) and Saint Joseph University, run by the Jesuits.[17] Paradoxically, for Tawfiq Huri the French Mandate was a sort of golden age, since Muslim protest was taken up by associations that complemented one another efficiently, "unlike what is taking place now"—a reference to the current fragmentation of the Sunni scene in Lebanon, where no religious authority is capable of centralizing and distributing Muslim donations.

At the end of the war, reporters from a religious publication interviewed Tawfiq Huri regarding the best means of revitalizing the Muslim presence in Lebanon. The director of Imam al-Awza'i took the debate over whether it was legal to nominate deputies to the first post-Taif parliament as a pretext to question the legitimacy of that parliament itself: "The press is divided between those who favor nomination and those who oppose it, but at bottom the problem is that the parliamentary assembly fails to respect Islam's injunctions *(la yaltazim bil-Islam)*. Whether or not the deputies are nominated, in fact the question is irrelevant to what Muslims are requesting."[18]

The director of studies at Imam al-Awza'i, Shaykh Kamil Musa, is a well-respected figure in Palestinian religious circles. Born in 1949 in a village of Bazal, in the underprivileged Akkar region, Musa obtained a doctorate in comparative Islamic jurisprudence *(fiqh muqaran)* from al-Azhar University in Egypt, where he completed all his higher education. He returned to Lebanon for good in 1980 and devoted himself to religious education. He taught classes in the sources of Islamic jurisprudence *(usul al-fiqh)* in the literature department at Tripoli Lebanese University and at BAU's law school, where he taught Shari'a. After four years, he left BAU, along with many of his colleagues, and devoted himself fully to Imam al-Awza'i Institute. In 1979, he had been the first instructor to teach a class there titled "The Holy Qur'an and Its Insights." In 1989, when he was fifty, he crowned his religious career with a further academic promotion—the title of professor, granted by two illustrious ulema from Damascus University's department of Shari'a: Nur al-Din al-Atar and Ahmad al-Hajji al-Kurdi, both of whom studied at al-Azhar University.[19]

Shaykh Kamil Musa teaches at Imam al-Awza'i Institute two days a week. He spends the rest of his time training preachers in his native region, Akkar, where he heads a Center for Islamic Preparation and Training. Kamil Musa is one of the Lebanese figures highlighted by the editors of *al-Hidaya,* the newspaper put out by young Palestinian Islamists in Ain al-Helweh. In fact, one of his former students, Abu Dia', now the preacher in an important Ain al-Helweh mosque, interviewed his professor on how he saw his center's mission.[20] Shaykh Musa explained that his mission is to connect Islam with reality "in every form" and to fight a distorted vision of Islam that is reduced to worship alone: "It is now clear that the problem, for Muslims, resides essentially in their having distanced Shari'a from the center of power. It therefore becomes a duty incumbent upon all workers of Islam, as a group or individually, to strive to restore Islam to power; if the current generation doesn't manage to do so, it will become the task of future generations, if God wills it."[21]

Still, Shaykh Musa sets himself apart from groups that advocate taking armed action and seizing power immediately:

> I criticize those who say: "I want God's rule here and now." We have to start by saying: "I am working to establish God's rule, anytime and anywhere, in order to be present when circumstances are most favorable to establishing God's rule." Muslims themselves constitute the first obstacle to attaining this goal. They have forgotten Islam, or misunderstood it and applied it wrongly, because for the past century or so they have been exposed to Western ideas and subjected to unbelieving regimes that have led them astray *(anzimat al-kufr wal-dalal)*.

According to Shaykh Musa, working to purify—that is, to "de-Westernize"—Muslims in Islamic lands is the first task at hand. The remedy, he maintains, requires the creation of an elite group of motivated Muslims who will be capable of directing a lengthy process of Islamic change: "I don't mean that we need to change every Muslim individual, through and through, in order to establish an Islamic regime, because that would be virtually impossible in practice; but it is necessary to create a solid vanguard *(tali'a matinat al-bina)*." In this Leninist vision of militant action, an active minority, owing to its organizational ability and intense convictions, takes the place of the masses, whose will has been alienated by Western ideas—Shaykh Musa repeatedly evokes the duty of self-abnegation incumbent upon Islam's "workers" and "cadres." In this framework, the institute's role is to train an Islamist elite, enlightened by its "acute political conscience" and capable of carrying out a "permanent jihad" that will protect the Islamic awakening from its worst enemy: the threat from within.

Shaykh Musa has a fundamentalist vision of Islam. According to him, it is necessary to "educate young people along the lines of the first generation of Islam, which lived in conditions far more difficult than ours, and which was the key to a complete change in the world, though it was made up of only 314 men [*sic*]. There are millions of us today, but where are we compared to them?" Shaykh Musa's most interesting views, however, concern the dramatic situation of Muslims in Lebanon that he conveys to his readers. When the publication's editor asked him to evaluate the "Islamic awakening" that Lebanon is allegedly experiencing, as well as the means of maintaining and strengthening that awakening, Shaykh Musa responded:

> No one can deny that the Islamic awakening is particularly vigorous at the current time, not only here in Lebanon, but throughout the Islamic world. Our awakening, however, is a special situation: Muslims in this country are engaged in a perpetual struggle against the entire world. Not a single unbelieving community is absent from Lebanon. Despite all the differences between them, they are all agreed on a single goal: that of fighting Islam and the Muslims. When it is taking place in such a difficult context, the Islamic awakening must increase in strength and intransigence.[22]

The vision of a minority persecuted by a coalition of hostile forces, of course, applies especially to Sunnis in Lebanon. But the religious dimension transcends Lebanon's borders: Shaykh Musa insists that jihad must not weaken anywhere in the region; efforts must be made throughout the geographical space of Greater Syria (Bilad al-Sham), the land of "citadels and fortified camps."[23] In this manner, too, "only jihad will liberate Palestine; not words and negotiations. The Crusaders occupied it for two hundred years, and militant Islam *(al-Islam al-jihadi)* liberated it. The same will happen again if God wills it, but only after we have truly returned to God Almighty. Liberating Palestine is not the responsibility of its people alone; it is the responsibility of every Muslim on this earth, because jihad becomes an absolute, individual duty *(fard ayn)* when a Muslim territory is occupied." The reference to Greater Syria is not purely rhetorical: Shaykh Musa also trained at Damascus's faculty of Islamic law, and his institute has a branch in the Syrian capital, at Abul-Nur Mosque, whose director was the former Syrian mufti, Shaykh Ahmad Kaftaro (who died in 2004). Shaykh Musa's reference space includes all of Greater Syria, which takes on its own identity thanks to its crucial geopolitical position in the fight to defend Islam against its many external and internal enemies.

Shaykh Abd al-Nasir Jibri created al-Da'wa College, the Islamic Preaching College, in 1989 with funding from the Libyan government, as noted. In the administrative office, visitors can admire a large picture of Shaykh Jibri shaking hands with Muammar Ghaddafi. Shaykh Jibri sees the role of the college as that of a "scientific and educational fortress," which should be capable of bringing Muslim students back together around a shared Islamic identity. He sees Western modernity as guilty of having separated fields of knowledge into a series of specialized, competing spheres of activity. According to him, religious thought, which has been "subtracted from the sciences and marginalized," must be restored to its dominant position, since religion is the "common ground" on which all Islamic civilization developed.[24]

The college's main mission is therefore to restore a sense of Muslim unity against the political and national divisions the West has created. Shaykh Abd al-Nasir Jibri clearly stakes a claim to this goal: "Our aim is to destroy what France has done to the region, or in other words to destroy the effects of imperialism. France made a mistake when it created Lebanon: they wanted to make a state for the Christians, next to the state for the Jews. Our efforts, carried out in a spirit of unity, must aim at erasing the boundaries between Muslim countries, starting with those separating Lebanon from Syria."[25]

Shaykh Jibri acknowledges that some Muslims oppose unity between the two states "because they would rather preserve the freedom that exists in Lebanon."[26] Ideally, he would like to see a Greater Syria subject to Shari'a, but he believes that people must adapt to their environment. Shaykh Jibri's discourse reproduces the cliché of Lebanon moving at two different speeds, with overdeveloped eastern—that is, Christian—regions and Muslim regions neglected by the Lebanese state. This is a common representation among Islamists in Ain al-Helweh, and is frequently repeated when one questions militants from the Lebanese Sunni petty bougeoisie, who thereby create a link, as they did during the civil war, between religious demands and social frustration.

Shaykh Jibri is a member of the Naqshabandiyya Sufi brotherhood, and his spiritual guide *(murshid)* was none other than Syria's mufti until 2004, the late Shaykh Ahmad Kaftaro. The Palestinians from the camp who attend classes at the college know that the director belongs to a Sufi brotherhood, though they do not share his allegiance; according to them, his orientations do not reflect overall faculty attitudes.

Finally, al-Azhar's Shari'a faculty (Kulliyyat al-Shari'a al-Islamiyya) depends directly on Dar al-Fatwa, the official authority for Sunni Muslims in Lebanon. The college was created in 1982 as an Islamic preaching college (Kulliyyat al-Da'wa al-Islamiyya) before acquiring its permanent title in 1990. According to Muhammad Nukkari, principal private secretary to the mufti of the republic, Dar al-Fatwa does not recognize diplomas granted by other Sunni religious institutions, "which appeared during the war, at a time when no state existed. These institutes teach general Islamic culture, but are not specialized in the religious sciences, as we are. We want to remain legal, and we would like to control the institutes that train individuals who do not have a spiritual relation to the sacred texts."[27] It is necessary to add, however, that some Dar al-Fatwa graduates do in fact have more than a "spiritual relation" with their religion; for example, Shaykh Yusuf Tuhaybash, a Palestinian preacher who graduated from Dar al-Fatwa's training center, also belongs to Usbat al-Ansar in Ain al-Helweh. Other shaykhs of Palestinian origin teach in the framework of Dar al-Fatwa, like Shaykh Husayn Dawud, the secretary of the League of Ulema for Palestine, who teaches at one of the al-Azhar Institute's branches in Tyre, in southern Lebanon.

Who Attends the Religious Institutes?

In the academic year 1995–96, there were 636 non-Lebanese and 353 Lebanese students at Imam al-Awza'i out of a total of 989 students.[28] For the 1997–98 year, the institute had 913 students of 21 different nationalities (312 at the bachelor level; 564 at the master or fifth-year level; and 37 doctoral students). Because the administrations were reluctant to provide the number of students of each nationality, it has been impossible to obtain data on the exact proportion of Palestinian students enrolled at the institutes. Downstream, one can observe that, with the exception of a few autodidacts (especially in Ain al-Helweh), almost all the religious figures in the Palestinian camps were educated at one of the institutes (principally al-Da'wa or al-Awza'i). One can also say with certainty that the student body at al-Awza'i is made up of a majority of foreigners, with a very high proportion of Syrian and Palestinian students. This tendency has been confirmed since the college's creation, in 1979: as early as 1992–93, there were 552 non-Lebanese students out of a total of 977, or 56.5 percent. That number represents a remarkable increase compared with the 1982–83 academic year, when there were only 36 foreigners out of a total of 135 students (26.7 percent).[29] Although the administration would like to attract "engineers, physicians, or students specialized in other fields," the students' social origins remain modest: 24 percent of them have illiterate mothers, and only 8 percent have parents who received higher education.[30] The students from Ain al-Helweh who take classes at al-Awza'i estimated that at least half the student body was of Palestinian origin, which would correspond to 300 or 400 individuals. If that is indeed the case, the figure is quite high (and does not even include those who study at al-Da'wa College, where education is free, whereas registration fees are $450 a year at al-Awza'i). For comparative purposes, during the 1998–99 academic year, around 475 Palestinian students were enrolled in the social sciences at Saida Lebanese University, the only university in all southern Lebanon.

Given the lack of official figures, to obtain reliable data on the students at al-Da'wa it was necessary to collect information from the lists posted at the gates to the school. Such lists provided the names, geographical origins, ages, and nationalities of students sitting for exams in February 2001. According to the lists, that year the college had around 350 students, with foreigners making up half the student body. There was a high proportion of Palestinian and Syrian students (a little more than fifty Palestinians, or one student in seven), but also Algerians (a dozen) and other students from the Indian subcontinent. That year, Palestinian students who attended classes at al-Da'wa were mainly from the refugee camps and came from all over Lebanon (Rashidiyyeh in the south, Wavel in the Beqaa, Saida and Ain al-Helweh, Nahr al-Barid and Baddawi near Tripoli).

In the Ain al-Helweh camp, two preachers are graduates of Imam al-Awza'i Institute. One of them, Shaykh Abu Fulan (a pseudonym), a young imam at an important salafist mosque in the camp, described the conditions in which he enrolled at Imam al-Awza'i Institute in 1986, and the bad experience he had with the administration of Dar al-Fatwa. He differentiated "official Islam," on the one hand, from "Islam as a movement," on the other:

> Initially, I wanted to study in Saudi Arabia, at the Islamic University in Madina. My application was accepted, but the professor who was in charge of admissions was fired, and I never heard from them

again. Then I went to the religious university of Dar al-Fatwa. I sat for an interview, which was a real interrogation. The questions had to do with politics and security issues. I immediately realized that their Islam is an official religion, not Islam as a movement *(ka haraka)*. They also discriminated against Palestinian students. They turned me down. At al-Awza'i, on the other hand, there is a warm atmosphere and no discrimination against the students.[31]

Dar al-Fatwa, it may be noted, attracts far fewer students than the two other institutes: in 2000, there were only a dozen first-year students enrolled.[32] But the student body also included a high proportion of Palestinians. Musa, for instance, enrolled around the tenth grade, when he was sixteen. Now eighteen, he has been studying at Dar al-Fatwa's al-Azhar College for two years. He spends half the week at the institute's boarding school (arriving in Ain al-Helweh on Thursday and returning to Beirut on Saturday). In the camp, he takes classes in religion at al-Nur Mosque with Shaykh Jamal, and sees no contradiction between what he learns in Beirut and what he learns in Ain al-Helweh. Shaykh Jamal encouraged him to study religion, and he received a fellowship from al-Nur Mosque's *zakat* committee. The subjects he takes are the same as those taught at Imam al-Awza'i Institute: Qur'an, *tafsir*, dogma, Islamic history, Arabic language, grammar, English, and mathematics. He does not feel his Lebanese professors discriminate against him at all—some, indeed, visit the camp regularly—but he has observed anxious reactions from his Lebanese peers: "They thought the camp was a dangerous place; they had the image that the media gives. They changed their opinion when they came to visit me."[33] He has Lebanese Sunni friends and concedes that, like them, he is "persecuted" in Lebanese society:

Muslims are the objects of suspicion here in Lebanon. We are asked to get out of the car at checkpoints. There are often arrests. The state doesn't take care of Muslim neighborhoods. In Sabra, which is a

Lebanese neighborhood, not a Palestinian one, there are no state services: it's a poor area. In Tariq al-Jadidah, it's the same situation.
When there is a sale of land among Lebanese, and the buyer is a
Muslim, it causes a scandal in the whole country. Bishops go on television to protest. This happened when some land was sold east of
Saida. Muslims are not even second-class citizens. They are third- or
fourth-class.[34]

Student Writings

The titles of theses and dissertations defended at Imam al-Awza'i
Institute are a good indicator of the "research agenda" favored
by professors supervising graduate students. Sample titles include
"Preachers and the Call to Islam: Between Present Reality and Desired Goals" (1998); "Constructing the Contemporary Islamic Personality" (1996); "The Unbeliever's Personality" (1998); and "The
Effects of Controversy and Divergence on the *umma*'s Unity"
(1998).

The content of these works offers an idea of the concerns of students who attend the institutes. Most of the works are based on a
binary opposition between an idealized religious past and a present
marked by decline. The students blame this decline on the fact that
religion, reduced to a weekly ritual, no longer infuses social life.
Historical distance is presented as moral distance. To restore original dynamism, Muslims must follow the example of the first believers, who faced conditions more dire still than those obtaining
today. A thesis by a Palestinian student titled "The Elements of Victory in Light of the Qur'an and the *Sunna*" (1997) follows this
model.[35]

Starting from a comparison between the situation of Muslims at
the time Muhammad was preaching and the reality of the current
situation, marked by decline and division, the student author—who
later became a shaykh in the Palestinian camp of Rashidiyyeh—

sought to highlight the reasons for the victory of original Islam, and the lessons Muslims must derive from this experience if they are to realize in the near future the conditions necessary for Islam's victory. Contemporary Muslims, for example, should give "military training the importance it merits," because the Prophet himself "trained his companions in a unique manner, which cannot be compared with anything taking place at the time." He prepared them "for all sorts of confrontations, in all possible conditions," until they "became experienced enough to engage in combat both inside and outside the Arabian Peninsula."[36] If they wish to increase their chances for success, Muslims must start by acting on the "domestic front" by building an efficient information network, for espionage is key to victory over the enemy: Muhammad himself could not have triumphed over Quraysh had he not known their intentions in advance. Similarly, by demonstrating a keen interest in the scientific inventions of his time, whose possible military applications he perceived immediately—as he proved during the battle of Badr—the Prophet demonstrated the importance of technological advancements and their application to the military field. In modern times, Iraq paved the way by carrying out technological innovations before the Gulf War. Consequently, "despite all the subsequent errors and drawbacks, Muslims in all Islamic countries are duty-bound to follow the Iraqi experience in the domain of military industry."[37]

Contrary to the claims of those ulema who betray Islam, the Prophet's experience does not have an exclusively religious dimension, according to the author of this thesis: believers must pay equal attention to all of the Prophet Muhammad's accomplishments, especially in the political and military fields. By rediscovering prophetic inspiration in all paths of existence, Muslims will be able to revive military and political victory over the enemies of Islam.

Exaggerated sectarianism recurs frequently in students' writings. Under the pretext of seeking to overcome past divergences between Islam's two main religious communities, the author of "The Elements of Victory" engaged in a standard attack on the Shi'ites, through a critique of their collective practices and ceremonies (like Ashura), which commemorate the founding event of this branch of Islam:

> On the question of the caliphate, after more than a millennium and several centuries, despite all the time that has passed, there are still merchants of discord *(fitna)* from cruel communities who like to stir up trouble. They open this question disloyally, to damage Muslim unity, destabilize them, and tear this unity asunder . . . Again, they place the question of the caliphate first on their list of priorities, only to conclude that the caliphate was forcefully seized from the Prophet's family. They live in the memory of Husayn's death, without trying to renew his work . . . It is truly surprising to see that this deceitful propaganda still exists today, and still has partisans who cling to it stubbornly, despite the considerable distance that separates us from [the time of] the caliphate, which increases the intellectual discord between Sunnis and Shi'ites.[38]

Iran, according to the author, is barred from aspiring to the status of Muslim power, since the country "applies a republican regime, which is forbidden in Islam." Implicitly, the bases for reconciliation as the author lays them out do not allow for the religious otherness of Shi'ism to be recognized. Rather, they require its suppression, pure and simple, since over time the commemoration of the pain and sense of injustice caused by the loss of the imamate has become one of the foundations of Shi'ism as a religious belief. To give up the memory of this event, which for the purposes of his argument the author relegates to distant history, would mean, in essence, to stop being Shi'ite.

In another thesis, written by an Iranian student and titled "Shura and Democracy: Between Shari'a and Positive Law" (1996), one can read, for example, that "democracy is against Islam, since it gives the people the right to legislate, which is God's exclusive right.

Even the Prophet did not have the right to legislate on his own initiative, without a revelation from God. To act differently is a reprehensible innovation, since it constitutes an infraction against God's rights." Furthermore, "democracy posits itself as an alternative to Islam," whereas "Islam is a complete construct, which lacks nothing, and which requires Muslims to live within it in every detail. At the same time, it is forbidden to introduce polluting elements in this fortified *(muhassan)* house, in order that Muslims may breathe pure *(naqi)* air. Now, the expression 'democracy' is one of those that poison the atmosphere of the Muslim house, and it incites weak Muslims to doubt Islam's ability to resolve humanity's difficulties." Along with a series of similar binary oppositions, all of which place the divine Islamic city above democratic society, which remains imperfect because of its all-too-human foundations, one can also read a more empirical denunciation of political practice in the Arab countries.[39] These countries, according to the author, "transform democracy into its opposite," for leaders "manipulate the elections to obtain 99 percent of the vote" and the secret service "controls state institutions." Of course, the examples given by the author relate to the Egyptian political system; the Syrian model is not mentioned, though it offers an equally obvious example of such practices.

The fact that Shaykh Abdallah Hallaq, another student at al-Awza'i Institute, is close to Hezbollah, an Islamist organization that participates in elections, does not prevent him from considering democracy a "corrupting" regime for Muslim faith. The Islamists *(al-islamiyyin)* who agree to participate in elections bear a grave responsibility, since they lead Muslims astray. Furthermore, by closing down Islamic radio stations, removing religious education from the public school curriculum, and allowing the media to sully Islam's image on a daily basis, the Lebanese political regime has proven itself an enemy of religion. Consequently, according to Shaykh Hallaq, Muslims must not compromise themselves by going to the polls, where they would have to renounce their essential religious values:

> It has become clear, and indeed it is axiomatic of political life in Lebanon, that those who hold political and financial power exploit their influence to accumulate the country's political and economic resources. This has become even clearer since the Islamists entered parliament. The question we must ask is: where were the Islamists in parliament when it was necessary to oppose the exploiters' aggression? Was their role as important as was required? We must ponder the answer at length . . . I say that we do not need their democracy to attain security, justice, and individual happiness.[40]

Would the alternative be to "open fire" on the regime? Prudently, Shaykh Hallaq impugns the option of violence and preaches a long-term strategy that consists of training an Islamic elite in all social sectors and "preparing popular public Islamic opinion" to warn it against the dangers of the current situation. Thanks to this work, when the time comes the "Islamic movement" will be able to retrieve political power. The established regime will fall like a ripe fruit, since by moving away from Islam it will have provoked the inevitable conditions of its own collapse. In the meantime, the "Islamic movement" must consort with intellectuals, politicians, journalists, and military men to show them that solutions exist to the crisis besetting the country. When the crisis becomes insurmountable, the Islamic movement will mobilize its supporters and establish itself as the only authority capable of saving the country.[41] Activists must work from the outside, to distance Muslims from political institutions, while infiltrating the state apparatus from the inside in order to seize power when a "great crisis" breaks out. At no point does Shaykh Hallaq take into account the obstacle that Lebanese society's sectarian nature could pose; unlike Sayyid Fadlallah, Hezbollah's former spiritual guide, who during the war wrote about the situation of non-Muslim minorities in the "Islamic

Republic," he does not devote a single line to the status of non-Muslim communities in his model Islamic state. They are not Muslim; therefore, they do not exist.

The theses and dissertations defended by students at Imam al-Awza'i Institute share the same characteristics, on the whole: the students cobble together their arguments by searching the religious corpus for any element likely to reinforce preexisting political attitudes. Religion comes across as an aside: its role is to confirm a political vision that pits Islam against the rest of the world. They remain faithful to a vision dominated by the clash of great cultural blocs and refuse to make the slightest concession to historicity—except when they are mocking the belief system of Shi'ite Islam, for instance. The exercise encourages a mixture of genres: the gloss of a famous medieval traditionist is immediately followed by extracts from the memoirs of a former head of the American or Israeli secret service.

One might also note the significant proportion of Syrian students attending the institute: between 1985 and 1999, thirty-one of the ninety-three master's theses written at Imam al-Awza'i Institute were defended by Syrian students.[42] The Awza'i Institute and the Preaching (al-Da'wa) College certainly have institutional or religious ties with Shaykh Kaftaro's center. But a radical critique of the social and political order is difficult to imagine in Syria.[43] Religious institutes in Lebanon therefore serve as a pressure valve of sorts: Syrian students enjoy a relative degree of free expression on topics that remain taboo in Syria.

Faculty Attitudes

To the extent possible, I attempted to observe interactions between faculty members and students during dissertation and thesis defenses held at Imam al-Awza'i Institute. My aim was to find out whether professors took responsibility for their students' work, given that some of the students—especially those nearing the end of their graduate studies—do not take regular courses during the academic year. By classifying the remarks and suggestions made by members of dissertation committees, it is possible to reconstitute a fairly faithful image of the faculty's religious orientations.[44]

On the delicate question of *takfir* (accusing a Muslim of apostasy), the professors expressed discomfort and refused to extend their rejection of positive law to society as a whole. Not a single member of the defense committee accepted the conclusions of a Saudi student who argued that modern Turkey could be considered the contemporary equivalent of Constantine's empire, and as such belonged to the "Realm of War," or *Dar al-Harb*.[45] Assimilating the two in this way could have grave consequences, since, according to the student's argument, all Turkey's population would thereby find itself in a situation of apostasy, and therefore subject to a collective death sentence. The head of the committee, Shaykh Kamil Musa, insisted on noting that it was necessary to distinguish political regimes, on one hand, from societies, on the other: "Turkey," he said, "is a Muslim land. One should not confuse the people with the regime. Positive law in Turkey is secular, as it is in most of the Arab regimes. The Turkish government is unbelieving; the same goes for the Arab regimes. One cannot see any difference between them."

The institute's members impose an Islamist opinion in other fields as well: professors forbid their students from pronouncing the word "Israel," and only the expression "occupied Palestine" can be used to indicate that state. Some no longer make the distinction—which is fundamental to Arab nationalist discourse—between anti-Zionism and anti-Semitism. During one defense, an instructor at the institute, Nayif Ma'ruf, commented on the candidate's assertion that, among the first four caliphs, two had been assassinated by Jews, and suggested that this may have been the case for all four. Shaykh Musa criticized a female student who had mentioned women's "right to freedom" *(haqq al-hurriyya)* in her thesis, exclaiming:

"What does that mean? Freedom like in the West? You shouldn't write such things!"

The committee's final evaluation of the dissertation submitted by the Palestinian Islamist shaykh Abdallah Hallaq—"The Causes of the Islamic Awakening: Stages in the Establishment of an Islamic State," defended on March 16, 1999, at the institute—sheds light on faculty attitudes toward this type of discourse. Hallaq's declaration that the Lebanese (and Arab) political system was illegitimate was met with ambivalence within the committee: its director, Shaykh Kamil Musa, focused his critique on the work's religious aspects, while praising the student's energy and strong convictions. The session was turbulent at times, especially when the candidate reasserted that, from a religious perspective, all the Arab regimes are impious. This comment aroused the objections of a (secular) member of the committee. The same professor also pointed out to him that *al-Wa'i*, the Liberation Party's publication, was cited too often in his bibliography and was not a worthy source for an academic work; he added that Hallaq's dual position, as shaykh and student, created a certain confusion, which undermined the quality of his research. Despite these remarks, made by a secular professor (while the head of the committee, Shaykh Kamil Musa, remained silent), Shaykh Abdallah Hallaq received a grade of "very good"—just below that of "excellent"—for a fairly mediocre compilation, a pamphlet rather than a doctoral dissertation, in which fundamentalist lampoons coexist happily with various citations and radical opinions.

There are at least two reasons for the academic recognition the institute conferred on Shaykh Abdallah Hallaq, one practical and the other ideological. First, Shaykh Hallaq serves a pivotal function, with immediate benefits for the institute's administration: he plays a crucial role in recruiting students. As Murshid's academic adviser, he helps advertise Imam al-Awza'i Institute in all Lebanon's Palestinian camps, encourages his students to continue their studies at the institute, and asks other shaykhs to do the same. The institute, for its part, accepts the diplomas conferred by Murshid. Consequently, accreditation from Shaykh Hallaq opens the institute's doors to applicants.[46] Since the increase in the number of students is largely due to the Palestinian element, the administration of Imam al-Awza'i Institute has no choice but to accept the situation and reward Shaykh Hallaq for his enthusiastic recruitment. His efforts in spreading information about the institute have been productive: all the young people of Ain al-Helweh's Islamist milieux know about the college. The best of them obtain scholarships from Murshid and "go up" to Beirut to complete their religious training. Though Shaykh Hallaq displays ideological convictions that some professors may challenge, his opinions are in sync with those of the most influential people in the institute's administration.

Imam al-Awza'i Institute, like the other religious colleges, may therefore be seen as one of the rare socialization milieux—in the sense of a "structured social community in which inculcation takes place"—open to young Palestinians in Lebanese society.[47] This community, which has already played a significant role in training the preachers who are active in the camps and in some regions with a high Palestinian population, helps establish ties that transcend and marginalize national identities, emptied of their political content.[48] The college thus appears as a locus for the construction of "ideological citizenship," bringing together young people who have been excluded from the social system for various reasons, but have in common a feeling of alienation from the state and the official political system.

Imam al-Awza'i Institute subscribes to a fundamentalist brand of Islam, defined essentially by its opposition to the West and Western values. It marks out cultural boundaries within the religious tradition itself, transmitted as a "mutilated and mutilating" tradition, to cite Professor Mohamed Arkoun. Among students and faculty alike, the same mythical construct functions systematically, with an

original golden age, imaginary historical continuity, a rupture provoked by European intervention in Oriental societies, and the duty
of "true believers" to bring about renewal by struggling against
Western influences and to return to "authenticity" at every level of
existence. This discourse cannot give rise to critical thought, since it
is based on an opposition between an Islam that is essentially above
and beyond history and a West (or Christianity) that exists only in
history.[49] Undoubtedly, the administration does not advocate violent action against the establishment, just as it would not accuse
Lebanese Muslim society of apostasy, but it spreads attitudes of
rejection with regard to official political space. More seriously,
through its negative view of non-Muslim communities, and of non-
Sunni groups at the narrowest level, it refuses the values of coexistence that are guaranteed, in theory, by the Lebanese political pact.

These dissertation defenses dramatize the complex, ambiguous
relationships between a faculty of ulema and some of their student
audience. The fact that these religious leaders have no ties with the
regime—nor even with the Sunni political elites—allows them to
criticize the Lebanese social and political system freely, in the name
of a divine order contained in the Shari'a. Classical Muslim jurisprudence is extremely rich and provides abundant fodder for dissertation topics: students have only to pick a religious institution (such
as marriage, *waqf*, or *zakat*) and compare it with contemporary realities (which no longer have much to do with it, if indeed they were
ever practiced under the conditions that doctrine dictates) in order
to adduce additional proof of the decline of Muslim societies. Although the main faculty members challenge the constitutional principles of political life in Lebanon and wish for complete implementation of the Shari'a, they do not condone taking violent action as a
radical mode of effecting political and social change.[50] The situational logic that allows peripheral ulema to question the political
order simultaneously prohibits them from extending such approval,
at the risk of incurring legal sanctions and the closing down of their

establishments. Young people in the camps or in Sunni popular neighborhoods have less to lose than their professors do, and, in their case, situational logic no longer necessarily counterbalances the power of meaning. The contradiction may only be transcended by an attempt at introspection with regard to the relationship between violence and religion, and such an attempt has yet to be made.

An examination of the student population that attends these centers reveals an ideal type different from that of the young Islamist graduate produced by a secular education system, discussed by Gilles Kepel for the 1980s.[51] The students at the Islamic centers never received a secular education; they judge Lebanese society, and Arab political regimes in general, on the immediate basis of religious knowledge they absorbed at private institutes. They cobble together their ideas not from a haphazard, undirected reading of religious texts, but from within the Islamic tradition, studied in a very formal and superficial way. These Islamist militants choose relatively small, insignificant centers of education, whose main quality, in their eyes, is their independence from Dar al-Fatwa and the mufti. They see Sunni Islam's official representative organization in Lebanon as an example of "state Islam," embodied in an official—Mufti Qabbani—who, according to the most indulgent analyses, is a prisoner of his institutional position. Other, less tolerant Islamists see him as the conscious instrument of those who seek to degrade his religion. The institute, which draws young people from popular backgrounds, for the most part, and includes a high proportion of non-Lebanese Arabs, offers its students tools for a radical critique of the political system, which could lead them to take violent action.

The proliferation of training centers and Islamic institutes in all of post-war Lebanon's Sunni regions, it seems, signifies that certain segments of Sunni Islam are rejecting the political order and feeling increasingly suspicious of political organizations, even those claiming an Islamic identity. The only Islamist organization that has voting power at the national level is the Jama'a Islamiyya, and it lost much of its credibility when it began advocating integration into the institutional political system—especially since that system's latent function, for the past decade, has been to discredit just such program-based parties. To preserve a political audience on the ground, Jama'a militants are forced to speak the language of salafist Islamism, even when doing so places them in a precarious position with regard to their public commitments. Young Islamists would rather mobilize in the framework of informal networks structured by teaching centers that are often very small, rather than put up campaign posters for candidates who, if they are elected, seem unlikely to implement Shari'a starting from the Place de l'Etoile, where the Lebanese parliament holds its sessions.

Through religion, a community of values has been sketched out between a population that is still very politically conscious and the proletarianized segments of Lebanese society. For Palestinian Islamists, the existence or absence of discrimination against them is a test that measures the intensity of religious sentiment among their Lebanese coreligionists.[52] For Lebanese Islamists, giving relevance to political identities developed by the West would be tantamount to betraying a religious allegiance superior to any human construct.

In the Palestinian camps, the time of the self-taught shaykhs is definitely over. It was phased out in three stages: initially, religious personnel in the Palestinian camps had no university-level training; piety, individual authority, or membership in a Sufi brotherhood (as in the case of Shaykh Ghunaym) was sufficient to bring candidates to the fore. This was the profile of al-Nur Mosque's first preacher in the 1960s: he was chosen for the task because he knew the Qur'an by heart, but he had never received formal schooling, whether secular or religious. The generation that took over in the 1980s—in its fifties today—was a hybrid: some of its members went to secular universities (as in the ideal of the Islamist militant with scientific or technical training, educated in a secular university, like Shaykh

Jamal Khattab), while others were already graduates of Lebanese Islamic institutes (as in the case of Shaykh Ali Abbas), heralding the current crop, whose only frame of knowledge is that taught in Middle Eastern Islamic universities and institutes. For instance, Shaykh Ahmad, a Palestinian, enrolled in a master's and then a doctoral program at Imam al-Awza'i Institute; these degrees capped his previous religious training, undergone in Saudi Arabia. He is originally from the Nahr al-Barid camp, in the Akkar region. At the age of thirty-eight, he has never come in any contact whatsoever with secular education: at the secondary level, he spent six years studying jurisprudence *(fiqh)* in Tripoli, at the Islamic Teaching and Training College (Kulliyyat al-Tarbiyya wal-Ta'lim al-Islami). Then he left Lebanon for four years, from 1981 to 1985, which he spent studying at the Islamic University of Madina, in Saudi Arabia, in the faculty for preaching and religious principles.

In Shaykh Ahmad's case, the intellectual continuity of the education he received at different religious centers, from the University of Madina to Lebanon's educational institutions, more than made up for the geographical discontinuity in his personal curriculum. Shaykhs who graduated from the Islamic University, or were exposed to the intellectual influence of ulema who emerged from it directly, have thus transplanted the salafist vision of history and the world, as taught within that system, throughout the region.

Today, this tendency is growing stronger: Islamic institutes, shunned by the children of the Sunni middle class whom the founders initially hoped to attract, have been taken over by young Palestinians who have just finished middle school or high school. In the camps, they are encouraged to continue their education in the capital, even if that means commuting back and forth between Beirut and Saida (which only takes an hour). If one takes into account the demographic structure of Lebanon's Palestinian population—43 percent of the population is below the age of sixteen—the phenomenon will inevitably have consequences for the internal equilibrium of the camps.

CHAPTER 7

Underground Jihad
in Sir al-Diniyeh

On December 31, 1999, the Lebanese population was preoccupied with preparations for New Year's Eve. Lebanon's Muslims had also been celebrating the month of Ramadan for the past ten days. Thus the serious clashes that occurred between army units and militant Sunni Islamists in the steep mountains of Sir al-Diniyeh, thirty miles northeast of Tripoli, came as a shock. The battle, which lasted for six days and threw the country back into the psychosis of civil war, left more than thirty people dead: eleven soldiers, including one officer; five civilians; and fifteen fundamentalist militants.

In the meantime, tensions had also reached the Lebanese capital, after a Palestinian from Ain al-Helweh, Ahmad Abu Kharrub, attacked the Russian Embassy, on the Mazraa coast road, in the upscale Verdun neighborhood. Abu Kharrub declared his "solidarity with Chechnya" before dying under a volley of shots fired by four hundred members of the Internal Security Forces (FSI). This was the first operation directed against Russian interests outside Federation territory since the war in the Caucasus had begun in 1994. On the day of the attack, the media had covered an explosion near the Lebanese military checkpoint, at the northern entrance to the Ain al-Helweh camp. Combatants from the Usbat al-Ansar group gathered near the army checkpoint but did not provoke a clash. On New Year's Eve, the body of a sister of the Maronite Antonine order was found on the outskirts of Beirut, stunning the population, and particularly the Christians, once again. The public was outraged by the particularly odious nature of the assassination. Although no one could link these various events, they had the cumulative effect of creating a nationwide sense of insecurity. As was the case during certain phases of the civil war, the series of events stirred collective memories and made it impossible to understand what was going on objectively.

Although no one could provide an immediate explanation for the Diniyeh clashes, local political observers could not resist linking them to the peace negotiations that had begun fifteen days earlier between Israel and Syria in Washington. On December 12, 1999, before the Diniyeh "events"—the euphemism was a misleading reference to the 1975 "events" that marked the beginning of the civil war—several hundred alleged Liberation Party (Hizb al-Tahrir) members had been arrested, first in Homs, and then in other Syrian cities.[1] Rumors circulating after the fact suggested that Syrian security services and the Lebanese army might have taken collective action against the presumed enemies of a regional peace deal that seemed to be in the offing. The Muslim Brotherhood's London branch, voicing its opposition to the arrests, stated: "Hafiz al-Asad's regime is more considerate toward Barak than toward its own citizens."[2] Often seen as an extension of Syrian space—some Syrian Muslim Brothers took refuge in Tripoli during the 1978–1982 war against the regime—the Sunni capital of northern Lebanon also suffered a campaign of preventive repression, with more than 160 arrests, according to the Saudi newspaper *al-Hayat*.[3] After the battle, some journalists wondered why none of the various "internal security" forces, whose role was reinforced considerably after General Lahoud took power in November 1998, had been able to locate an Islamist underground and training camps in the Diniyeh region, a zone that has also been under the control of the Syrian army and intelligence services *(mukhabarat)* since 1976.

These events can be seen as the dramatic outcome of ideological dynamics that had been under way since the end of the civil war, in Lebanese society and the Palestinian camps alike. The Diniyeh clashes confirmed the existence in Lebanon of a form of jihadist Islamism that differed from other known forms of Islamic radicalism in terms of its functioning, its understanding of the struggle, its priorities, and its doctrinal references.

Basim al-Kanj: Profile of a Professional Jihadist

The leader of the Sir al-Diniyeh insurgents was found dead after the battle of January 2000. Basim al-Kanj (Abu Aisha) was born in 1964 in Azqa village, in the Diniyeh region.[4] He graduated high school with a technical diploma in Qubbeh, a poor neighborhood of Tripoli, and in 1985 received a scholarship from the Hariri Foundation, which allowed him to go to the United States and continue his studies in Boston. There, he was very influenced by conferences and meetings about jihad in Afghanistan, and he helped raise funds for the "freedom fighters" who were benefiting from the support of the Reagan administration. At these meetings, Basim al-Kanj came to know several Lebanese expatriates, including Khalil Akkawi, who was also working toward a technical degree in the United States. In Orlando, where Akkawi lived, a preacher of Palestinian origin, Shaykh Tamim al-Adnani, was encouraging young people to go on jihad in Afghanistan. He provided useful information to those who showed an interest in making the trip by sending them to al-Farook Mosque in New York.[5]

Basim al-Kanj married an American who later converted to Islam. As a result, he lost his residency in the United States, as stipulated in the internal regulations of the Hariri Foundation's student mission. He was forced to leave the United States in 1989. With logistical support from the Service Bureau for Arab Combatants, which Abdallah Azzam headed, Kanj went to Pakistan for the first time, with his wife and daughter. He settled his family in Peshawar, on the border between Pakistan and Afghanistan.

After several military training sessions on Pakistani territory, Basim al-Kanj, then twenty-five, went off to fight the Soviet troops with the other Arab *mujahidin*. The young Arabs were bound by ties of solidarity and guided by the same religious ideals. In Peshawar, Basim al-Kanj joined Khalil Akkawi, who had arrived in Pakistan two years before. Thanks to Akkawi, he met another Lebanese, Hilal Ja'far, who had emigrated to the United States and was Akkawi's roommate in Orlando, where he was pursuing a degree in mathematics begun at the American University of Beirut. He left for Peshawar in 1987, following the same route as his friend. A few years later, these volunteers would form the core of Kanj's Lebanese network in Tripoli. Kanj also met Osama bin Laden and Ayman al-Zawahiri during this period. He was wounded in fighting against the Soviets, and in 1990 was taken to a hospital in Peshawar. Then he left the Indian subcontinent for good, traveling back and forth between the United States and Lebanon. After having returned to his native country once between 1991 and 1994, he pursued the path of an "international jihadist" in Bosnia-Herzegovina, and then left the Balkans after the Dayton Accords were signed in 1995. He volunteered to go and fight in Chechnya, but, for reasons that remain obscure, the director of the Service Bureau for Arab Combatants in Chechnya, located in Azerbaijan, refused to give him a permit. He returned to the United States, where he lived alone for two years before moving back to Lebanon and joining his many children in his native village of Azqa in 1996. In the United States, at the global Islamic congress held in Chicago in 1995, Basim al-Kanj had met Qasim Dahir, a former Tawhid sympathizer who lived in Canada and whose main activity in North America consisted of fundraising for Afghanistan. Basim al-Kanj convinced Dahir to direct his funds toward Lebanon. While in London, Dahir met Abu Qatada, an Islamist shaykh of Palestinian origin whom Basim al-Kanj had met in Peshawar.

After his return to Lebanon, two concerns guided Kanj's actions: renewing ties with the former comrades he had met in Peshawar, and setting up a solidarity network within Lebanese society, which he had left in the mid-1980s. His recruitment strategy focused on two particularly receptive environments: the Ain al-Helweh camp and the poor quarters of Tripoli.

The Ain al-Helweh Encounter

During his 1994 stay in Lebanon, Basim al-Kanj had met demobilized Afghan veterans who had returned to their homeland. Thanks to one of them, Ahmad al-Qassam, whom he had met in Peshawar—and who was executed on March 24, 1997, for having participated in the assassination of Nizar al-Halabi, the head of al-Ahbash—he met Usbat al-Ansar leaders for the first time in the Ain al-Helweh camp. He met the group's emir, Abu Mahjin, and his lieutenant, Abu Ubayda, also known as Jihad Mustafa, the head of the clandestine organization's military wing. The members of Usbat al-Ansar saw Basim al-Kanj's visit as an acknowledgment of their importance on the local scene of jihadist Islamism. It also offered an opportunity to gather information about the situation of Muslims on the various jihad fronts.

In terms of experience, however, the two categories of jihadists had nothing in common at first sight. The Afghan veterans were activists who had spent more than a decade participating in radical global Islam. They had moved from America to the Indian subcontinent, occasionally stopping over in Europe or Latin America to raise funds for a jihad that changed with the wind, theorized in Peshawar and applicable virtually everywhere else. Compared with these professional, itinerant jihadists, Ain al-Helweh's salafist groups were static, urban actors confined to a small physical space. Since the mid-1980s, they had been rebelling against the PLO, the quasi-state organization that claimed to represent them, and since the early 1990s they had been engaged in a multifaceted struggle against the "enemies of Islam" in Lebanese society. In the mid-1980s, the war against the Soviets in Afghanistan provided a new ideological model for militants of Palestinian origin who were engaged in combating the PLO influence in Ain al-Helweh. At stake now was the definition of the refugee population's very identity. In that context, the war in Afghanistan gave the new religious entrepreneurs the opportunity to implant a network of symbols, images, conflicts, and figures within the camp. As noted, the way had been paved for this encounter with an "Arab Afghan" several years earlier, when the war was idealized for the camp's younger generation, whose members were expected to identify with the heroic figure of Abdallah Azzam.

Besides acknowledging the role of Usbat al-Ansar in the field of radical Islam, the arrival in the camp of a key participant in the Afghan war—someone like Basim al-Kanj—had practical implications, in terms of the exchange and sharing of weapons, logistical resources, and volunteers. For instance, Basim al-Kanj gave Abu Mahjin software that allowed him to transmit information via a secure Internet connection.

In a country as small as Lebanon, an encounter between militants like Basim al-Kanj and Usbat al-Ansar was almost inevitable, even if Usbat al-Ansar members were still relatively unknown outside the restricted circles of salafist-style Lebanese Islamism. When the meeting took place, at any rate, Basim al-Kanj was with people involved in the fighting against the Ahbash. He was escorted by Umar Yi'ali, a friend of Ahmad al-Qassam who was working at the Association for Guidance and Goodwill (Jam'iyyat al-Hidaya wal-Ihsan).[6] In Tripoli, the salafist shaykh Da'i al-Islam al-Shahal headed the organization, which was dissolved in 1995 after a decision taken in the Ministerial Council. Abu Mahjin took advantage of Umar Yi'ali's visit to the camp to request that the salafist association send shaykhs to give religion classes to the young inhabitants of Ain al-Helweh. Umar Yi'ali agreed, and even suggested that young people from the camp be sent to Tripoli to take classes. This exchange subsequently took place. Such details indicate that the takeover of the camp was not a unilateral process; it also resulted from an appeal directed toward the outside world.

The process of resocialization through religion is vital to our understanding of how the symbolic rupture with Palestinian national space occurred in practice. The appeals that Ain al-Helweh activists made to shaykhs whose knowledge was renowned in religious circles correspond to a phenomenon familiar from the case of the GIA in Algeria in the mid-1990s: militants with poor religious culture turn to ulema whose knowledge of the traditional corpus enables them to interpret the concrete circumstances of the struggle in an Islamic light. This explains the presence in Ain al-Helweh of collections of texts by Abu Qatada, a Palestinian shaykh living in London, who served as the religious expert for the GIA in Algeria in the 1990s.

After Basim al-Kanj left for the United States in 1995, Ahmad al-Qassam appointed people close to him to develop ties with Abu Mahjin's group. Umar Yi'ali commuted between Tripoli and Ain al-Helweh, exchanged religious cassettes and pamphlets with the Usbat al-Ansar emir, and, thanks to the members of the Islamist militia, learned how to use a Kalashnikov. Ihab al-Banna, formerly an anchor on the Voice of Islam radio station, which broadcast from Beirut, also went back and forth between Ain al-Helweh and the capital to maintain ties with Usbat al-Ansar. After Ahmad al-Qassam was executed in 1997 for the assassination of Shaykh al-Halabi, Basim al-Kanj, who was now settled in Beirut, asked Ihab al-Banna to become the main liaison with Ain al-Helweh. Banna went to the camp at least once a month to give religion lessons to Abu Ubayda and talk about the situation of Muslims in Lebanon. Thanks to these contacts, Basim al-Kanj was able to ensure that the members of Usbat al-Ansar shared the same salafist leanings and the same understanding of religious action as his own circle.

For Ain al-Helweh's jihadists, Basim al-Kanj represented a gateway to the Lebanese religious scene and a means of projecting their influence beyond the camp. Two Afghan *mujahidin* veterans of Libyan origin were supposedly even sent to Tripoli to convince Kanj—unsuccessfully—to fuse his network with Usbat al-Ansar. Despite these power struggles—the stakes were control of the jihadist movement in Lebanon, with the symbolic and financial advantages that went along with such a position in external relations—the two groups continued to cooperate. Basim al-Kanj, accompanied by Ihab al-Banna, regularly visited Abu Ubayda, spending the night and leaving the next day. In early July 1997, the two men even planned an armed operation to free their companions who had been sentenced to death in the Nizar al-Halabi affair and were leaving Rumiyyeh Prison to undergo medical tests in a Beirut hospital. The project was aborted for reasons that remain unclear.

In early 1998, Basim al-Kanj began to set up training camps in the Diniyeh region, north of Tripoli. To that end, he used the logistical services of Palestinians in Ain al-Helweh. These camps had a provisional vocation: they combined religious instruction and military training, and their function was to recruit volunteers in order to expand existing Islamist networks.

Young People in Tripoli

The speed with which Basim al-Kanj carried out his recruitment activities in certain popular circles in Tripoli is noteworthy. By canvassing young men who attended small mosques and religious institutes, he allegedly was able to recruit more than two hundred partisans in less than a year.[7] This success was inherently a disavowal of the existing Islamist organizations in Tripoli (Jama'a Islamiyya and Tawhid), which were largely discredited owing to their participation in elections.[8] They no longer had any influence on young people, whom they were incapable of integrating into state networks or parastate services. Without these resources, their ideological discourse was running on empty. At each new clash with the authorities, they had to give in, thereby eliciting disdain from disenchanted young people.

For the most part, recruitment took place in the popular quarters of the old city's eastern sectors: Abu Samra, Qubbeh, and Bab al-Tabbaneh. At the outset of the war, Abu Samra had produced its own Islamist neighborhood militia, Jund Allah (God's Soldiers), with a hundred or so young combatants, recognizable by their black military fatigues and light weaponry handed out by Fatah.[9] The inhabitants of Tripoli's poor neighborhoods lived in conditions similar to those that prevailed in the most urbanized Palestinian camps, and their experience of the war is comparable to that of Ain al-Helweh's Palestinian refugees. In both cases, a political organization strongly identified with an urban space defined itself in relation to a far larger regional entity, which it integrated into its field of action thanks to its military means. Through Fatah and the other Palestinian factions, Ain al-Helweh thus came to "rule Saida" between 1976 and 1982, just as the Tawhid imposed itself on all of Tripoli, starting with "its" neighborhoods—Abu Samra, Qubbeh, and Bab al-Tabbaneh—from 1981 to 1986. Several times, local concerns matched regional struggles, exacerbating the violence of clashes and placing those zones that were rebelling against Syria under heavy fire from Damascus's allies in Lebanon or the Syrian army itself. Tripoli's Islamist neighborhoods, in a preview of what would happen in the Palestinian camps, found themselves besieged by armed militias supported by Syria. They were forced to negotiate a surrender in 1986, when Syrian troops entered the city. Because these neighborhoods were outside Syrian control, and because, at various points in the conflict, they constituted an opening through which Fatah could act freely in Lebanon, they were directly exposed to attacks by the Syrian regime and its proxies in Lebanon.

The neighborhoods of Tabbaneh and Qubbeh are the most densely populated of Tripoli, with 34,908 and 42,172 inhabitants, respectively, out of a total population estimated at 221,592 (that is, 15.75 percent and 19.03 percent of Tripoli's population).[10] Tabbaneh and Qubbeh, "where the deterioration of dwellings and the lack of infrastructure are more marked than anywhere else in the city," also have the greatest number of individuals per family: 7.78 in Qubbeh and 6.94 in Tabbaneh.[11] The number of unskilled unemployed workers is even higher in these two neighborhoods than in the rest of the city. Half of Qubbeh's inhabitants are originally from the Akkar or Diniyeh. Over the years, as the Christians left, the neighborhood became exclusively Muslim.

Individual stories can give a face to such data. Isma'il Isma'il, who died at the age of twenty-six in the Diniyeh battles, was born in 1974 in Qubbeh. He was the youngest of seven siblings, three of whom were already married but too poor to rent apartments, and thus forced to remain in the family house along with their children. All told, then, about a dozen family members lived under the same roof. Isma'il's father was a coffee peddler in the streets of Tripoli. His seven children all dropped out of school before the ninth grade. Some of them received technical training before finding work as manual laborers on construction sites. After leaving school, Isma'il earned a living by making shoes with one of his brothers. At the same time, he attended Shari'a classes in the old city's mosques. No one knows how the salafist network connected with Isma'il, but in 1999, when Basim al-Kanj decided to divide Tripoli into five sectors—each sector named after the neighborhood in which its members lived—Isma'il was integrated into the Qubbeh sector (headed by Abdallah Hazim, Basim al-Kanj's assistant) as a matter of course.

Abdallah Hazim came from the same neighborhood and the same social universe as Isma'il Isma'il. He was older, however, and was involved in politics during the Lebanese war. Born in 1964 to a family of ten children, he left high school and worked several small traditional jobs, such as carpentry. During the war, when he was still a teenager, Fatah recruited him. He later left the organization and joined the ranks of Tawhid, the Islamist militia led by Shaykh Sha'ban that dominated the Qubbeh neighborhood starting in 1983. He split off from the movement in 1986, shortly after Syrian troops entered the city. Like many other Islamist militants of the time, he was arrested by the Syrian security services and spent five years in a Syrian jail on charges of belonging to Tawhid. When he was released, he sought to reestablish ties with his comrades-in-arms, who had taken refuge in the Ain al-Helweh camp. He was arrested again and jailed for five more years. In 1998, he helped found Basim al-Kanj's network, in which he was responsible for military supplies. Abdallah Hazim was accused of throwing grenades at the church in his neighborhood in October 1999. He fled into the Diniyeh mountain, provoking the subsequent New Year's Eve clashes with the Lebanese army.

Confrontation with the Lebanese Army

On December 29, 1999, Basim al-Kanj ordered his men to take over the building that housed the radio station of al-Hidaya wal-Ihsan, a salafist association that had been disbanded. The building was in the village of Assoun, a few miles from the training camp that the group had set up in the neighboring mountainside. The radio station's employees immediately informed the association's president, Shaykh Da'i al-Islam al-Shahal, that thirty armed men in military uniforms were occupying the building without due cause. The operation confirmed rumors that had been circulating for a few months about the existence of one or even several "Islamist underground movements" in the Diniyeh region. The situation in Tripoli had been tense since the previous October, when the city's churches had come under grenade attack. Military security had arrested several dozen young men. Fearing that the situation would spiral out of control, Islamist figures from Tripoli and the surrounding region, among them Shaykh Da'i al-Islam al-Shahal, approached the Jama'a Islamiyya deputy Khalid Dahir and asked him to mediate between the armed groups and the Lebanese army. The army was preparing to intervene in order to apprehend the perpetrators of the Tripoli attacks, whom it suspected of having taken refuge in the region. A delegation made up of Dahir and the vice-president of Diniyeh municipality, who had close ties to the Jama'a Islamiyya, went to the camp, following army orders.

According to Khalid Dahir's testimony, the rebels were opposed to the way Muslims were being treated in Lebanon and to the humiliation and arrests meted out by the Lebanese army, especially in the wake of demonstrations that had broken out in Abu Samra when Tawhid's radio station was closed down in 1996.[12] The delegation of Islamist notables, who claimed to have official guarantees, offered judicial immunity to all combatants who agreed to lay down their arms, with the exception of two individuals who were accused of having fired on an army patrol the previous October and who were implicated in attacks on churches in Tripoli. Basim al-Kanj received the delegation and requested a twenty-four-hour delay before responding. The delegation returned the following day, with a representative sent by Shaykh Sha'ban. Basim al-Kanj was absent, having joined the group occupying the building, and so the delegates spoke with his aid, Abd al-Hakim Jazzar. The camp was placed on alert after an army patrol passed nearby, immediately ending the negotiations. The delegation's members were accused of complicity and briefly taken hostage. During the evening, Abd al-Hakim Jazzar let the three emissaries go, after having informed them that a battle had broken out between the army and Basim al-Kanj's group around the Assoun radio building. Previously, the group inside the building had attempted unsuccessfully to interrupt a program of Qur'an verses to broadcast their own message and seize a platform from which to explain their aims publicly.

On the morning of December 31, 1999, a routine army check-point was set up several hundred feet from Assoun Radio. Soldiers who were inspecting a suspicious vehicle found themselves under fire from Islamists who had gathered outside the radio building. When the clash ended, four soldiers were dead, and the insurgents, who had sustained only a few wounded, had taken two hostages: an army officer and a staff sergeant. Abu Aisha was put in contact with Major Hasan Mirqabawi, head of intelligence for the northern region. The rebel leader threatened to decapitate the two military men unless he was given two cars in which to evacuate his fighters to a neighboring village. On the evening of December 31, without waiting for a reply, he decided to leave the building with his group and the two prisoners. After a two-day march through the snow toward Uyun al-Samak village, the group, made up of eight Islamists as well as the two hostages, reached the Christian village of Kfar Habu on January 2, 2002. The Lebanese army, which had subdued the last pockets of resistance around the rebel camp the previous day, encircled them rapidly, and the assailants stormed the house of a military policeman. The officer was wounded but managed to escape, while his wife and mother-in-law were killed in the shoot-out. The next day the army stormed the house. All the insurgents were killed, along with one of the hostages, Lieutenant Colonel Milad al-Nadaf. The coroner found that he had been tortured before dying in the confrontation.

What Did They Want?

According to the official interpretation, the insurgents were attempting to establish an Islamic state based in northern Lebanon. This was the version of events made public in the prosecutor general's investigation:

> Basim al-Kanj's principal objective was to set up an Islamic state in Lebanon, with the Qur'an as its constitution. He felt there was no

need for consultation regarding the establishment of this state, since such a project is related to the incontestable postulates of faith for Sunni and salafist Muslims. The creation of an Islamic state constitutes a duty for every Muslim, even if he must perish in carrying it out. Basim al-Kanj believed that an Islamic regime had to be born in the north because this region, more than any other, is propitious terrain, given the weight of the Islamic presence there and because its young Sunni Muslims are both zealous and committed.[13]

This version, however, does not seem credible. The camps, which had been set up intermittently starting in 1998, were not designed to constitute the embryo of an Islamic state or emirate. Their function, at once more modest and more pragmatic, was to accustom volunteers to the use of weaponry to prepare them for the Islamist cause of the time, serving in Chechnya. Combatants for the Caucasus had already been trained in Ain al-Helweh, and Basim al-Kanj wanted to set up an equivalent branch in the north to utilize the idle young Islamists in Tripoli's neighborhoods. Evidence suggests that Diniyeh's Islamist leaders, with Basim al-Kanj at their head, did not seek a direct confrontation with the Lebanese army. They detested the army, certainly, for its "impious" character, but Basim al-Kanj, as a veteran, knew that a confrontation with the state was premature, given the modest means available to the "believers" compared with a modern army. On the other hand, propagating jihadist ideology among Tripoli's young "hittistes" was a way of helping them emerge from the social and political prison in which they were confined, and of reviving their taste for action. The imaginary landscape of jihad required a prior *hegira* (voluntary exile) to the mountains of Diniyeh, where those who had already experienced combat in Afghanistan could instruct the younger members, in a space free from the city's influence and dangers.

Moreover, Lebanese Sunni radicalism was subject to the same difficulty besetting the militants in the Palestinian camps in the late

1980s: it remained impossible to carry out an armed jihad against an enemy—Israel—that occupied a piece of Lebanese territory at the time, less than 120 miles from Tripoli. Political exclusion was therefore accompanied by strategic exclusion, with a front in the south occupied by Hezbollah, which represented a despised Shi'ite version of Islam, and access blocked by two regional powers, Iran and Syria, neither of which had any interest in giving free rein to armed Sunni Islamism in Lebanon.[14]

Excluded from the political system at the national level, young Sunnis from Tripoli's underprivileged neighborhoods may have been searching for a way to inscribe their religious identity within a regional space. In contrast with the Maronites, Shi'ites, and Druzes, the three other main communities in Lebanon, Sunnis do not have a specific space for themselves. As Roger Nab'a remarked in the early 1980s, "there has never been Sunni unity at the Lebanese level, along the lines of Druze or Maronite unity, especially because there is no Sunni territory. The Sunnis are in the cities of the Sahel; they're scattered: Tripoli, Beirut, and Saida. There are very few Sunni mountain dwellers."[15] The activists saw Tripoli's hinterland as a geographical territory that could serve as the material base for a collective representation that would encompass the whole Sunni confession. In that sense, radical Sunnis dreamed of creating a "mountain refuge" more than a mile high, fairly inaccessible, separated from the other communities, and designed to become a center for the identity of young urbanized militants in search of religious purity.

In this hypothesis, taking up arms was less a way of defying state authority than of affirming the existence of a religious identity, like the Shi'ite militants of Amal or Hezbollah in the regions the militias controlled. These groups understood that the Weberian "rational-legal" model of the state, exercising a monopoly on the means of violence throughout national territory, was not applicable in Lebanon, where only the militia of the Lebanese Forces was really forced to lay down its arms after the war. In order to succeed, however, such a plan had to be articulated within the national and regional political system rather than standing out from it, even in abstract terms. Framed by Syria, that system could not allow an exaggerated form of Sunni religious sentiment to develop a geographical expression. This refusal might explain why some of the Sunni ulema were so indignant after the prosecutor general published his report, which ascribed to the insurgents the desire to establish an "Islamic emirate" in Lebanon. Against this interpretation, the community's intellectuals protested against the discriminatory treatment to which Sunnis were allegedly subjected, more so than other Muslims in Lebanon. Unlike Amal and Hezbollah, the two Shi'ite militias that ruled over neighborhoods and regions where the Lebanese army could only intervene after negotiations and the militias' final approval, Sunnis were unable to take over spaces that the regime—defined essentially through its army and security bodies—did not control. While the "state of Hezbollah" has been able to develop its "Islamic society" outside—or, rather, beside—state institutions, the Islamicized segments of the Sunni community have not been given the same right, even in those regions neglected by the Lebanese state since independence. The roadblocks at the entry to the Palestinian camps, and the legal exclusion of the refugee population of Palestinian origin, may be seen as an extension of this policy.

The clandestine activities pieced together with the help of the prosecutor general's report point to a process that transcends the immediate police matter at hand. This profoundly original development can be seen as the creation of a network in which two categories of activists from two different universes come together. The Lebanese militants who led the Diniyeh insurrection developed their political and religious identity outside Lebanon and, more generally, outside the Middle Eastern religious scene and the global Arab political system. Sent to the United States for graduate studies in technical fields during the 1980s, almost all of them experienced a militant awakening in this American exile, when they began to identify with the *mujahidin* who were fighting the Soviets in Afghanistan after the 1979 invasion. The enthusiasm aroused by the Afghan war motivated their involvement in nongovernmental organizations. Basim al-Kanj was still on a Hariri Foundation scholarship when he became enamored of the *mujahidin* cause; Hilal Ja'far was completing his studies in science in Orlando and collecting donations for the victory of the Afghan jihad at the same time. The vast majority of jihadists spent time in the United States, which confirms America's importance as an indispensable "passageway" for transnational religious networks.

Time spent in Pakistan or Afghanistan was the next significant stage in these militants' itineraries. The experience influenced their interpretation of Islam to a considerable degree. In one way or another, all those who spent time in the Indian subcontinent returned bearing a "Pakistani version" of radical Islam, in which "Islamism is no longer content with being a call to Shari'a, but also contains nostalgia for a caliphate."[16] For Lebanese militants and activists of Palestinian origin alike, the construction of a new identity involves recourse to a totally new element. Making a detour via the Indian subcontinent modified Basim al-Kanj's conception of jihad; for Usbat al-Ansar, the voyage was imaginary, but it nonetheless produced very real effects in Palestinian camp society.

These processes gradually gave rise to a Lebanese-Palestinian conjunction, although these two groups, seen collectively from the time of Lebanon's creation and the emergence of the Palestinian cause, have had different histories, experiences, and political trajectories that occasionally intersected during some episodes of the Lebanese war. The paths are different, but they converge upon a single militant reality. The feeling of participating in a holy war in the mountains of Diniyeh mobilized Muslims of Palestinian origin just as it did Muslims of Lebanese nationality. The phenomenon, which affected the younger generation, produced an original combination of alienation and integration. Whatever their national origin, these militants felt alienated from their political system and the "national" values it produced, which they perceived as a betrayal of Islam's higher values (paradoxically, national allegiance was no doubt more effectively internalized, under PLO guidance, by the Palestinians—deprived of a homeland—than by the Lebanese religious militants, who were nostalgic for the Sunni preeminence of Ottoman times). In parallel, the same actors sought integration into globalized religious networks, free of any national roots and offering a far more intense feeling of belonging and identity.

For at least some of these militants, alienation was more ideological than social, more "imagined" than actually experienced. It mainly worked in relation to the political scene, where it expressed the weakness of national sentiments among certain segments of the Lebanese population, especially the Sunnis. Such shared feelings of social frustration may partly explain the move toward global Islam, given the social experience of failure—whether in the underprivileged Sunni neighborhoods of Beirut and Tripoli or in Ain al-Helweh—but they do not tell the whole story. Another explanation, more subversive because it is less reassuring, comes from the growing gap between "local" social reality and the wider ideological universe in which activists evolve. One can be a high school teacher with a degree in higher education, make a monthly salary above the national average, and still feel an almost complete (and, unfortunately, often justified) lack of interest in Lebanese political life, where nothing is at stake and where the cadence is provided by elections in which the need to form alliances to get a seat in parliament blurs the religious identity of the parties involved.

The War in Chechnya and Lebanese Reality

Before the Caucasus, the Balkan war in Kosovo had mobilized activists throughout the Muslim world. Ethnic cleansing of Muslims in the province of Kosovo by the Serbian government in Belgrade gave rise to a chain of official and private efforts in support of the refugees, while provoking harsh criticism of NATO action among Islamists. According to Shaykh Jamal Khattab, all forms of violence at the end of the twentieth century were directed against Muslims alone. The preacher argued in his sermons that the West was preventing Muslims from having a state in the heart of Europe, while in Indonesia, East Timor was moving toward secession with help from the United Nations, simply because its inhabitants were Christians and their separation would weaken a Muslim state. In Kosovo, according to Shaykh Jamal,

> Muslims are caught between NATO and the Serbs, all Crusaders. All of them strike at the Muslims. The Serbs slit throats, kill, and rape, while NATO bombs trucks of refugees. NATO is the reason that the Muslims who remained in this region—95 percent of which was Muslim—have been expelled . . . No one is in a hurry to save them or even hear their cries for help. All this, my brothers, is because enthusiasm is dead, religious fervor has died out in people's hearts, and faith has become lukewarm.[17]

In the months preceding the Diniyeh clashes, the war in Chechnya, on which al-Jazeera provided daily news bulletins, had gradually become another Afghan war in the minds of the pious Sunni Muslims in Tripoli, Saida, and Beirut. An "emotional cause" was born and maintained through Friday sermons, fundraising for "Islam's fighters," and videotapes showing Commander Khattab fleeing Russian fire through the Chechen mountain ranges, pitting the strength of his faith against hi-tech weaponry. A considerable part of this audience found itself literally immersed in jihadist Islamism, and identified with the population of Grozny as it suffered daily bombardments from Russian troops. In the Diniyeh mountains, the imbalance of power, and perhaps even the topography of the battlefield, evoked the struggle of the jihad combatants in the Caucasus. In the fevered imagination of those who were following the battle in Ain al-Helweh, the fight against the Lebanese army was an extension of the Chechen jihad against the Russians. Significantly, young members of Usbat al-Ansar believed that the Lebanese army might attack the camp, and thus they were preparing themselves for "another Grozny" to take place. The religious factor buttressed this reading of the events, as demonstrated by "analyses" that emphasized the religious identity of the soldiers sent to Diniyeh: according to such narratives, all of them were from "hateful *asabiyyas* [solidarity groups]," as a shaykh from the camp put it. In Ain al-Helweh's radical circles, the soldiers were often described as "mainly Christians and Shi'ites." This would explain the determination and "hatred" shown by the Lebanese troops.

Ahmad Abu Kharrub's Sacrifice; or, How the Voice of Truth Covered the Voice of Palestine

During the Diniyeh confrontation, links with Ain al-Helweh were dramatized in the suicide operation carried out by a Palestinian from Saida camp, Ahmad Abu Kharrub, on the Russian Embassy in Beirut, situated on the busy Mazraa beachfront road. The thirty-year-old Palestinian was killed in an attack by the Internal Security Forces—which also lost a policeman in the clash—so it was not revealed whether he was acting on his own or under orders from Usbat al-Ansar.

Ahmad Abu Kharrub's family was originally from the village of Na'ameh, to the extreme north of Palestine, in the zone of "seven villages" that was Lebanese in 1920 and became Palestinian after the 1923 convention was signed, laying down the Lebanese-Palestinian border between the two mandatory powers of the time, France and Great Britain. After the civil war, the Lebanese government began asserting its sovereignty over these villages, which are today in Israeli territory. In 1994, it issued a decree offering Lebanese nationality to the seven villages' "Palestinian" inhabitants. Taking the opportunity to benefit from minimal legal security at a time when legislation on the status of Palestinian refugees in Lebanon was growing harsher, the Abu Kharrub family immediately provided proof of their geographical origins to show their right to nationality (the family was registered in the Marjayun municipal office in southern Lebanon). The uncertainties of modern Middle Eastern history and the whimsical borders traced by the mandatory powers resulted in odd classifications within the family. The father, who is deceased, became Lebanese in the mid-1990s, along with two of his sons, while their respective wives, who were not taken into account by the decree, remained Palestinian as far as Lebanese law was concerned. For religious reasons Ahmad, the youngest of the brothers, preferred not to file a request, since he refused to establish even a functional link with a state whose legitimacy he did not recognize, even if this meant compromising his children's future. They would keep their father's nationality, and thereby be deprived of the rights their cousins enjoyed.

The family's history in Lebanon is also instructive. After 1948, they sought refuge in the Nabatiyyeh camp in the south. The Israeli air force destroyed the camp in 1974, and the father was forced to move to the Metn area, populated by Christians. He settled in Bikfaya village—incidentally, the cradle of the Jumayyel family. The move was practical since the father had worked as a nurse in the village hospital, run by nuns, since the early 1960s. At the outbreak of the war in 1975, Bikfaya's *mukhtar* (mayor) advised the family to leave, as they were the only Palestinians in the village. Despite friendships made over a period of eighteen years, the notable told the father that he could no longer guarantee the family's safety at a time when the cycle of collective reprisals against civilians was fueling hatred in the two camps. The family had to return to Nabatiyyeh.

Salam, Ahmad's older brother, born in 1959, received technical training and found work as a technician on the PLO's radio station, Voice of Palestine, in 1980. Thereafter, his work as a sound engineer ensuring the high quality of broadcasts was his main contribution to the Palestinian cause. Four times—in Beirut in 1982, and then in Saida in 1986, 1987, and 1990—he barely escaped Israeli bombardments intended to eradicate the Voice of Palestine's technical capabilities. At the end of the Lebanese war, Salam, who had become blind, settled on the outskirts of Ain al-Helweh, in the Lebanese-Palestinian neighborhood of Ta'mir, before moving to the slum of Sakka in 1996. He lived in a modest, whitewashed single-storey dwelling with a corrugated tin roof, next door to his brother Ahmad.

Ahmad is nine years younger than Salam—he was born in 1968—and did not experience the beginning of the "Palestinian revolution" in Lebanon. He was still a schoolboy during the war of the camps, when he was taken prisoner for several days by Amal militiamen who were chasing down Palestinians in Nabatiyyeh. In 1989 Ahmad joined Shaykh Maher Hammud's small Islamist militia in Saida, which was dissolved when the Lebanese army returned to the region in 1991.[18] Having obtained certification as an electrician, Ahmad Abu Kharrub found work at Shaykh Hammud's radio station, Voice of Truth (Sawt al-Haqq), while taking classes in religion at several of the city's mosques.

Ironically, Salam and Ahmad had the same type of technical training, but they utilized their skills in the service of diametrically opposed causes: Ahmad seemed to be a re-Islamicized version of Salam. Their differences can by no means be attributed to their levels of education, their professions, or their religious devotion—Salam himself is very pious but refuses to see the world from an exclusively religious vantage point. The brothers' individual perspectives might be better explained by reference to socialization, for they were both exposed to very different influences.

Salam experienced his first political stirrings at the beginning of the Lebanese civil war, at a time when the PLO exercised uncontested hegemony over the refugees collectively and, more generally, over Muslim society in Lebanon, in the camps and elsewhere. He was actively involved in the many debates that took place within the central committee, and most of his political training was directly related to his professional responsibilities, which included broadcasting the PLO's political vision in Lebanon and the region for the duration of the war. In a way, his work tools were the main vector of his socialization. He was familiar with the Palestinian nationalist rhetoric broadcast on Voice of Palestine, and so he was able to differentiate among the PLO's various political actions at a very early stage. He was also able to justify the organization's local initiatives in terms of strategy and political survival. His professional trips abroad—to Tunis or Belgrade—broadened his worldview, while his brother never had the opportunity to leave Lebanon, or even to spend several months in another part of the country. Ten years later, when Ahmad became an adult, the PLO was weakened by its defeat at the hands of the Israeli army in 1982. Even in the refugee camps, its natural bases, it could no longer ensure the political socialization of young Palestinians; this was even more obvious in the case of those living outside the camps. During the same period, Hezbollah, still in its infancy, became exclusively responsible for resisting Israel in the south. It took up the slogans of the 1970s, adding a religious dimension, while the Palestinian leadership was already on the road to realist diplomacy, translated in the implicit recognition of Israel at the 1988 Palestine National Council meeting in Algiers, which put an end to the utopian project of a return to 1948 Palestine through armed struggle.

The socialization effect also had a geographical and territorial dimension. Ahmad was not exposed to the same influences as his brother was, and he came of age in a narrower social space. At an early stage, he was included in Saida's Islamic society, with its shaykhs, its mutual assistance networks, its special interests, and its specific vision of the regional order. Keeping one's distance from a beaten and discredited PLO was a means of integrating oneself into the local Islamic world. For a young and very politically aware Palestinian, searching for an activity outside the camps meant obtaining local protection. Religious leaders, who had been mobilized during the war of the camps, provided most of this protection in the form of jobs, social assistance, and intervention for Palestinians harassed by Amal militiamen.

The combined result of a generation gap and personal experiences can explain the differences in the two brothers' political perceptions. As an adult, Ahmad became fascinated by distant conflicts—in Afghanistan, then Yugoslavia, and finally the Balkans. He engaged in increasingly tense discussions with Salam, who had gone to Yugoslavia on work before the civil war, and who felt that, contrary to the speeches being given in most of Lebanon's mosques, "there were no visible differences between Muslims and the other inhabitants." Salam's direct, first-hand experience (of Christians in Bikfaya and Bosnian Muslims in the former Yugoslavia) clashed with Ahmad's ideological, religious knowledge, mediated through the words of religious leaders in Saida and the surrounding area.[19]

These leaders had gathered at the funeral of the Lebanese shaykh Muharram al-Arifi, one of the main figures of Islamism in Saida since 1985. It so happened that on the same day Shaykh Arifi was buried in Saida, Ahmad Abu Kharrub was buried in Ain al-Helweh. The words of homage paid to the deceased deliberately played on the contrast between a shaykh who fought the real enemy—Israel—and the lost souls of Diniyeh, who preferred to exacerbate internal divisions and make enemies during a delicate phase in regional politics. But this opposition was artificial, for the most part, and might have served to illustrate a specifically Lebanese tragi-comedy: Shaykh Muharram al-Arifi, who had set himself the mission of combating PLO influence in the camps, was one of Ahmad Abu Kharrub's former teachers, and images of the deceased shaykh covered the walls of Ain al-Helweh just after his death. Ahmad's main fault was to have taken too seriously an opportunistic shaykh who had reaped political profits from the time he had spent in Israeli jails, and had become the instrument of Hezbollah's policy in Saida's Sunni Islamist networks after he was set free. All Ahmad wanted was to apply the exhortations of a shaykh who had made a career of official resistance in Lebanon, and for that reason his death was shrouded in indignity. That same week, by contrast, representatives of the president and the prime minister attended the funeral of the "militant shaykh" Arifi, an event that brought together all Saida's notables.[20]

The destiny of the Abu Kharrub family provides an example of how volatile individual identities can be, and how allegiances can fragment and divurge in many directions, even though individuals initially share the same family context. Salam was a member of the PLO, while Ahmad chose radical Islam to the extent of making the ultimate sacrifice. A third brother served in the Lebanese army.

Ahmad Abu Kharrub's tragic destiny shows the complex relationship between emotional causes such as the Chechen conflict, as broadcast by al-Jazeera and commented upon in Lebanese mosques, and local Islamist mobilization in Lebanon. Influenced by events taking place many miles away, and wishing to act upon them, the more radical Islamists followed a single-minded logic of moving as far as possible from any military presence, in the hope of finding a space empty of state influence. Mobile militants *chose* Sir al-Diniyeh for its geographical isolation and its proximity to Tripoli, where certain neighborhoods could serve as reservoirs of young activists. But this was not a case of inhabitants defending their town and their religion; nor was it a case of "neighborhood *asabiyya*" of the Bab al-Tabbaneh variety, studied by Michel Seurat in the early 1980s in Tripoli, even though some young men were from these quarters. The neighborhoods offered no "security" and produced no "urban militias." Had that been the case, Tripoli's poor urban neighborhoods would have been the main theater of clashes with the Lebanese army.

This "separation of time and space" that characterizes globalization, according to the sociologist Anthony Giddens, appears as the main feature of the Diniyeh events. According to Giddens, "in conditions of modernity, place becomes increasingly phantasmagoric: that is to say, locales are thoroughly penetrated by and shaped in terms of social influences quite distant from them. What structures the locale is not simply that which is present on the scene; the 'visible form' of the locale conceals the distanciated relations which determine its nature."[21] In the same way, family relations and context, tradition, and religious ceremonies no longer determine the quality of social links; instead, personal relations and ideological systems play that role. Ties of trust among the networks' main activists were established outside of Lebanon, in exile in the United States or in the valley of Peshawar in Pakistan. They were then extended to other individuals, in the clandestine climate created by the struggle against the Ahbash brotherhood after Shaykh Nizar al-Halabi was assassinated. Basim al-Kanj placed his trust, sight unseen, in the leaders of Usbat al-Ansar because the Lebanese state had condemned them. For him, that condemnation served as a guarantee that they were sincere in their commitment to jihadist Islam.

Salafist Networks in the North: The Case of Nahr al-Barid

In the Nahr al-Barid camp, nine miles north of Tripoli, one finds similar examples of emigration from the camps and severance from Palestinian national symbols. Religious networks inspired by salafism work together with the Lebanese networks in the Akkar, and local preachers challenge the regional and domestic order with the same intensity, and on the same terms, as in the mosques of Ain al-Helweh. But in contrast to what has taken place in Ain al-Helweh, the camp's religious groups have avoided violence, leaving it up to militants from Tripoli to attack the city's churches, night-clubs, and even military and other official institutions, and to bear the consequences in terms of repression and official opprobrium.

The activists' refusal to take violent action is due to the camp's location in an area controlled by Syria, as well as to the inhabitants' desire to continue reaping the material benefits they derive from this situation, rather than living under a blockade similar to that ex-perienced by the camps in the south.

Salafist-type networks were predominant in Nahr al-Barid: at least four mosques out of eight—Khalid Ibn al-Walid, Palestine, al-Hawz, and al-Awda—were centers of salafist influence. Some of these (Khalid Ibn al-Walid and Palestine, for example) were not in-side the camp's walls. Their position on the fringes of Nahr al-Barid served a dual purpose: to attract as wide an audience as possible in the Akkar, including Palestinians as well as Lebanese; and to regis-ter the mosque with Dar al-Fatwa, which is impossible on land rented by UNRWA. For the same reasons, one of the camp's salafist shaykhs built a mosque at the camp's northern extremity. The loca-tion, at the crossroads of three adjacent regions, was chosen delib-erately to radiate over as wide a space as possible, far beyond Nahr al-Barid's physical limits.

It is interesting to discover the circumstances in which the camp's preachers acquired their religious knowledge. In 1981, more than fifty young Lebanese and a few young Palestinians from the Nahr al-Barid camp went to Saudi Arabia to study at the Islamic Univer-sity of Madina, where they enrolled in the faculty for preaching and religious principles (Kulliyat al-Da'wa wa Usul al-Din). Their trip was the result of close ties between the Lebanese shaykh Salim al-Shahal, the most prominent salafist in northern Lebanon, and the prestigious Saudi shaykh Ibn Baz. One of these young Palestinians, Shaykh Ahmad, had helped set up an Islamist militia, the Nucleus of the Islamic Army (Nuwa al-Jaysh al-Islami), in 1980, when he was still a teenager. Salim al-Shahal and his son, Da'i al-Islam, who was very close to Ahmad, created the militia, which was suspected of having blown up churches in Tripoli's Zaharia neighborhood during the war.

Shaykh Ahmad's sojourn to Saudi Arabia, where he joined his friend Da'i al-Islam, who had been there for a year, was a turning point in his religious journey. At the time, the University of Madina painted a picture of lively student life, with young people of diverse origins comparing the situation of the different Islamic movements in their respective countries. Discussions were especially candid because, according to the testimony of alumni, there was no trace of the Saudi state or its agents on campus.

According to Shaykh Ahmad, the Islamic University trained some of those who later became leaders of the most radical Islamist groups, and thereby changed the identity of the Muslim world:

> There were students of all nationalities. The Filipino students from back then are those who are fighting the United States today; there was also a large number of Pakistani students . . . I would say half the students were from Pakistan or India. They are the ones who created the madrasas from which the Taliban emerged. During my stay there, I discovered the existence of many Islamic organizations throughout the world, which I had never heard of before. Shaykh Zayd, then vice-president of the university, even gave a few hundred Syrian students special permission to go train in Iraq to fight the Syrian regime. They disappeared for six months and came back after the Hama events in June 1982.[22]

In 1985 young Ahmad, bachelor's degree in hand, returned to Lebanon via Cyprus with help from a young militant with ties to Shaykh Minqara, the Tawhid emir who controlled the port region of Tripoli at the time. A few days after his return, the Syrian security services arrested him on the basis of an accusation, made by a resident of Nahr al-Barid, that he was conspiring with the Syrian Muslim Brotherhood. He was released after being detained in Damascus for three months in a tiny underground cell in Palestine Branch Prison (Far' Falastin), specially designed for Palestinians. He left for Libya, where he taught Arabic for two years, and then returned to Nahr al-Barid. In 1992, after the war ended, Shaykh Ibrahim Ghunaym put him in charge of preaching in al-Quds Mosque, but the young shaykh's zeal soon put an end to that experience. In the context of the first post-war legislative elections, during the summer of 1992, a debate over the opportunity for Lebanese Muslims to participate in the elections—a controversy whose novelty in Lebanon shows just how far the most radical salafist ideas have progressed—divided Islamist circles. Shaykh Ahmad, influenced by his Saudi education, considered such participation a flagrant violation of religious law. His Friday sermons thus targeted Fathi Yakan, the spiritual guide of the Jama'a Islamiyya and himself a candidate for the elections, who naturally encouraged political participation. This radical attitude, however, immediately resulted in Shaykh Ghunaym's asking him to leave, for fear that young Ahmad's excesses might harm his own political alliances outside the camp.[23]

After Shaykh Ahmad was told that his services were no longer required at al-Quds Mosque, he taught at the center run by Da'i al-Islam al-Shahal, the Association for Guidance and Goodwill. When the Lebanese government closed the center in 1996 amid charges that it was "inciting religious fanaticism," Ahmad found work as an Arabic teacher in an UNRWA school in Nahr al-Barid. His preaching activities continued, however: the same year, Dar al-Fatwa's local administration for religious foundations appointed him preacher in a village in the Akkar. Thereafter, he also preached once a month in the Baddawi camp, where he made it his goal to establish the salafist movement, which had not yet taken root. Not surprisingly, Shaykh Ahmad enrolled as a doctoral candidate at Imam al-Awza'i Institute. There, he found an education in line with what he had learned in Saudi Arabia.

Nahr al-Barid's other shaykhs had life experiences fairly similar to Shaykh Ahmad's, and they make up a generation that has now reached middle age. The imam of al-Hawz Mosque, Shaykh Ahmad al-Hajj, also had his "Saudi moment," when he was a member of the student delegation sent to Saudi Arabia in 1981. Those who were not on the trip were exposed to similar influences: Shaykhs Haytham al-Sa'id and Ahmad Mithqan, who organize activities at Khalid Ibn al-Walid Mosque, studied with salafist shaykhs from the Shahal family at their center, al-Hidaya. After the center was closed down, Ahmad Mithqan spent a year studying at Shaykh Hallaq's Murshid center so that he could subsequently enroll at Imam al-Awza'i Institute. As for Haytham al-Sa'id, he graduated from al-Da'wa college in Beirut. At the end of the 1990s, the shaykhs of Khalid Ibn al-Walid Mosque invited fifteen Saudi clerics each year to come give seminars at their center in Nahr al-Barid.

As in Ain al-Helweh, the socialization work carried out by the new generation of clerics in Nahr al-Barid relocated the enemy inside the camp, as religious groups increasingly drew their material resources and symbolic values from outside the traditional networks of "Palestinian society" in Lebanon. The version of the Diniyeh events propagated by the camp's religious circles translated this exit from a Palestinian space of reference, since the militants immediately reappropriated the account of a "conspiracy against Islam," which circulated in the Islamist mosques of Tripoli and the Akkar. According to this version, young men *(shabab)* who were harassed by the army went into the mountains to escape Lebanese repression and prepare themselves to assist their persecuted brothers in Chechnya. The tragic outcome of the whole affair could be blamed on the behavior of "Maronites, who threw grenades into churches themselves." A Lebanese shaykh, Zakariya al-Misri, expressed this version as early as November 1999, suggesting in a tract that parties other than the Islamists might be behind the explosions, "as was the case after an investigation into explosions at

Sa'idat al-Najat Church in Juniyeh revealed that Samir Geagea of the Lebanese Forces had been involved."[24]

Islamist solidarity was demonstrated against the state and Fatah alike. After the clashes of August 15, 2002, which pitted Fatah combatants against insurgents from Sir al-Diniyeh who had taken refuge in Ain al-Helweh, religious figures in Nahr al-Barid accused Fatah of seeking to cooperate with the United States in their fight against terrorism after the attacks of September 11.[25] During this episode, the main salafist representatives and sympathizers once again endorsed the version of events described by Zakariya al-Misri, according to which, "on the morning of August 15, 2002, Fatah killed a young member of the Diniyeh group, just after he had finished praying in the camp, in order to light the fuse of confrontation between the parties, with the aim of arresting these young men and turning them over to the government."[26] This version illustrated the fractures dividing the refugee camps once again, and demonstrated the propensity of religious actors to endorse an account of events compatible with Syrian interests, if not suggested directly by Syria itself.

Perception of the Islamist Threat

When the Lebanese army overcame the last pocket of Islamist resistance on January 3, 2000, after a week of fighting, the Lebanese media posed a question that generated speculation among a population accustomed to such an exercise. The question might be summed up as follows: How could an Islamist underground exist just a few miles from Tripoli without provoking an immediate reaction from the Lebanese and Syrian military authorities? The question was particularly pressing since the region was familiar ground for Syria: large numbers of Syrian laborers worked there; historical ties existed between Tripoli and its Syrian hinterland; and the Syrian leadership had experience of local society since the mid-1970s, when Syrian troops entered the country. Paradoxically, intelligence services were vigilant when it came to local society precisely because of Tripoli's "Syrian character."[27] Tripoli, as the largest Sunni city in Lebanon, escaped the effects of the Israeli occupation of south Lebanon (which Saida did not). As a result, it was long seen as a threat to Syrian power, as a refuge for the political opposition—most often linked to the Muslim Brotherhood—and as a hub for those who, contesting Syrian policies in Lebanon, did not hesitate to denounce the religious foundations of the regime that emerged from Hafiz al-Asad's 1970 coup d'état. Given all these circumstances, the unusual laxity of the security forces appeared as a curious anomaly.

Such negligence, however, may be analyzed on the basis of how Syrian security, and its Lebanese subcontractors, defined the menace within Lebanese society after the end of the war. In the ten years that followed the conflict, the threat was linked mainly to two groups, who were guilty of having ties to Israel at various points in their history. The first—the Lebanese Forces—was linked to Israel during certain periods of the civil war, while the second, Fatah and Yasir Arafat, had "broken the ranks of Arab solidarity" (read: emancipated itself from Syrian tutelage) and attempted to negotiate sovereignty with the "Zionist entity." The memory of the conflict with the Islamists in Tripoli faded, because most of the Sunni preachers internalized their defeat at Syrian hands (like Shaykh Sa'id Sha'ban, who survived the reoccupation of Tripoli thanks to Iranian intercession) or refused to go along with the insurrection led by the Syrian Muslim Brothers and accept money from Yasir Arafat (like Fathi Yakan, the spiritual guide of the Lebanese Jama'a). Others were marginalized on the local political scene: such was the case with Shaykh Kan'an Naji, one of the founders of the small Islamist group Jund Allah.

The Syrian regime found it more expedient to transcend the memory of the 1982 clashes. It understood the benefits it could derive from religious mobilization within Syrian Muslim society, as long as that society's anger was directed against Israel and, in the local vocabulary, its new "allies"—Egypt, Jordan, and the Palestinians. In Friday sermons, the "Arab regimes" were habitually denounced; the expression served to designate those Arab governments that had signed peace agreements with Israel.[28] The declaration of solidarity with Iraq went hand in hand with denunciations of the West, broadly inscribed within the framework of a "culture clash." Furthermore, such mobilization maintained religious tension that allowed Syria to act as a permanent regulator of the Lebanese social and political scene. A vital function of Muslim religious leaders—Sunnis and Shi'ites alike—was to systematically transform the question of Syrian-Lebanese relations, when it was raised, into one of inter-Lebanese relations, thereby preventing the creation of a national coalition directed against Syria. Soon after Maronite bishops demanded the negotiated retreat of the Syrian army from Lebanon in September 2000, Hezbollah organized a mass demonstration on the occasion of Ashura in the capital's southern outskirts. Hasan Nasrallah, the Shi'ite organization's secretary-general, declared that those who sought the Syrians' departure were "speaking in their name alone," and that "most Lebanese [had] a different point of view."[29]

In the Middle East, religious activists are acutely aware of the *umma*'s weakness to outside aggression. The Syrian regime sought to present itself as the last Arab regional power capable of protecting the Muslim community, and in so doing it skillfully mingled Islamic and nationalist concerns. Michel Seurat showed how Damascus was able to take on various roles and political identities according to the beliefs and positions of those with whom it negotiated. To create "an image acceptable to all parties," he wrote, "the Syrian regime could allow itself to engage in dialogue with Kamal Jumblatt's progressive coalition in the name of 'progressive Arabism'; with Yasir Arafat in the interest of the [Palestinian] cause; and with the Lebanese Phalangists on the implicit basis of minority solidarity—before clubbing them brutally, each according to their measure and in their own time. It was a marvelous application of Pascal's sentence: 'If he exalt himself, I humble him; if he humble himself, I exalt him.'"[30]

The Syrian leadership's ability to create common interests with the most diverse groups did not wane with time: since September 11, 2001, Syria has presented itself as a state engaged in close cooperation with the United States in the effort to track down al-Qa'ida networks, while simultaneously mobilizing Muslims in Lebanon against the patriarch and the Christian opposition of Kurnat Shahwan, accused of seeking American protection against Syria (that is, against "the Arab and Muslim *umma*") in the framework of the U.S. invasion of Iraq.[31]

The ability of Islamic movements to express opposition, then, has not been eliminated; it has merely been externalized in response to the needs of Syrian regional policy, and in order to create immunity from possible repression within its ranks. The new equation explains why Syrian and Lebanese intelligence sources remained relatively indifferent to radical Sunni Islamism and its rhetorical excesses, as long as the Islamists continued to denounce the new regional order—from which Syria remains excluded—in their sermons. These preachers, deprived of any strategic base, served as platforms from which to denounce the regional and global order. As Bertrand Badie has remarked, this function was "an astounding antidote to the imbalance between the powers: when a confrontation occurs between two states of very unequal power, it is clear that the least powerful of the two has no chances against the other, which leaves it with only one weapon: that of fighting not on the turf of power and classical warfare, but on that of social dynamics and social movements."[32] The Syrian regime replaced the terrorist violence of the 1980s with verbal violence, which it used to its own advantage. Under the Syrian tutelage imposed on post-war Lebanon (1990–2005), Lebanese authorities essentially served as sub-contractors for their Syrian colleagues, and so chose to act against all those who had been tied to Israel or the "Arafatists"—presented as more or less the same in the official discourse—in any way. The arbitrary, political definition of the threat, the regional usefulness of Islamism as a platform with no visible consequences for domestic stability, and the desire to let past clashes lie: these are the reasons the Syrian-Lebanese security forces did not react at first to the mobilization of Islamic activists in al-Diniyeh.

An additional explanation lies in the behavior of the innumerable Islamist militants responsible for informing Syrian agents about possible threats to the regime. These Islamist informants probably did not think that the camps improvised in the Diniyeh mountains with the sole aim of training combatants to carry out jihad in Chechnya constituted a threat to the Syrian regime's interests in the region. Forced to resort to subterfuge with their Syrian correspondents and with each other, these militants must have limited their intelligence work to what was strictly necessary. They were accustomed to answering specific questions about whether a given group or individual was straying from the allowable margin, and they saw no point in divulging information about a military reality that had no direct relation to regional and local strategies as defined by Damascus.

Far from constituting a *deus ex machina* manipulating all the sources of authority in Lebanese society, the Syrian services depended heavily on their Lebanese informants in grasping local realities, especially in a region like Diniyeh, which, unlike Akkar and Tripoli, they did not control directly. The December 1999 clashes took them by surprise: they were also the victims of their means of information-gathering, which was based on a static view of the situation and indirect knowledge of the religious state of affairs in certain regions. This knowledge was mediated by individuals who carried out their task—identifying explicit opposition to Syrian policies and the Syrian regime—without completely abandoning their personal convictions and specific interests.

After the Diniyeh events, the Syrian authorities changed their policy on Islamism and attempted to exercise stricter control over the various radical Sunni movements. This reevaluation was in itself a disavowal of the official version of the Islamist movement, which sought to circumscribe the phenomenon by attributing it to an external conspiracy. This was also a sign that the leadership in Damascus had realized that Lebanon's Sunni Muslims were suffering from latent dissatisfaction.[33] This new policy of tighter control was enforced on Lebanese territory as a whole, in every city or region with a high Sunni population.

In early 2000, the former Tawhid emir of the port (mina) of Tripoli, Hashim Minqara, was released from the Syrian jail where he had been held since 1983. He immediately challenged Bilal Sha'ban, the son of Shaykh Sa'id (who had died in 1998), for leadership of the movement. In Tripoli, Shaykh Minqara benefited from all sorts of material amenities (a site for his activities, weapons permits, recruitment of volunteers, and so on) and from the support of several dozen members of Tawhid who had been freed from jail a few months after him.[34] Further north, Colonel Muhammad Muflah, Ghazi Kan'an's representative in Halba, in the Akkar region, brought notoriety to the then fairly unknown Union of Akkar Ulema (Ittihad Ulama al-Akkar), a group that united all the shaykhs of the region.[35] After September 10, 2000, when an assembly of Maronite bishops published a document denouncing the effects of Syria's presence in Lebanon at the political and economic levels, the members of the Union strongly criticized the patriarch's position, accusing him of serving Israeli interests and of pursuing "isolationist" projects. Syrian instructions also passed through Dar al-Fatwa. A Palestinian shaykh from a village in the Akkar received a call from the administrator of religious foundations in the north, expressly requesting that he attack Patriarch Sfayr's positions in his

Friday sermon. As the shaykh explained: "To avoid negative reactions to me as a Palestinian, I said in the mosque that, on that point, I was speaking under official instructions from Dar al-Fatwa."[36]

In Beirut, the inhabitants of Tariq al-Jadidah, a popular neighborhood, once again saw posters announcing the Murabitun, an organization that had disappeared. Ibrahim Qulaylat, its leader, was in exile in Paris. Similarly, tracts signed by the "February 6 Movement" were distributed in the capital. The Syrians thereby sought to reactivate Sunni militias that they—and Amal, the Shi'ite group headed by Nabih Berri—had eliminated in the mid-1980s.[37] These groups were allowed to exist once again as long as they legitimized Syria's actions. In the same way, the Jama'a Islamiyya attacked the positions of the "eastern camp" and demonstrated total solidarity with Syria on the Chebaa Farms. In the Iqlim al-Kharrub region, Damascus apparently encouraged the creation of Sunni militias to increase the pressure on Walid Jumblatt. Jumblatt was to ally with the Kurnat Shahwan group before transforming himself into the main opponent of Bashar al-Asad's policy in Lebanon after the extension of President Lahoud's mandate in September 2004 and the assassination of former Prime Minister Rafiq al-Hariri on February 14, 2005.

The Syrian policy of the time had several objectives: it aimed to prevent possible anti-Syrian mobilization in radical Sunni groups; domestically, it prevented the alliance forged between Walid Jumblatt and the "Christian camp" in 1999 from spreading through other communities; and finally, it threatened the Christians with a minority position should the Lebanese system be desectarianized.

Conclusion

Since 2005, Lebanon has been at the heart of international current events: Rafiq al-Hariri was assassinated on February 14 of that year; massive anti-Syrian demonstrations took place on March 14; Syrian troops withdrew on April 26, twenty-five years after their arrival on Lebanese territory; an international U.N. commission was formed to investigate the murder of the former Lebanese prime minister; and a new majority, largely hostile to the Syrian regime, took power.

Despite the scope of the changes that have taken place, however, Lebanon has undergone an aborted political revolution. Supported by the United States and France, which proposed a host of Security Council resolutions aimed at reestablishing the authority of the Lebanese government and disarming Hezbollah, the new political majority—the "March 14 national gathering," as it is called, organized around Rafiq al-Hariri's son and his former minister of finance, current Prime Minister Fuad Siniora—has proved unable to integrate the Shi'ite militia definitively within the Lebanese political system, despite numerous concessions. Hezbollah, powerfully armed by Iran and Syria, has preferred to maintain its regional alliances, invoking religious, political, and strategic reasons to buttress its position. The Shi'ite militia, which Iran's leadership sees as an extension of the Khomeini revolution in Lebanon, provides Iran with a border contiguous with Israel on Lebanese territory. For the Iranian regime, this easy access to Israel is an ace with which to discourage the international community from resorting to military sanctions should it continue its nuclear program.

In this uncertain situation, Lebanon settled gradually into governmental paralysis during the first months of 2006, against a background of economic crisis, conflict with its neighbor, Syria, and tension between Sunnis and Shi'ites fueled by the deterioration of the situation in Iraq.

These problems were at the root of the war the Israeli army launched against Hezbollah in summer 2006, after a July 12 commando operation by the Shi'ite militia resulted in the kidnapping of two Israeli soldiers and the death of three others. Inspired by the precedent of NATO's war in Kosovo in 1999, the Israeli army's massive reprisals against regions under Hezbollah control combined intensive air strikes and ground operations in the villages of southern Lebanon and the Beqaa. Nonetheless, the bombardment did not succeed in ending the Shi'ite militia's rocket strikes against cities in northern Israel. Many observers saw the conflict between Israel and Hezbollah as the precursor to a wider regional clash between the United States and Iran.

The scale of destruction—more than eighty bridges were destroyed, roughly one hundred roads were rendered impassable, and the industrial sector was devastated—suggests the worst for the economic future of this disaster-stricken country. On the political level, the Lebanese regime has agreed to deploy its army on the borders with Israel for the first time in forty years, but the Lebanese army, which for the most part is made up of Shi'ite soldiers and officers from the villages of southern Lebanon, does not seem capable of disarming Hezbollah, as Resolution 1701 requires it to do. Since the arrival of a multinational U.N. force with a mandate to end the conflict and support the Lebanese army, four military and political entities—Israel, UNIFIL (the United Nations Interim Force in Lebanon), the Lebanese army, and Hezbollah— have been watching one another warily. Each of them interprets Resolution 1701 in a different way.

Let us now consider how the changes that have taken place in Lebanon have directly affected the groups examined in this book.

The Withdrawal of Syrian Troops

Throughout the 1990s, the Lebanese state's political authority was undermined from within by the creation of a Syrian-controlled security apparatus that gave itself the authority to define areas where only it had the right to intervene. This dispossession was obvious at the highest levels of the Lebanese state hierarchy: the Council of Ministers, which according to the Taif Accords is the country's executive authority, could never discuss the question of the Palestinians in Lebanon. This very sensitive issue was tied up too closely with Syria's regional interests. During the fifteen years of Syrian control, the various Lebanese ministers of state—interior or foreign affairs, for instance—played no role in defining policy on Palestinian refugees in Lebanon. This institutional paralysis made it impossible for Lebanon to develop guidelines for the social and political opportunities available to refugees; deprived the state of knowledge that would have been extremely valuable for the future; and left expertise on the refugee question to foreign research centers.

Apart from administrative questions related to displacement, the Lebanese government's role ended precisely where Syrian security interests made themselves manifest in Lebanon. Thus Lebanon's main security bodies—General Security, headed by Jamil al-Sayyid, or military intelligence services—were restricted to performing subordinate functions dictated by the Syrian authorities wielding power at the time. From 1990 to 2000, Syrian General Ghazi Kan'an over-saw Syrian security from his base in Anjar, a village in the Lebanese Beqaa Valley. His adjutant and successor after 2000, Rustum Ghazaleh, had headquarters at the Beau-Rivage Hotel in Beirut; there, he set goals and issued orders that his many Palestinian contacts were responsible for carrying out in the camps. Ultimately, nothing could be achieved without the approval of the Syrians, who had two aims: to maintain demands for the right of return in order to participate in regional negotiations with Israel; and to prevent Yasir Arafat's Fatah from extending its influence in the camps.[1]

Jamil al-Sayyid's policy was justified by the desire to make Palestinians ineligible for full integration into Lebanese society *(tawtin)*. But the long-term effect of such a policy was to make the younger generation unqualified to emigrate, owing to the drastic decline in education levels caused by the long list of restrictions to which Palestinians were subjected. Even now, after the Syrian withdrawal, the Palestinian question in Lebanon has retained a regional dimension, since only a renewal of the Palestinian-Israeli peace process can ward off the possibility of *tawtin,* by allowing the refugees to be represented by a Palestinian state and to benefit from legal guarantees that will let them work, in Lebanon or elsewhere.

The Palestinians and Resolution 1559

Hezbollah is aware that the camps represent a "weak link" in the implementation of U.N. Resolution 1559, calling for a complete disarmament of all militias in Lebanon. Enforcing 1559 in the Palestinian camps could create a dynamic of disarmament from which Hezbollah could hardly escape. For this reason, it intervened among Palestinians to guarantee a position hostile to Resolution 1559 on principle, in the name of solidarity against a Middle East dominated by the United States and Israel. Hasan Hudruj, the member of

Hezbollah's political bureau who is in charge of the Palestinian question, was given responsibility for contacting all the Palestinian groups in Lebanon. Hezbollah and Syria also attempted to reach Fatah's Palestinian leaders, in a bid to short-circuit the influence of Mahmud Abbas, the president of the Palestinian Authority, elected shortly after Yasir Arafat's death. The Shi'ite party leaders thus sought to prevent direct coordination between the Lebanese government and the various Palestinian organizations. Fuad Siniora, the Lebanese prime minister, tried to counter this attempt by breaking Hezbollah's monopoly on the question and renewing ties with the head of the Palestinian Authority.[2]

As these measures were being taken, on June 3, 2005, Trad Hamadeh, the Lebanese minister of labor close to Hezbollah, decided to ease the draconian measures blocking the labor market for Palestinians. Without modifying the exclusion on principle of Palestinians in Lebanon, this initiative may be seen as an attempt to encourage Palestinian organizations to pursue the channels of cooperation opened up by Hezbollah.

This strategy of coordination with Hezbollah was echoed among some Palestinian factions (like the PFLP and PDFLP) and Hamas. Both in Lebanon and in Palestine, Palestinian elites who "speak" Hezbollah's language in this way have renounced their capacity to define the meaning of their struggle, to the benefit of an organization that shares neither their interests nor their strategic goals. Solidarity with Syria and Iran has thus distanced the Palestinians from the international system, at the very time that the system appears to be their only means of avoiding an unequal confrontation with a state as powerful as Israel. This reality also illustrates the fact that, despite past conflicts, Lebanese and Palestinians share a common destiny. For both parties, access to sovereignty depends directly on the involvement of the international community and the moderating effect it can exercise on their aggressive neighbors.

Finally, Hezbollah has also improved its negotiating capabilities by refusing to allow the Lebanese army to disarm pro-Syrian Palestinian militias outside the camps without prior political arrangements.

The Religious Environment in the Palestinian Camps

Despite their hostility toward Shi'ite Islam on a theological level, jihadist preachers in Ain al-Helweh and Nahr al-Barid called on their followers to oppose the international community's intervention in Lebanon, and announced their solidarity with Hezbollah on the question of disarmament. The priority, for them, was to foil the American project to encircle the *umma*: already engaged on its eastern flank, in Iraq and Afghanistan, the Americans are now concentrating on the western flank, on the territory of Bilad al-Sham. The Syrian regime is presented as the ultimate source of resistance to this plan, and Sunni Muslims are called upon to offer it their support, lest they be called traitors. The camps' preachers thus presented Syria's withdrawal as the loss of external protection for the Palestinian refugees. On that occasion, they preached fear, exploiting the memory of the trauma inflicted by the Lebanese war. The liberation of Samir Geagea, former head of the Lebanese Forces, gave the preachers the opportunity to evoke the massacres at Sabra and Shatila in justifying their refusal to disarm the camps in the face of new threats from the Christian regions. Resolution 1559 provided them with the opportunity to mingle ideological convictions and tactical interests in their sermons, and to clothe in Islamic cultural codes their rejection of a text whose application would destroy the material conditions of their influence in Palestinian camp society.[3]

Solidarity with the Syrian regime necessarily led to a tactical alliance with Hezbollah. Salafists, however, as the self-declared owners of original Islam, identify themselves primarily in opposition to Shi'ism, which according to them represents a rejection of the sources of Islamic legitimacy, whether at the individual or the political level. Considerations linked to survival, then, are behind the salafist shaykhs' tendency to borrow the language of Hezbollah regarding the resistance and its role in countering Western and Israeli threats. From within the salafist mosques in Ain al-Helweh and Nahr al-Barid, Hezbollah is seen as a hypocritical organization that monopolized the southern Lebanese front for its own interests by applying an "Islamic" label to a resistance limited to Lebanese Shi'ites alone. Such behavior was confirmation of Shi'ite duplicity, which medieval Sunni tradition denounces. But this type of confessional polarization, widely maintained within religious circles, must not leak out, for nothing should hinder Islamic solidarity with the main adversary of the United States in Lebanon. Sectarian disputes disappear before the imperatives of survival.

To avoid renouncing their own principles, the shaykhs are therefore obliged to introduce a distinction between theology and strategy: Shi'ites are still despised when it comes to religious identity, but the urgency of regional struggle justifies striking a pact with Hezbollah—even implicitly—aimed at putting paid to Western plans for the region. This is why Ain al-Helweh's salafists denounce international resolutions like 1559, 1680, and, since the summer of 2006, 1701, all of which require Lebanese and Palestinian militias to lay down their weapons; it is also why, in the name of defending Sunni identity, they have been careful to prevent Hezbollah from gaining influence in the refugee camps.

Depending on what is at stake and where the struggle is taking place, then, the jihadist shaykhs choose to emphasize different aspects of their religious identity, each of which corresponds to a specific strategy. From the camp mosques, they challenge the regional order, advocate the reestablishment of the caliphate, and condemn the Arab regimes that cooperate with the United States. This utopian and radical regional perspective depends on maintaining the local status quo, however, because for these shaykhs the point is to preserve their positions and avoid being arrested by the Lebanese police. As sites for preaching activities and recruitment of jihadist militants, the camps must remain outside the purview of the state, even if that means striking a tactical alliance with Hezbollah. On the other hand, the shaykhs encourage their followers to fight Shi'ites as long as the fight takes place in Iraq. From the cities of Iraq's "Sunni triangle," these Islamists can finally reconcile the different aspects of their religious identity by fighting a grab bag of enemies: U.S. troops, Nuri al-Maliki's government, Sunnis who have chosen to participate in politics, and Shi'ite Iraqi civilians. In fact, volunteers from Ain al-Helweh joined the ranks of Abu Mus'ab al-Zarqawi's group, and several dozen of them have already been killed since Saddam Hussein's regime fell in April 2003. In the clandestine underground in Lebanon's camps and in Iraq, jihadist militants choose to exaggerate their religious identity as Sunnis, whether against their non-salafist coreligionists or against Shi'ite Muslims; in their relations with their immediate environment, however, they know how to blend in with the anti-Western Islamic consensus to stay in the good graces of Hezbollah and the Syrian regime.

This Islamic brand of Machiavellianism contains inevitable contradictions and fuels divisions and controversies. To avoid explosion, the shaykhs seek to ensure that violence, formulated at a rhetorical level and occasionally directed against certain individuals, does not upset the status quo they helped create. This is why they work to limit its impact to more distant fronts like Chechnya in the late 1990s and Iraq today. As for the Syrian regime, it constitutes a corridor to Iraq, and as such enjoys immunity. The radicals' predisposition to displaying solidarity with a regime whose infidel character they condemn in other situations is due to their desire to preserve a situation that has lasted for more than fifteen years and provided them with a means to win over some young people and prepare recruits for new battles.

But this balance may be impossible to maintain. It has become difficult to transcend contradictions in light of the growing polarization between Hezbollah, Iran, and Syria on one side, and the government of Fuad Siniora backed by Hariri's family, the United States, and France on the other. The current crisis is dividing the ranks of Sunni jihadist groups. Some of them hold Rafiq al-Hariri responsible for the policy of exclusion targeting Palestinian refugees during the 1990s (although General Security and the presidency, both institutions closely linked with Syrian intelligence, had the exclusive prerogative to define that policy). Others prefer to focus their hatred on Hezbollah, in the name of defending their religious identity. The latter might take up arms against the Shi'ites if a confessional civil war were to break out in Lebanon, while the former could be responsible for violent attacks against the new U.N. force or leaders tied to the new political majority, aimed at weakening the Hariri team from within.[4] The same tension exists in Lebanon as was manifest in Iraq when al-Qa'ida operative Ayman al-Zawahiri asked Abu Mus'ab al-Zarqawi to suspend anti-Shi'ite actions in the name of the struggle against the United States and its regional allies.

The Interplay between Global and Local Jihadism

Whatever the nature of the ties between Islamists in Lebanon—or some of them—and Osama bin Laden or Ayman al-Zawahiri, the salafist-jihadist phenomenon exists autonomously: its development does not depend on "international terrorist networks." The thousands of anonymous militants who embody it today have realized that the Muslim states are incapable of modifying regional and global power relations, and so they have privatized utopia and violence in their own way. Benefiting from impasses in the regional peace process, local Islamists have exploited the corrosion of Arab and Palestinian unity in order to advance the cause of jihadist Islamism. Their methods have been made credible because they exist outside state and regional politics. The war in Afghanistan provided the ideological matrix for the movement, by allowing religious militants to legitimize their actions through reference to the earliest Muslims, and to resurrect medieval traditions that interpreted armed jihad as an obligation for "true believers."

The spread of jihadist Islamism from Afghanistan to Ain al-Helweh was made possible by new, rapid means of communication. Globalization alleviated the frustration that camp inhabitants felt about their local situation by providing them with models of behavior that could be adapted in different places and situations. Islamists who were thousands of miles apart were able to reappropriate the ideological universe formed in the late 1980s by Peshawar's "jihadists," without having been directly associated with that cause. They were able to do so because the usual means of socialization were no longer working, whether in the framework of the family, or in the political and strategic framework of the PLO: the organization, divided into rival clans and facing a situation that threatened its very survival, was incapable of offering a vision to its people, who were dispersed throughout the camps of the Middle East. In Ain al-Helweh, the jihadist movement was borne by idle teenagers who had been resocialized by radical religious networks. These young people did not want to follow in their fathers' footsteps; they had seen the men around them demobilized after a war fought in Lebanon against "too many enemies"—a war that had led to nothing.

Escaping into a transnational movement is a way for Islamists in the Lebanese camps to avoid the national situation. Their new links with global Islamism actively discourage local human interactions and communication with other religious groups. In times of peace such links encourage the logic of ghettos that marked the lowest points of the civil war. But introversion is no longer a survival mechanism, as was the case during the war; on the contrary, the re-fusal to "mingle" *(ikhtilat)* has become voluntary. In some regions of the Akkar, for instance, local Islamists have stronger ties with a Saudi university than with the Christian villages in their immedi-ate area. The same can be said of Ain al-Helweh, where some mosques seek out the influence of a London-based preacher, while their shaykhs now refuse to speak with PLO militants.

The Centrality of the Palestinian Question

Salafist jihadism must be fought with tangible political goals, with a state—and therefore a territory—for the Palestinians. True, the re-sumption of the Palestinian-Israeli peace process will not prevent religious militants from devoting all their efforts to mocking its re-sults and weakening people's faith in its effectiveness, as they did in the Palestinian camps throughout the 1990s. This destructive ob-session, however, was also the militants' way of expressing fear of a process which, if successful, would challenge the credibility of their preaching and the basis of their grip on the refugee popula-tion. If, however, nothing is done to resume Palestinian-Israeli ne-gotiations, Ain al-Helweh might become the vanguard of a salafist-jihadist militancy that would spread in the Palestinian territo-ries, break through nationalist barriers, and change the scale of the struggle, the better to strike "the serpent's head"—that is, in jihadist parlance, the West in general. The best-informed representatives of jihadism in the camps are doing their utmost to destroy the nation-alist tenets embedded in the PLO's political legacy. Though they are capable of carrying out targeted assassinations, their role is also to control those among them who are too ready to use violence in settling accounts with the PLO. As careful readers of Ayman al-Zawahiri, the al-Qa'ida operative, they know that the "distant enemy"—the West—must be targeted as a priority. By contrast, the "nearby enemy"—Arab regimes or quasi-state organizations like the PLO—can be overcome easily once belief in its legitimacy collapses. This is what has taken place in the past few years, as certain segments of the population in Lebanon's camps have turned away from the PLO.

Islamists who lay claim to such an ideology are not fighting to liberate a particular territory and are not integrated into a national political scene. Their terrorism is different, in nature, from that of liberation movements, which alternate between terrorist violence and negotiations in their attempts to secure political independence. The lack of territory has produced a type of terrorism that is subordinated to no particular demand. What is really at stake, in this case, is the ability to impose on Muslims—wherever they may be—a sense of religious belonging and political loyalty.

When faced with such a threat, the international community failed to meet its moral and political obligations. Instead, the humiliation meted out to Arafat and the concomitant destruction of the Palestinian Authority's institutions shattered the national framework. They opened up the Palestinian question to a congeries of regional influences, from Tehran and Damascus as state actors to the limits of Waziristan, Pakistan, for non-state figures like Bin Laden and Ayman al-Zawahiri. Both groups were able to benefit from the Bush administration's refusal to revive the Palestinian-Israeli peace process. At a time when Arab satellite channels are showing images of Palestinian suffering, the United States' enemies in the region understand the importance of a conflict that American neoconservatives have systematically refused to see as anything other than a pretext for Arab dictators trying to make up a legitimacy deficit. American and European responsibility is certainly stronger for this question than for any other, since a peace process that anchored Palestinian identity around a territory and a viable state, with East Jerusalem as its capital, would have given the Palestinian side and the Arab regimes the means of fighting the jihadist forces within their own societies—by the sheer force of conviction.

Notes

Introduction

1. There are no reliable statistics regarding the precise number of Palestinians in Lebanon, just as no one knows how many Palestinians were killed during the Lebanese civil war, what (no doubt large) proportion left Lebanon after the Israeli invasion of 1982, or how many were naturalized in 1994 under less than transparent circumstances. Not all the refugees—whether those of 1948 or those of 1967—were registered with UNRWA, and many left the country while maintaining their registered status.

2. These figures come from a study carried out by the Norwegian Institute for Applied Social Sciences (FAFO) in February 1999, using a representative sample of all Palestinian camp dwellers. See FAFO, *Living Conditions of Palestinian Refugees in Camps and Gatherings in Lebanon*, February 2000.

3. I held additional interviews in the camps in August and September 2002. Two earlier articles, based on this work, appeared in *Maghreb-Machrek*: "Le destin mêlé des Palestiniens et des Libanais au Liban" [The Mixed Destinies of Palestinians and Lebanese in Lebanon], issue 169 (July–September 2000), ed. Bernard Rougier and Elizabeth Picard; and "Dynamiques religieuses et identité nationale dans les camps de réfugiés du Liban" [Religious Dynamics and National Identity in Lebanon's Refugee Camps], issue 176 (Summer 2003), ed. Jean-François Legrain. Finally, a more recent article takes into account the political changes that have occurred since 2005: "Les camps palestiniens

283

du Liban. La Syrie, le Hezbollah et le nouveau pouvoir libanais face aux attentes internationales" [Lebanon's Palestinian Camps. Syria, Hezbollah, and the New Lebanese Regime: International Expectations], in *Transcontinentales,* issue 1 (2005).

4. For an overview of the Palestinians' role in the war in Lebanon, see Rosemary Sayegh, *Too Many Enemies: The Palestinian Experience in Lebanon* (London: Zed Books, 1994). On the PLO's strategy during the conflict, see Rex Brynen, *Sanctuary and Survival: The PLO in Lebanon* (Boulder, Colo.: Westview Press, 1990). On the causes of the war and the dynamic of the conflict, see Samir Kassir, *La guerre du Liban: de la dissension nationale au conflit régional (1975–1982),* [The War in Lebanon: From National Dissent to Regional Conflict (1975–1982)], 2nd ed. (Paris: Karthala, 1994).

5. The expression "Black September" refers to the occasion on which the troops of Jordan's Hashimite monarchy crushed PLO combatants in September 1970. Despite a compromise struck between King Hussein and Yasir Arafat, the Jordanian army destroyed the remaining pockets of Palestinian resistance the following year.

6. In his memoirs, former president of the republic Elias Hrawi recounts that he had to buy back from Samir Geagea, then the head of the Lebanese Forces militia, an arms shipment docked in the port of Beirut on its way to Yugoslavia, in order to allow the Lebanese army, which was lacking munitions, to continue its operations against the PLO in July 1991. The purchase was made for "five million dollars" thanks to Rafiq Al-Hariri, who transferred the money to a Swiss bank account. See the daily *al-Hayat* of June 24, 2002. That anecdote aside, the former president's account also reveals that Hikmat al-Shihabi, then head of the Syrian joint chiefs of staff, opposed an attack by the Lebanese army on the Palestinian camps. Hikmat al-Shihabi is said to have warned the Lebanese president that such an operation "would cause an uprising in the Arab and Islamic world."

7. This figure comes from Palestinian sociologist Suhayl Mahmud Al-Natur, *The Situation of Palestinians in Lebanon* (in Arabic) (Beirut: Dar Al-Taqaddum Al-Arabi, 1993), p. 59.

8. The Palestinians' right to work is regulated—or rather, suppressed—by the general arrangement applying to foreigners residing in Lebanon; they must obtain a work permit, delivered by the Ministry of Social Affairs, and enjoy no special status. A December 1994 decree barred non-

Lebanese from practicing more than seventy professions, from that of CEO or engineer to that of guard or cook. In the few sectors of the economy that remain open to Palestinian workers—construction, low-ranking service jobs, agriculture—they have to compete with the thousands of Syrians who have arrived in Lebanon since the end of the war.

9. The literal translation of *juzur amniyya* is in fact "security islands," but, insofar as the Arabic expression designates places outside state control, it is more meaningful to convey it as "security-free islands," or indeed "islands of insecurity."

10. Demographic pressure is not the only reason the total number of mosques in Ain al-Helweh has doubled since the end of the Lebanese war, leaping from three in 1990 to six today. The same phenomenon can be observed in Nahr al-Barid, the biggest refugee camp in the north.

1. From Iranian Influence to Sunni Affirmation

1. "We energetically condemn all this corruption; we say to you that it is Israel that is leading your reform program. Each time you seek to establish a program in the country, whatever it may be, you extend a humiliated hand in Israel's direction. You bring military experts from Israel into this country, and in exchange you send students to them. We tell you, sir, that this way of doing things is immoral. Do not go against the people's sentiments on this point, for, with God, the people can turn against you" (speech delivered by Khomeini in Qom, addressing the shah). See Amin Mustafa, *Iran and Palestine* (in Arabic) (Beirut: al-Markaz al-Arabi lil-Abhath wal-Tawfiq, 1996).

2. The *khums* (fifth) is a specifically Shi'ite institution. Believers must calculate their revenue for the past year. If they have made a profit, they must give one-fifth of it to a charitable organization or a *sayyid*, a religious figure who can trace his genealogy back to the Prophet Muhammad.

3. See Mustafa, *Iran and Palestine*, p. 56.

4. See *The Palestinian Cause in the Words of Imam Khomeini* (in Arabic) (Damascus: Iranian Embassy, 2000 [1420 A. H.]), p. 109.

5. Waddah Sharara, *The State of Hezbollah: Lebanon, a Muslim Society* (in Arabic) (Beirut: Dar al-Nahar, 1996), p. 109. The Da'wa Party was formed in Najaf, Iraq, in the late 1950s on the initiative of one of

Shi'ite Islamism's main theoreticians, a jurist and theologian named Muhammad Bakr al-Sadr, who waged an all-out struggle against the Baa'th regime and was finally executed in 1980. The organization's Lebanese branch is at the roots of Hezbollah and trained some of the political leaders who headed Iran after the 1979 revolution.

6. See Gilles Ménage, *L'oeil du pouvoir: Face au terrorisme moyen-oriental, 1981–1986* [The Eye of Power: Face to Face with Middle Eastern Terrorism, 1981–1986] (Paris: Fayard, 2001), pp. 59–60.

7. As Salim al-Lawzi, a Lebanese journalist, wrote in November 1979 in the weekly *al-Hawadith:* "The leadership of the Palestinian Resistance has realized that the southerners are so unhappy that they have taken up arms to defend their homes and land, not only against Israel, but against the Palestinians as well. This means that the breaking point is drawing closer and closer, which is what the Palestinian leadership is currently attempting to avert, by intervening in Lebanon and Iran simultaneously" (*al-Hawadith,* November 16, 1979).

8. See Francis Grimblat, "La communauté chiite libanaise et le mouvement national palestinien, 1967–1986" [The Lebanese Shi'ite Community and the Palestinian National Movement, 1967–1986], *Guerres mondiales et conflits contemporains* [World Wars and Contemporary Conflicts] (July 1988), no. 151, PUF / quarterly historical review.

9. Interview with Muhammad Hasan, July 2001, Saida. At the time, Sayyid Hasan al-Amin was voicing his support for the Palestinian cause in a periodical—"Dignity" *(al-'Ird)*—to which another Shi'ite ulema, Sayyid Hani Fahas, also contributed.

10. Cited by Augustus Richard Norton, in *Amal and the Shi'a: The Struggle for the Soul of Lebanon* (Austin: University of Texas Press, 1988), p. 43.

11. See Sami Zubian, *The Lebanese National Movement: Past, Present, and Future. A Strategic Perspective* (in Arabic) (Beirut: Dar al-Masira, 1977), p. 334.

12. Interview with Muhammad Hasan, Saida, July 2001.

13. Ayatollah Khomeini vehemently condemned the Saudi peace plan because, by accepting Resolutions 242 and 338, it implicitly recognized the state of Israel. See *The Palestinian Cause in the Words of Imam Khomeini,* pp. 174–175.

14. See the congregation's informational booklet written by Shaykh Ali Khazim (Beirut: Dar al-Ghurbat, 1997 [1418 A. H.]).

15. Ibid.

16. Interview with Shaykh Muharram al-Arifi, September 1998, Saida.

17. Shortly after Shaykh al-Arifi's death in January 2000, his associates put together a CD-Rom about his life, which also included a series of sermons recorded in Saida, as well as some religion lessons. The citations from his sermons are taken from this CD-Rom.

18. Joseph Maila, "Réflexion sur la violence au Liban" [Reflections on Violence in Lebanon], in Les conférences de l'ALDEC [Conferences of the Lebanese Friends for Cultural Development], *La guerre du Liban au regard des sciences humaines* [The War in Lebanon as Seen by the Humanities] (Beirut: Saint Joseph University, Faculty of Literature and Humanities, 1985), pp. 43–55.

19. *Al-Hidaya* (October 1990), no. 11. In the late 1980s, Islamist militants from Ain al-Helweh began publishing a periodical of a dozen pages titled *al-Hidaya*—a religious term that refers to guidance in God's path. *Al-Hidaya* tells us a great deal about the way these militants interpret the world around them. It also gives some insight into the Islamist networks in the camp and the various currents that cut through them. When writers for this publication interviewed Lebanese religious figures, they sought acknowledgment of the inherent contradictions between the demands of Islamic legitimacy, on the one hand, and Lebanese political reality, on the other. They thus deliberately exaggerated Lebanon's contradictions.

20. See Gilles Kepel, *Jihad: Expansion et déclin de l'islamisme* (Paris: Gallimard, 2000), p. 225. Translated as *Jihad: The Trail of Political Islam* (Cambridge: The Belknap Press of Harvard University Press, 2003), pp. 210–211.

21. Ibid.

22. This is the case for forty-eight-year-old Nazih, who has been disabled since he was wounded in the Israeli bombardments of 1982. He and his mother, his wife, and his four children survive on less than $100 a month, which he makes selling objects found on Saida's trash piles; they live in two humid, unhealthy rooms in one of the camp's houses. Nazih goes to Shaykh al-Zayn's mosque every Friday because he believes that the shaykh "is better trained than the others."

23. Bertrand Badie has developed the notion of "social vacuums," which he defines as "social spaces that escape the state's authority." See "Ruptures et innovations dans l'approche sociologique des relations inter-

nationales" [Breaks and Innovations in the Sociological Approach to International Relations], *Revue du monde musulman et méditerranéen,* 2–3, nos. 68–69 (1993).

24. In the Congregation of Muslim Ulema's publication, *al-Wahda al-Islamiyya* [Islamic Unity], of October 9, 1987, see "The only solution to the question of the camps will be an Islamic solution."

25. See Abdallah Hallaq, *Jihad and Change [al-Jihad wa at-Taghir]* (Beirut: al-Dar al-Islamiyya, 1985/1406 h), p. 126.

26. Ibid., p. 128.

27. *Al-Hidaya,* August 1990.

28. See Samir Kassir, "La Nakba recommencée?" [The Nakba, Take Two?], in *Revue d'études palestiniennes* [Palestinian Studies Review] (Fall 1998), no. 17, pp. 59–65. Samir Kassir was assassinated in Beirut in June 2005.

29. Abdallah Hallaq, "The Islamic Awakening: Programs, Schools, and Movements" *(al-Sahwa al-Islamiyya. Manahij, Madaris, Harakat)* (Beirut: Dar Sabil al-Rashad, 1999), p. 371.

30. Interview with Shaykh Abdallah Hallaq, Saida, April 7, 1999.

31. See Shaykh Abdallah Hallaq's dissertation, defended on March 16, 1998, at the offices of Imam al-Awza'i.

32. The expression was used by Ze'ev Schiff and Ehud Ya'ari in *Israel's Lebanon War,* ed. and trans. Ina Friedman (New York: Simon and Schuster, 1984).

33. According to Rashid Khalidi, the camp's defense was led by Muslim shaykhs and galvanized by young "cubs" (*ashbal* was the term used to designate young combatants) wielding anti-tank RPG-type weapons in close proximity to Israel's armored vehicles. See *Under Siege: PLO Decisionmaking during the 1982 War* (New York: Columbia University Press, 1986), p. 51.

34. For example, he was one of the speakers at a gathering in Beirut that echoed the "anti-conference" held in Tehran to denounce the peace process inaugurated by the Madrid talks in October 1991. See the weekly newspaper *al-Bilad,* November 2, 1991.

35. Interview with Shaykh Ghunaym, January 2001.

36. See *al-Nahar* daily newspaper, December 18, 1991.

37. See Chapter 2.

38. On August 7, 1989, Ayatollah Khomeini proclaimed that the last Friday of each month of Ramadan would be "World Jerusalem Day," dur-

ing which "all Muslims are called upon to hold ceremonies expressing their support for the rights of the Muslim Palestinian people."

39. Khalid Islambulli was the name of the man who killed Anwar al-Sadat in 1981. Nasrallah made this speech at a demonstration organized by Hezbollah against the "agreement on capitulation and humiliation." The demonstration was held on the southern outskirts of Beirut, in Harat Hrayk, on November 1, 1998. Fatah's newspaper in Lebanon, *al-Quds*, replied to Hezbollah's secretary-general in the following terms: "Yes, Hasan Nasrallah, we have many Khalid Islambullis; but all of them remain loyal to the symbol of the revolution and the state that will be born: President Yasir Arafat. Even those with whom we disagree politically are forbidden, by their hearts and their allegiance, from doing what your hate-filled words demand."

40. See Hezbollah's weekly newspaper, *al-Ahd* ("The Promise") (Friday, October 9, 1998), no. 769.

41. *Al-Ahd* (October 1998), no. 768.

42. *Al-Ahd* (October 1998), no. 769.

43. See *al-Quds* and its defense of the Palestinian Authority's position in Lebanon (1998), no. 39, p. 11.

44. Ibid.

45. Editorial titled "The Blackmail Battle," *al-Quds* (July 1998), no. 39, p. 3.

46. Interview with members of the DFLP, Ain al-Helweh, May 25, 2000.

47. Interview with a Palestinian militant in the Lebanese Jama'a, Saida, January 1999.

48. Interview held in Saida, April 1999.

49. According to one of its leaders, al-Quds hospital—the only hospital in Ain al-Helweh—is a center for Shi'ite proselytizing: "They give aid, but under certain conditions . . . Free of charge for the families of Islamic Jihad martyrs. They close the hospital for Jerusalem Day, which Khomeini decreed. They close it during Iranian national holidays. Have you ever heard of a hospital closing on a national holiday?" (interview with a Sanabil leader, Saida, April 1999).

50. Interview with a salafist militant, Ain al-Helweh, May 25, 2000.

51. Shaykh Yusif's sermon at the Hisham Sharaydi Mosque, Ain al-Helweh, Friday, April 16, 2001.

52. See *Minbar al-Da'iyyat* (October 1998, no 42, p. 17), a newspaper published by Shaykh Qatarji and distributed in Ain al-Helweh's

Islamist bookstores. Some of the camp's religious figures contribute to this publication.

53. Interview with Abdallah Hallaq in *Al-Wahda al-Islamiyya,* October 9, 1987.

54. See Murshid's informational booklet, 1993 (1414 A. H.), p. 7.

55. Abu Dia', the young shaykh at Omar Ibn al-Khattab Mosque in Ain al-Helweh, is one of those who followed this path: he was able to register for a master's degree in Islamic law for the 1998–99 academic year thanks to financial help from Murshid.

56. *Al-Hidaya* (March 1991), no. 16.

57. Speech made by Shaykh Hallaq to his students within the framework of the Murshid educational network, Ain al-Helweh, Friday, February 16, 2001.

58. Interview with Shaykh Hallaq, Ain al-Helweh, April 15, 2001.

59. Murshid's influence is also felt in the northern camps. In the early 1990s, a Palestinian student at Imam al-Awza'i Institute could compare religious life in the camp with what it had been previously: "For example, if we compare how many people go to mosque today with what the situation was in previous years, in the past, the four mosques were barely full, and most of the people who went regularly were elderly, there were almost no young people. Today, more and more people attend the six mosques regularly, especially on Fridays, and most of those who attend regularly are young people." It is apparently in response to this growing demand that two additional mosques were built: al-Quds Mosque and the Mosque of Devotion (Masjid al-Taqwa), adding to the four that already existed. The camp's mosques are placed under the dual control of the Islamic *waqf* administration in the Akkar and of Murshid (the Supervisory Council on Religious Affairs). See Mahmud Raja Husayn Za'rura, *Memorandum on the Demographic and Economic Situation of Palestinians in the Nahr al-Barid Camp,* 1993 (1414 A. H.) (Library of the Imam al-Awza'i Institute).

60. Marcel Gauchet provides this definition of socialization within the framework of school in "Essai de la psychologie contemporaine, un nouvel âge de la personnalité" [Essay in Contemporary Psychology: A New Age of Personality], *La démocraties contre elle-même* [Democracy against Itself] (Paris: Gallimard, 2002), pp. 207–263.

61. During the summer of 1998, reconstruction work was carried out in

the camp of Burj al-Shamali, near Tyre, although the camp was under "blockade" as far as construction materials were concerned.

62. Interview with Shaykh Ghunaym, February 3, 2001, Nahr al-Barid.

63. *Al-Hidaya* (April 1991), no. 17.

64. In one of his sermons, Shaykh Jamal Khattab contrasted Sultan-Caliph Abdul-Hamid II's resistance in the face of Zionist pressure with the current cowardice of Arab leaders, "who receive salaries from the American Mukhabarat [intelligence] and are selling the Islamic nation very cheap."

65. *Al-Hidaya* (April 1991).

66. The Syrian-Lebanese people, according to Lebanese historian Edmond Rabbath, remembered Jamal Pasha only as *al-Saffah,* the Bloodshedder. *La formation historique du Liban politique et constitutionnel: Essai de synthèse* [The Historical Formation of Political and Constitutional Lebanon: An Essay in Synthesis] (Beirut: Lebanese University Press, 1986), p. 262.

67. Interview with a Palestinian teacher at Nahr al-Barid, summer 2002.

2. Islamism from Peshawar to Ain al-Helweh

1. See *al-Hidaya,* November 1991, no. 22 (1412 A. H.). The citations are taken from the same issue.

2. Sayyid Qutb (1906–1963) is still one of the Islamist movement's main intellectual sources. An Egyptian schoolteacher, this Muslim Brotherhood member opposed the Nasser regime and was hanged in 1966. In a massive Qur'anic exegesis (*In the Shadow of the Qur'an*) and theological-political works (*Social Justice in Islam; Signposts*), he renewed the concept of *jahiliyya* (the state of ignorance in which Arabia dwelt before prophetic revelation) and applied it to contemporary Muslim political systems, which he judged guilty of preferring the sovereignty (*hakimiyya*) of men to that of God.

3. In Ain al-Helweh, an average family consists of 6.5 members, whose living space is less than 485 square feet.

4. The Muslim Student Union was created in the late 1950s by Mustafa Tahan, a Muslim Brotherhood sympathizer of Syrian origin who was studying in Turkey at the time. The Union had branches in all Pakistan's universities, and its president, a Jordanian national, enthusiastically supported Shaykh Azzam's activities.

5. Contemporary Islamism has annexed the work of Ibn Taymiyya, a theologian of the thirteenth and fourteenth centuries (1263–1327), because of the central importance of jihad in his doctrine. An event from this Hanbali judge's career makes this retrieval especially relevant: during the siege of Damascus in 1300 by Mongols converted to Islam, Ibn Taymiyya called on the city's inhabitants to go on jihad against the authorities, whose conversion he considered superficial and opportunistic. He explained to the people that they were allowed to kill him if he joined the opposing camp, "even if [he] bore on [his] head a copy of the Qur'an." Cited by Louis Pouzet, a Jesuit priest, in his *Damas au VIIe – XIIIe siècle. Vie et structures religieuses dans une métropole islamique* [Damascus in the Eighth–Thirteenth Century: Life and Religious Structures in an Islamic Metropolis] (Beirut: Dar al-Machrek, 1986), p. 300. Paradoxically, the second siege of Damascus claimed several hundred lives, while the first claimed virtually no victims, though the impious army that led it in 1260 had destroyed the Baghdad caliphate only two years before. On the doctrine and life of Ibn Taymiyya, see Henri Laoust, *Essai sur les doctrines sociales et politiques de Taki-Din-Ahmad B. Taimiya* [Essay on the Social and Political Doctrines of Taqiyy al-Din Ahmad Ibn Taymiyya] (Cairo: Institut français d'archéologie orientale, 1939). For an English-language source, see Rudolph Peters, *Jihad in Classical and Modern Islam: A Reader*, 2nd ed., updated and expanded (Princeton: Markus Wiener Publisher, 2005).

6. Interview with Uzaifa Azzam, Amman, May 2004.

7. *Al-Mujahid,* issues 5 and 6 (April–May 1989; Ramadan-Shawwal 1409). The publication also denounced the way Shi'ites, in Afghanistan and elsewhere, sought to impede jihad. *Al-Mujahid*'s editors argued that "massacres of old people, women, and children, carried out by Shi'ite militias in Lebanon's Palestinian camps, are an almost perfect illustration of the hostility that the *rawafid* have always felt toward the Sunnis, while the Palestinians expected the Shi'ites to take their side against the Jewish invaders." All the prominent figures of contemporary salafism—Abd al-Aziz Ibn Baz, Muhammad Ibn al-Uthaymin, Nasir al-Din al-Albani, Abu Bakr al-Jaza'iri—have also written articles and given interviews in *al-Mujahid.*

8. See "Islamic Preaching," under the pen name Sadiq Amin (published in Arabic in 1982 under the title *al-Da'wa al-Islamiya*).

9. Abdallah Azzam, "The Muslim People's Jihad" (in Arabic) (Sanaa: Maktabat al-Jil al-Jadid; Beirut: Dar Ibn Hazm, 1992), p. 25. This book is a collection of op-ed pieces published in *al-Jihad*.

10. *Al-Jihad* (May 1986), nos. 15–18.

11. Interview with a Service Bureau veteran, Amman, March 2004.

12. *Al-Jihad* (June 1985), no. 7.

13. The idea that the expulsion of Jews and Christians from the peninsula was one of the prophet's last wishes, expressed "four days before he died," was taken up in *Nectar Sealed*, a life of Muhammad, by the winner of a competition for the best prophetic hagiography, organized in Madina by the World Islamic League in 1979. The author, a Pakistani citizen named Safi al-Rahman al-Mubarakpuri, worked at the Center for Research on the Life of the Prophet Muhammad, at Madina's Islamic University. The book was distributed globally in several languages, including Arabic, English, and French.

14. This point is corroborated by the former president of the Muslim Student Union in Pakistan, who stated that Azzam "wanted to create his own jihadist school" (interview, Irbid, Jordan, July 2004).

15. Interview with Abu Tariq, Ain al-Helweh, Saturday, December 18, 1999.

16. See *al-Hidaya* (January 1990), no. 2, p. 1.

17. See *al-Hidaya* (April 1990), no. 6, "The Islamic Movement and Its Current Priorities," p. 3.

18. See *al-Hidaya* (April 1990), no. 16, p. 6.

19. Muhammad Daud was the first president of the Republic of Afghanistan, having abolished the monarchy in a coup d'état in 1973. He was overthrown in 1978 by the Afghan Communist Party, of which the main figures were Nur Muhammad Taraki, Hafizullah Amin, and Babrak Karmal. On Hafizullah Amin's initiative, the Khalq faction of the Communist Party implemented an authoritarian policy, in particular by marginalizing the other faction, Parcham, led by Babrak Karmal. The Soviets intervened in December 1979 after Hafizullah Amin assassinated Taraki, his former comrade. Babrak Karmal was president of the revolutionary council from 1980 to 1986. On Afghanistan's recent history, see Barnett R. Rubin, *The Fragmentation of Afghanistan* (New Haven: Yale University Press, 2002).

20. See *al-Jihad* (June 1986).

21. See *al-Hidaya* (February 1991), no. 15, p. 4.

22. In 1997, Muhammad Khalid al-Itani, a Lebanese national, met a friend of Abu Muhammad al-Masri's in Germany. Through this contact, he met Abu Muhammad al-Masri in the Ain al-Helweh camp; the two men agreed that it was necessary to bring young Arabs together and set up an organization capable of striking "Jewish and American interests" in the region. In 1998 and 1999, the group is said to have smuggled arms out of Ain al-Helweh and Shatila to Beirut, whence they would be taken secretly to Jordan to be used in attacks. It would thus seem that Abu Muhammad al-Masri, through his nephew, managed to organize a meeting between Bin Laden and Muhammad al-Itani during the summer of 1999, at which the two men supposedly planned operations in Europe, which were to be carried out with weapons obtained from Ukrainian arms dealers (see *al-Safir* newspaper, May 20, 2000).

23. The *hijab* covers only the hair, whereas the *niqab* covers the entire face.

24. Shaykh Taqiyy al-Din al-Nabahani, a secondary school teacher, created the Islamic Liberation Party (Hizb al-Tahrir) in Tulkarm, in the north of Transjordan, in 1953. Although its origin is exclusively Palestinian, the party developed a pan-Islamist ideology devoted to the reestablishment of the Islamic caliphate and the destruction of the Arab regimes within their current borders. Severely repressed by the Jordanian regime in the 1960s, the party still has clandestine cells scattered throughout the Middle East, in England, and in Central Asia. Its members devote themselves almost exclusively to publishing tracts and communiqués, but have not crossed the threshold into violent action.

25. In theory, this institution depends on Islamic Jihad. In reality, it is directly linked to the Iranian Embassy. Its current head is Shaykh Sa'id Qasim, who took over for Shaykh Barakat after he retired to Beirut's southern outskirts, in the Shi'ite neighborhood of Harat Hrayk.

26. For instance, during the demonstrations surrounding the World Trade Organization (WTO) meeting in Seattle, in November 1999, the censor at al-Nur Mosque stopped transmitting whenever a woman appeared.

27. The very day of the assassination, members of Usbat al-Ansar handed out candy to passers-by in the streets of Ain al-Helweh, to celebrate their revenge on the man considered responsible for the murder of the shaykh who founded the movement, Hisham Sharaydi.

28. A week after the event, a member of Usbat al-Ansar, Hisham Shahabi, was killed while he was trying to rob a bank in Dammur. Details of the

investigation that were leaked to the press indicated that Shahabi was part of the group that had killed the judges in Saida.

29. Interview with a leader of Usbat al-Ansar, *al-Nahar,* October 26, 1998.

30. Results of the statistical survey carried out by FAFO, *Living Conditions of Palestinian Refugees in Camps and Gatherings in Lebanon,* February 2000.

31. Interview conducted at the office of a humanitarian association in Ain al-Helweh, summer 1998.

32. *Al-Nahar,* March 9, 1995.

33. The January 26, 1995, issue of *al-Nahar* reported that "unknown assailants blew up a shop selling alcohol and cigarettes near al-Qanaya Church, on the road to Saida. The owner had already faced gunfire during the two previous years." Several other liquor shops were blown up in the region (see *al-Nahar,* August 1, 1997, and May 12, 1998). In 1998, a vendor was assassinated and another person wounded (*al-Nahar,* August 31, 1998).

34. *Nida'ul Islam,* a magazine published in Australia, devoted one article to the Lebanese regime's "assassination," on March 14, 1997, of three militants who had received death sentences for the murder of Nizar al-Halabi. In another issue, later removed from the Internet edition, the magazine offered low-cost computer equipment, with revenues going to jihad fighters worldwide. Among the beneficiaries, in addition to "Chechnya's Muslims" and those of Ogaden, were the "Muslims" of al-Nur Mosque, in Ain al-Helweh. See *Nida'ul Islam* online at http://www.islam.org.au.

35. Shaykh Jamal Khattab, sermon of February 5, 1999, delivered at al-Nur Mosque, Ain al-Helweh. Implicitly, Shaykh Jamal was thus admitting that, at least in terms of organization, Westerners are closer to the model of original jihadist Islam than Muslims are today.

36. Shaykh Jamal, ibid.

37. Interview, April 9, 1999, Ain al-Helweh.

38. *Al-Nahar,* October 26, 1998. By contrast, the only Palestinian member of the Jama'a Islamiyya's political bureau, Osama Abbas, considers the Taliban "a caricature of Islam" whose members owe their success to American aid, which is given because the United States wants to help project a "deformed image" of Islam as a religion.

39. See Anonymous, *Imperial Hubris: Why the West Is Losing the War on Terror* (Washington, D.C.: Brassey's Inc., 2004), p. 77. The author, Mi-

chael Scheuer, an expert on terrorism and on U.S. intelligence in Afghanistan and South Asia, previously wrote *Through Our Enemies' Eyes: Osama Bin Laden, Radical Islam, and the Future of America* (Washington, D.C.: Brassey's Inc., 2002).

40. For example, the camp as a whole is subjected to checkpoints at entrances and exits, systematic vehicle searches, a prohibition on bringing in construction materials, and a prohibition on the use of motorcycles.

41. See Michel Wieviorka, *Sociétés et terrorisme* (Paris: Fayard, 1988), pp. 15–34.

42. Ibid.

3. The Struggle against al-Ahbash

1. Nizar Hamzeh and R. Hrair Dekmejian, "A Sufi Response to Political Islamism," *International Journal of Middle East Studies,* 28 (1996), pp. 217–229. The word *ahbash* means "Ethiopians" in Arabic.

2. Interview with Muhammad Nukkari, the mufti's principal secretary, in charge of Dar al-Fatwa's general administration, Beirut, Dar al-Fatwa, May 13, 2000.

3. See *Sarih al-Bayan* [The Explicit Declaration], Shaykh Abdallah al-Hirari, Jam'iyyat al-Mashari' (Beirut, 1990), p. 195.

4. The battlefield in the confrontation with the Ahbash is occupied almost exclusively by salafist shaykhs. See, for example, *Al-Habashi, Shudhudhu wa Akhta'uh* . . . [Al-Habashi, His Aberrations and His Errors. A Succinct Depiction of al-Habashi's Principles, and Warning against the Threat to the Sunnis from His Faction], by Shaykh Abd al-Rahman Dimashqiya (the pamphlet bears no date or place of publication). See also one of the last fatwas (no. 19606, 1418 A. H.) issued by the grand mufti of Saudi Arabia, Ibn Baz, describing the Ahbash as a "deviant faction."

5. According to the Jesuit priest Henri Lammens, when the Qur'an refers to the "face" or the "hand" of God, Ash'ari takes these expressions in their literal sense. Lammens believes, however, that it is possible to avoid accusations of anthropomorphism by pointing out that such expressions do not entitle one to make analogies with the human body. It is therefore necessary to interpret *bila kayf,* which means without asking why or, in other words, without attempting to understand reasons or modalities. Here, modality is a mystery that transcends human un-

derstanding; the discussion must therefore be avoided. The formulas are intended to satisfy intellectuals and "simple believers." *L'islam. Croyances et institutions* [Islam. Beliefs and Institutions] (Beirut: Imprimerie catholique, 1926).

6. Henri Laoust defines the concept of *tafwid* as a mental attitude that consists in leaving the interpretation of certain verses to God. See *Essai sur les doctrines sociales et politiques de Taki-Din-Ahmad B. Taimiya* [Essay on the Social and Political Doctrines of Taqiyy al-Din Ahmad Ibn Taymiyya] (Cairo: Institut français d'archéologie orientale, 1939), p. 514.

7. Nizar Hamzeh and R. Hrair Dekmejian provide an example of such misinterpretation, arguing, for instance, that "there has been a convergence between the values, aspirations, and socioeconomic interests of the Sunni middle class and the contents of Shaykh Habashi's message—that is, sectarian accord and political stability; an enlightened Islamic spiritualism within a modern secularist framework; a Lebanese identity wedded to Arab nationalism; and an accommodating attitude toward the Arab regimes, particularly the Syrian government" (Hamzeh and Dekmejian, "A Sufi Response to Political Islamism," p. 224).

8. Since their birth in the laboratory of Syrian intelligence, in Anjar (Biqaa Valley), the Ahbash have offered information to intelligence services in the increasingly numerous countries where they are established, and especially in western Europe and the United States. Zacharias Moussawi, sentenced to life in prison by the American judiciary for his involvement in the attacks of September 11, 2001, has a brother who is frequently called upon to explain Moussawi's behavior to the media, and who is also, as it happens, a member of the Ahbash brotherhood.

9. On the history of the Muslim Brothers in Lebanon, see the dissertation of Dalal Bizri, "Les mouvements islamistes sunnites au Liban" [Sunni Islamist Movements in Lebanon] (Paris: Ecole pratique des hautes études en sciences sociales, 1984).

10. On that occasion, Shaykh Nizar al-Halabi's successor, Shaykh Husam Qaraqira, paid homage to the Syrian president for "protecting Lebanon's independence and sovereignty." As for Adnan Tarabulsi, he declared that "Lebanon today is more independent than it has ever been. Contrary to what some people think stupidly, independence does not mean placing brothers and enemies on equal footing." See the Ahbash's publication, *Manar al-Huda,* (December 1999), no. 82, pp. 44–49.

11. Letter from Lord Cromer to Lord Rosebery, 1886, cited by Hannah Arendt in *L'impérialisme* (Paris: Fayard, 1982), p. 157.

12. The Syrians, aware of such a risk, began to encourage another Sunni religious trend to establish roots in Lebanon. The Ahbab are tied to the mufti of Damascus, Shaykh Kaftaro, who is officially close to the regime and decidedly hostile to the Ahbash. In this way, a "frontline" has been created to neutralize dangerous comparisons. On the Ahbab movement, see *al-Shira'a*, a Lebanese publication, August 5, 1996.

13. Interview with the shaykh of Wadi Zayneh's Islamic center, March 2000. The neighborhood of Wadi Zayneh, seven miles north of Saida, is mainly populated by Palestinians, many of whom moved to the region during the war of the camps.

14. To celebrate the "election" of president Emile Lahoud in 1998 in their own way, the members of the organization put up billboards, especially visible in the western part of the capital, showing the Lebanese president (a general) proudly saluting Bashar al-Asad (who, at the time, was a colonel). At least the billboards identified the individual who was responsible for the "Lebanese dossier" until he succeeded his father to the presidency.

15. See the salafist magazine *Nida'ul Islam* (July–August 1997).

16. Acts of revenge have been added to the assassinations that make up the fabric of relations among the Palestinian factions: a Palestinian Ahbash shaykh, who taught in Ain al-Helweh, was killed in Saida (see *al-Nahar*, August 26, 1994); two bombs were placed in front of shops belonging to members of the brotherhood (*al-Hayat*, December 3, 1994).

17. Ernesto Laclau has developed the concept of "hegemonic victory": such a victory occurs "when the objectives of a particular group are identified with society at large." See Ernesto Laclau, *La guerre des identités. Grammaire de l'émancipation* [Identity Warfare. A Grammar of Emancipation] (Paris: La Découverte, "Recherches / Bibliothèque du MAUSS," 2000), p. 105.

18. The lecture was given on August 18, 1991, at al-Nur Mosque, Ain al-Helweh. See *al-Hidaya* (October–November 1991), nos. 21 and 22.

19. Ibid.

20. *Al-Hidaya* (November 1991).

21. Philip Khoury, *Syria and the French Mandate: The Politics of Arab Nationalism, 1920–1945* (Princeton: Princeton University Press, 1987), p. 83.

22. See Edmond Rabbath, *La formation historique du Liban politique et constitutionnel: essai de synthèse* [The Historical Formation of Political and Constitutional Lebanon: An Essay in Synthesis] (Beirut: Lebanese University Press, 1986), pp. 126–127.

23. After the decree was promulgated, Sami al-Sulh, the council president, fired the director-general of pious foundations, with whom he was in conflict.

24. The Maqasid Society is a charitable network founded in Beirut in 1878. Initially, it was responsible for providing primary education for orphans. The network later extended its educational and humanitarian activities to all Lebanon's cities, and, on the eve of the war, it had become the main purveyor of social services to Sunnis. It remained under the control of the Salam family dynasty for a long time, until the late council president Rafiq al-Hariri also sought to control it. Thanks to its resources, the society remains a formidable apparatus of political patronage.

25. See Adnan Ahmad Badr, *al-Ifta wal-Awqaf al-Islamiyya fi Lubnan: Madiyan wa Hadiran wa Mustaqbalan* [Dar al-Fatwa and Pious Foundations in Lebanon: Past, Present, and Future] (in Arabic) (Beirut: al-Mu'assassa al-Jamiya lil-Dirasat wal-Nashr wal-Tawzi', 1992). This book was originally a dissertation defended by the author, a lawyer by profession, at the Imam al-Awza'i Institute.

26. The mufti's visit was reported in the daily *al-Safir*, December 28, 1996. Before the election, a petition had circulated, protesting the modification of the January 1955 legislative decree to restrict the electoral body and exclude most of the ulemas from the vote. See the weekly *al-Shira'a*, December 30, 1996.

27. The *shaykh 'aql* of the Druze community and the president of the Higher Shi'ite Council have a far larger electoral base than the mufti's and are considered far more representative. The *shaykh 'aql* is directly elected by all Druze males age twenty-one and older. The president of the Higher Shi'ite Council is indirectly elected by a legal and an executive committee. The legal committee, made up of twelve ulemas, is elected by all the Shi'ite ulemas in Lebanon who have a degree in religious studies. The executive committee is made up of ex officio members—community deputies—and twelve civilians, elected from within a general committee, which in turn is composed of fifteen social-professional categories within the Shi'ite community (for example, civilian

judges, university professors, lawyers, local council directors, and so on).

28. Cited by Jakob Skovgaard-Petersen, "The Sunni Religious Scene in Beirut," *Mediterranean Politics,* vol. 3, n.1 (Summer 1998), pp. 69–80.

29. *Al-Nahar,* Monday, December 30, 1996.

30. After confrontations in Diniyeh, deputies, mayors, and "clerics" from Akkar addressed a complaint to the mufti in which they denounced his "excessive indulgence" and his inertia in the face of threats of infiltration and the establishment of control over religious functions by extremist groups (see the *Daily Star,* January 17, 2000).

31. Interview with Shaykh Abd al-Nasir Jibri, February 8, 2001, al-Da'wa College, Beirut. Reactivating grassroots religious networks to counterbalance the mufti's influence is nothing new in Lebanon. Reacting to the "mini-coup" that brought the Nasserist shaykh Hasan Khalid to the head of Dar al-Fatwa in 1966, Saudi Arabia immediately "turned toward religious institutions . . . and gambled on their reactivation after what most observers agreed had been a time of lethargy." Quote is from Waddah Charara, "Mosquée et quartier: une 'pratique du paysage social.' Une enquête sur un comité de mosquée" [Mosque and Neighborhood: "Social Landscape Practices." Enquiry Regarding a Mosque Committee], *Maghreb-Machrek,* January–March 1989, no. 123.

32. Excerpts from a live program aired on March 23, 1997, and titled "Open Forum," on Idha'at al-Fajr Radio, broadcasting from Saida after the three militants accused of having murdered Nizar al-Halabi were executed at Rumiyyeh Prison.

33. Joseph Maila, "Cruauté et société. Réflexion sur la violence au Liban" [Cruelty and Society. Reflection on Violence in Lebanon] Beirut: Saint Joseph University, Faculty of Letters and Humanities, 1985.

34. See Michael Johnson, *Class and Client in Beirut: The Sunni Muslim Community and the Lebanese State, 1840–1985* (London: Ithaca Press, 1986).

35. After the 2000 elections culminating in Rafiq al-Hariri's triumph countrywide, Elizabeth Picard described that victory, "which put an end (temporarily?) to the Sunni leadership's pluralism," as "that of a restoration of communitarian stakes in political mobilization. After all the other confessional groups, but in a more striking way and with graver consequences, Lebanon's Sunnis chose the solidarity of 'primor-

dial' identity to participate in political negotiations." See "Elections libanaises: un peu d'air a circulé . . ." [Lebanese Elections: A Little Fresh Air], *Critique internationale* (January 2001), no. 10.

4. The Struggle to Control the Camp

1. Following the 1993 Oslo Accords, Munir al-Muqdah, a former leader of Force 17, Fatah's elite battalion, led a military offensive against loyalist Fatah positions in Ain al-Helweh. When fighting broke out again in November 1994, he benefited from Usbat al-Ansar's logistical support and was able to restrict the "Arafatists" to Baraksat, in the camp's northern sector. After his nominal reintegration into the Fatah apparatus in 1999, he maintained external ties with Syrian and Lebanese backers. Confrontations between the different factions marked life in the camp during the postwar years, thus providing the Islamists with fuel for their condemnation of the PLO leadership's "moral and material corruption."

2. Interview with a merchant from Ain al-Helweh who belongs to a neighborhood committee made up of Safuriyya residents, Ain al-Helweh, summer 2002.

3. On the Diniyeh clashes, see Chapter 7.

4. Interview with Abu Tariq, December 18, 1999.

5. Paul Ricoeur, "L'idéologie et l'utopie: deux expressions de l'imaginaire social," *Du texte à l'action. Essai d'herméneutique II* [Ideology and Utopia: Two Expressions of Social Imagination, in From Text to Action: Essay in Hermeneutics, II] (Paris: Le Seuil, 1986), p. 424.

6. *Al-Quds* (the Palestinian Authority's newspaper in Lebanon) (1998), no. 39.

7. Interview with a Fatah leader, Rashidiyyeh, July 2001.

8. *Al-Nahar*, October 22, 2000.

9. *Nida'ul-Islam* (October–November 2002).

10. The Syrian regime chose to rise above the memory of the 1982 clashes, having understood the benefits it could derive from religious mobilization within Lebanese Muslim society, as long as the resulting anger was directed against Israel and, in the new local vocabulary, its new "allies": Egypt, Jordan, and the Palestinian Authority. In 1993, when Hezbollah leaders went to make the case (successfully, as it turned out) for a Hamas bureau to be opened in Damascus, Syrian leaders are said

to have told them: "We can tell the difference between those who are fighting Israel and those who want to confront the regime." See Hasan Fadlallah, *al-Khayar al-Akhar* [The Other Choice] (Beirut: Dar al-Hadi, 1994), p. 106.

11. Interview with a Hamas leader in Nahr al-Barid, August 2002.

12. *Nida'ul-Islam,* June–July 2002. See http://pandora.nla.gov.au/pan/31890/20031025/www.islam.org.au/articles/33/english/yasin(e).pdf.

13. Interview with Shaykh Jamal Khattab, Thursday, January 11, 2001, Ain al-Helweh, al-Nur Mosque.

14. See *al-Wala wal-Bara* [Loyalty and Separation], by Ayman al-Zawahiri, al-Qa'ida's main ideologue, posted online in December 2002. See also Gilles Kepel, *The War for Muslim Minds: Islam and the West* (Cambridge: Harvard University Press, 2004), pp. 134–139, 142.

15. Communiqué issued by the Palestinian Ulema League on October 5, 2000. The text's authors believed that "Palestinian demonstrations in Lebanon prove that Palestinians reject *tawtin* [naturalization in Lebanon] in any form, and consider the homeland the only option."

16. Tract distributed after a conference in Saida, November 5, 2000.

17. Interview with Shaykh Ali Yusuf, August 26, 2000, Saida.

18. Friday November 6, 1998, Ain al-Helweh.

19. See *al-Jihad* (November 1985).

20. See Henri Laoust, *Essai sur les doctrines sociales et politiques de Taki-Din-Ahmad B. Taimiya* [Essay on the Social and Political Doctrines of Taqiyy al-Din Ahmad Ibn Taymiyya] (Cairo: Institut français d'archéologie orientale, 1939), p. 125.

21. Various political figures gathered at the village of Metn, in the heart of Mount Lebanon, in April 2001, with the consent of the Maronite patriarch, Nasrallah Butrus Sfayr. The group, which included nine deputies, sought to form a moderate, legalistic opposition. The charter of Kurnat Shahwan—by metonymy, the name designates the village of Metn—called for the "redeployment" of Syrian troops and sought to deter amalgamation by reaffirming that Israel was still "the main source of danger" for Lebanon. This political initiative triggered many counter-demonstrations among Syria's main supporters, who grouped Kurnat Shahwan with other events taking place at the same time (debates over the Syrian Accountability Act in Congress, in addition to the International Maronite Congress, which was favorable to the draft and which was held in Los Angeles in June 2001) in order to give credit to the idea of a vast anti-Syrian coalition.

22. The text of the Syrian-Israeli peace plan as leaked to the Arabic-language press made explicit the principle of the war on "international terrorism." According to that version, "the two parties recognize that international terrorism in all its forms constitutes a threat to the security of all states. For this reason, they have a common interest in intensifying international efforts to solve this problem. Each of the two parties thus commits itself to forbidding all forms of violent activity that constitute a threat to the other, to its citizens, and to its assets. Each party will take the necessary measures to ensure that no action of this sort will be launched from its territory" (al-Hayat, January 16, 2000).

23. Interview in Ain al-Helweh, December 1999.

24. Quoted by Hassan Sabra, "an al-sahwa al-islamiyya fi lubnan" [About the Islamic Awakening in Lebanon], in al-Harakat al-islamiyya al-mu'asira fil-watan al-arabi [The Islamic Movement in Lebanon] (Beirut: Markaz dirasat al-wahdat al-arabiyya, 1987), p. 103.

5. Preaching Topics

1. Verses from The Holy Qur'an, English interpretation by Abdullah Yusuf Ali (Beirut: Dar al Arabia, n.d).

2. This statement is false, for the number of deputies was increased in relation to the arrangements initially made in the Taif Accords. The increase allowed the Syrian regime to place candidates on the lists of notables who already enjoyed local legitimacy.

3. This was the case in 2000, for example, after Hafiz al-Asad's death, when a preacher cast doubts on the late president's piety as a Muslim.

4. Conference recorded at al-Nur Mosque under the title "Civil Marriage: The Concept and Its Dangers," presented on March 22, 1998.

5. Islam institutes "milk ties" similar to blood ties between boys and girls who have shared a wet nurse. Shaykh Jamal once again transforms the difference between civil and religious spheres into an absolute, necessary opposition. Civil marriage must therefore be seen as transgressing divine prescription, since the Qur'an expressly forbids a man from marrying his wet nurse or his nursing sister (Qur'an, IV, 23).

6. According to Ali al-Halabi al-Athari, a salafist shaykh, "We cannot contradict ourselves by participating on the one hand while, on the other, we tell the masses at every opportunity that it is bad not to gov-

ern according to God's Law, and that every authority that fails to govern according to this law has no legitimacy." See "The Jurisprudence of Reality" [Fiqh al-Waqi'] (Jordan and Beirut, 1992 and 1996).

7. See, for instance, the interview with Zuhayr al-Ubaydi, a Jama'a deputy in Beirut, in al-Safir, titled "Al-Ubaydi: 'We Do Not Seek to Establish an Islamic State.'" The deputy noted: "We are in favor of suppressing a confessional political system, which poses an obstacle to the principle of equal opportunity and to the idea that competent officials must occupy relevant positions in state leadership . . . But we do not intend to establish an Islamic republic at the present time. We are and have always been opposed to this idea, because the conditions for its implementation are not present in Lebanon. Nevertheless, we believe that Lebanon can benefit from many rules and laws that conform strictly to Islamic Shari'a, without infringing on the principles and beliefs of the other communities" (al-Safir, September 2, 1992).

8. In most Lebanese soap operas, couples do not kiss, and friends greet each other somewhat awkwardly: with no physical contact, or in a "physically correct" manner, by pressing each other's hands while standing at a respectful distance.

9. Along the coast between Beirut and Saida, all the billboards that show naked bodies have been painted over, leaving only faces and brand names visible.

10. Philippe Braud, "Violence symbolique, violence physique. Eléments de problématisation," in Guerres civiles. Economies de la violence, dimensions de la civilité ["Symbolic Violence and Physical Violence: Elements for a Problematic," in Civil Wars: Economies of Violence, Dimensions of Civility], ed. Jean Hannoyer (Paris: Karthala, 1999), "Hommes et sociétés," pp. 33–45.

11. Sermon on the Prophet's companions and their flight to Abyssinia, delivered in Ain al-Helweh, 1997.

12. The expression "Sunni ultimatum" was used by the Lebanese political scientist Farid al-Khazen in his book The Breakdown of the State in Lebanon, 1967–1976 (London and New York: I. B. Tauris, 2000), p. 307.

13. Edmond Rabbath, La formation historique du Liban politique et constitutionnel: essai de synthèse [The Historical Formation of Political and Constitutional Lebanon: An Essay in Synthesis], 2nd ed. (Beirut: Lebanese University Press, 1986), pp. 607–608.

14. Quote from Shaykh Jamal Khattab is from an undated sermon at al-Nur Mosque. For a genealogy of the links between Arabism and Islamism, see Henri Laurens, *L'orient arabe. Arabisme et islamisme de 1798 à 1945* [The Arab Orient: Arabism and Islamism, 1798–1945] (Paris: Armand Colin, "U," 1993), p. 102.

15. The woman was none other than Madeleine Albright, then secretary of state in the Clinton White House.

16. François Georgeon, "Le dernier sursaut (1878–1908)" [The Last Tremor (1878–1908)], in *Histoire de l'empire ottoman* [History of the Ottoman Empire], ed. Robert Mantran, (Paris: Fayard, 1989), pp. 523–576.

17. This is also a driving idea in the ideology of the Liberation Party that has connections in the camp. In a Liberation Party bulletin, probably published in London on August 6, 1996, and addressing the "Lebanese province," Muslims are "asked not only to refrain from assisting the regime and participating in it, but also to change it. Change through the heart is possible for all Muslims."

18. See Efraim Karsh and Inari Karsh, *Empires of the Sand: The Struggle for Mastery in the Middle East* (Cambridge: Harvard University Press, 1999), pp. 100–101.

19. Sermon delivered on May, 11, 1418, A. H., at al-Nur Mosque, Ain al-Helweh.

20. Ibid.

21. See *al-Nahar,* April 30, 2001.

22. The expression is from Michel Dobry, *Sociologie des crises politiques* [Sociology of Political Crises] (Paris: Presses de la Fondation nationale des sciences politiques, 1986), p. 236.

6. The Role of Islamic Institutes in Lebanon

1. See Bassem Sirhan, "Education and the Palestinians in Lebanon" (paper presented at a conference on Palestinians in Lebanon, published in the *Journal of Refugee Studies*, 3, 10 [1997]).

2. When the study's authors refer to the adult population, they mean women and men over fifteen years of age. Thirteen percent of men are illiterate, compared with 26 percent of women.

3. See Sirhan, "Education and the Palestinians in Lebanon." These figures must be used cautiously: according to Sirhan, they show that at least

one-third of Palestinians registered with UNRWA in Lebanon left the country for good or obtained permanent residency in another country. The author concedes, however, that fewer and fewer Palestinians are able to enter secondary school. According to him, frustration and despair are dominant traits among Palestinians today, so that the general tendency is now to leave school as early as possible (between the ages of twelve and fifteen).

4. See Philippe Fargues, *Générations arabes. L'alchimie du nombre* [Arab Generations: The Alchemy of Numbers] (Paris: Fayard, "Documents," 2000), especially chap. 6, "L'école et les formes élémentaires de l'inégalité" [School and Elementary Forms of Inequality], pp. 147–170.

5. See Rashid Khalidi, *Under Siege: PLO Decisionmaking during the 1982 War* (New York: Columbia University Press, 1986). The author writes that, for the Palestinians of the 1917–1982 period, the Fakahani neighborhood, a half-mile area in central Beirut, was the closest thing since 1948 to a political, intellectual, financial, administrative, and spiritual capital (p. 100).

6. The breakdown of students by nationality for the academic years between 1987 and 1990 is derived from Fadia Abu Khalil Fadlallah's Ph.D. thesis in educational sciences, titled "The Birth and Development of Higher Education in Lebanon" (in Arabic) (Beirut: Saint Joseph University, Faculty of Literature and Humanities, Department of Arabic Literature, 1994), p. 726. The difference in the overall number of enrolled students is due mainly to the decrease in the number of Jordanian and Syrian students enrolled at Beirut Arab University.

7. They are therefore far less numerous than the 1,789 Egyptian students, 1,448 Syrian students, and 1,109 UAE students enrolled, and barely more numerous than the 645 students from the Sultanate of Oman. These figures were kindly communicated to the author by the BAU administration in June 2002.

8. The institute has also set up a media center where economic reports issued by roughly 125 banks worldwide are collected, as well as a data center providing information on the world's main cities—more than 850 cities in 160 countries.

9. The college, created in 1979, was officially recognized by the Lebanese state on October 15, 1986 (decree 3484), upon a request presented by the "Islamic Education Center" (al-Markaz al-Islami lil-Tarbiyya). The center had been established in 1976 and constituted as a pious founda-

tion for public welfare *(waqf khayri islami)* in 1979, according to a ruling of the Sunni religious court of Beirut, an institution that depends on the prime minister. The Islamic Center is the "mother institute." The college is part of a wider project, as yet incomplete, which aims to set up an Imam al-Awza'i Institute. Classes began at the college in 1979 (1 Muharram 1400 A. H.). *Source:* informational pamphlet put out by the college for the 1998–99 academic year.

10. In Lebanon, the Jama'a Islamiyya is the equivalent of the Muslim Brotherhood.

11. See Chapter 2. Notably, Fatah helped create Amal, a fact the Shi'ite organization's current leaders avoid mentioning. It is true that the organization turned against its founder less than ten years after its creation, during the war of the camps (1986–1988).

12. On the Sunnis' organizational capabilities in Lebanon, see Chapter 3.

13. See *al-Taqrir al-Islami,* October 12, 1979, issue 4.

14. See *al-Taqrir al-Islami,* December 1979, issue 7.

15. See *al-Taqrir al-Islami,* November 9, 1979, titled "The Dangers of External Financing for Islamic Society in Lebanon."

16. Interview with Tawfiq Huri, January 31, 2000, at the institute.

17. Interview published in *al-Ma'arij,* September 1991, issues 6 and 7, pp. 123–124.

18. Ibid.

19. The first teaches Qur'an and *hadith* sciences, the second jurisprudence.

20. "Dialog With Shaykh Kamil Musa," *al-Hidaya* (1991), issue 18, pp. 6–8.

21. Ibid., p. 7.

22. Ibid.

23. Bilad al-Sham designates Lebanon, Syria, Jordan, and Palestine.

24. Shaykh Abd al-Nasir Jibri, *L'enseignement religieux au Liban* [Religious Education in Lebanon], Islamic Conference on Education (Tripoli, Lebanon, 1996), p. 204.

25. Interview with Shaykh Jibri, February 8, 2001, Beirut.

26. Ibid.

27. Interview with Muhammad Nukkari, Dar al-Fatwa, Beirut, November 2, 2000.

28. In the same year, there were 710 male and 279 female students. See the data provided in *Le point sur le Liban* [Lebanon: Review], ed. Gérard Figuier and Louis Hanna (Paris: Maisonneuve et Larose, 1998), p. 194.

29. See *L'enseignement supérieur au Liban* [Higher Education in Lebanon],

ed. Adnan al-Amin (Association libanaise des sciences de l'éducation, 1997), p. 93.

30. *Les étudiants au Liban: pratiques et attitudes. L'héritage de la division* [Students in Lebanon: Practices and Attitudes. Inheriting Division], ed. Adnan al-Amin and Mohamed Fa'ur (Association libanaise des sciences de l'éducation, 1998), p. 100.

31. Interview, Ain al-Helweh, April 10, 1999.

32. For 1995–96, a total of 285 students were registered, with 201 Lebanese and 84 Palestinians. See *Le point sur le Liban.*

33. Interview, Ain al-Helweh, July 13, 2000.

34. Ibid.

35. See Ahmad Awad Abul-Shabab, "The Elements of Victory in Light of the Qur'an and the *Sunna,*" 1997, doctoral thesis, library of the Imam al-Awza'i Institute, Beirut.

36. Ibid., pp. 538 and 540.

37. Ibid., p. 503.

38. Ibid., p. 398.

39. For example, "democracy is a human regime, subject to error, while the Islamic regime rests on a divine quality." See Muhsin Baqir al-Hanari, "Shura and Democracy: Between Shari'a and Positive Law," 1996, doctoral thesis, library of the Imam al-Awza'i Institute, Beirut, p. 374.

40. Abdallah Hallaq, "The Causes of the Islamic Awakening: Stages in the Establishment of an Islamic State," library of the Imam al-Awza'i Institute, Beirut, p. 420.

41. Ibid., p. 277.

42. Among these ninety-three fifth-year students, there were forty-one Lebanese citizens, seven Palestinians, six Iraqis, three Algerians, and three Jordanians as well as one Saudi subject and one Iranian.

43. On the situation of Sunni Islam in Syria, and the relationship between Shaykh Kaftaro's networks and the regime, see Annabelle Böttcher's dissertation, "Sunni Islam under Hafez al-Assad: Coercive and Persuasive Strategies in the Politics of Islam" (unpublished translation of "Syrische Religionspolitik unter Asad," Freiburg im Breisgau: Arnold-Bergstraesser-Institut, 1998), p. 258.

44. Note that most of the faculty are graduates of the same institute. For the 1991–92 academic year, there were about thirty professors, of whom five were full-time instructors, nine were part-time lecturers, and sixteen were advisers. See Fadia Abu Khalil Fadlallah, "The Birth and Development of Higher Education in Lebanon."

45. The defense took place on February 8, 2000, at Imam al-Awza'i Institute. The student wrote his thesis, its title tinged with eschatological overtones ("The Signs of Victory for Islam and the Muslims in Light of the Qur'an and the *Sunna*"), under the supervision of the Lebanese salafist shaykh Zakariya al-Misri, whose attitude to the regime was hostile during the Diniyeh events. See Chapter 7.

46. A salafist shaykh from Nahr al-Barid, Shaykh Ahmad Mithqan, entered the institute after Shaykh Hallaq intervened on his behalf. Mithqan was a student at Da'i al-Islam al-Shahal's al-Hidaya Center. After the state closed the center, he studied at Shaykh Hallaq's Murshid institute for a year in order to enroll later at Imam al-Awza'i.

47. Philippe Braud, *Sociologie politique* (Paris: LGDJ, 1994), p. 214.

48. Such preachers include, for example, Shaykhs Ali Abbas and Abu Dia' in Ain al-Helweh, and Shaykh Ali Abdallah in Bur al-Shamali (where there is only one mosque).

49. For this argument, see Gustav von Grunebaum's critique of Ali al-Nadwi's work *Ce que le monde a perdu depuis le déclin des musulmans* [What the World Has Lost Since the Muslims Declined], published in 1951. See von Grunebaum, *Modern Islam: The Search for Cultural Identity* (Westport, Conn.: Greenwood Press, 1962), p. 252.

50. On relations among "peripheral ulema," the state, and recourse to violence in contemporary Egypt, see Malika Zghal, *Gardiens de l'islam. Les oulémas d'Al Azhar dans l'Egypte contemporaine* [Guardians of Islam: Al-Azhar's Ulema in Contemporary Egypt] (Paris: Presses de la Fondation nationale des sciences politiques, 1996).

51. Gilles Kepel and Yann Richard, eds., *Intellectuels et militants de l'islam contemporain* [Intellectuals and Militants of Contemporary Islam] (Paris: Le Seuil, "Sociologie," 1990).

52. In Saida, families that would rather not send their children to UNRWA schools generally opt for religious schools that are integrated in Lebanese Jama'a networks. Al-Iman secondary school, for example, readily accepts young Palestinians.

7. Underground Jihad in Sir al-Diniyeh

1. According to Liberation Party sources, Syrian security forces arrested more than 500 of the organization's members in several cities; the Islamist organization attributed the lack of reaction in the international media to peace negotiations between Israel and Syria: "Perhaps this is

because [the media] want to hide Syria's inhuman actions, as long as it continues to abandon Palestine and to recognize the Jewish usurpers' state . . . This is a crime of which the Syrian regime has often accused other states" (see the Liberation Party website: http://www.hizb-u-tahrir.org, January 9, 2000).

2. The communiqué was quoted in *al-Quds al-Arabi* newspaper, December 24, 1999.

3. *Al-Hayat,* January 6, 2000.

4. Information on the group's members and their life stories was obtained from the Lebanese media, which published the closing speech made by the prosecutor general for the Judicial Council. For a complete text of the accusations brought, see *al-Nahar,* July 11, 2000.

5. Shaykh Tamim al-Adnani traveled throughout the United States to collect donations and raise believers' awareness of the urgency of the jihad in Afghanistan. The Palestinian shaykh, who was originally from Jerusalem and had collaborated very closely with Abdallah Azzam in the Service Bureau, felt that for religious reasons he could not act within the framework of the PLO: "The orders they brandished publicly did not bear the banner 'there is no god but God and Muhammad is His prophet.'" Considered a religious obligation, the duty to engage in jihad wherever possible led Tamim al-Adnani to settle in Peshawar. See the interview with Shaykh al-Adnani in *al-Jihad,* issue 32 (1987).

6. The association was headed by the salafist shaykh Da'i al-Islam al-Shahal. It was dissolved in 1995 after a decision taken in the Ministerial Council. Umar Yi'ali was also a former member of the Society for the Propagation of the Faith (Jam'iyyat al-Tabligh), established in India in 1927. The society is a transnational, apolitical re-Islamicization movement that exhorts believers to return to imitating the Prophet Muhammad strictly in their daily lives.

7. See the analysis by Ibrahim al-Amin in *al-Safir* daily newspaper, Thursday, January 16, 2000.

8. The Islamic Unification Movement, or IUM (Harakat al-Tawhid al-Islamiyya), an Islamist organization, was established by Shaykh Sa'id Sha'ban in the early 1980s. The IUM (usually called Tawhid) took Fatah's side during the Syrian-Palestinian war of November 1983. Sa'id Sha'ban had links with Ayatollah Khomeini, whom he had met in Najaf, Iraq, in 1963, and this guaranteed his survival, as well as that of his organization, after the Syrian army took the city in 1986. For

an analysis of Islamist networks in Tripoli during the war, see the dissertation by Joumana al-Soufi (under the supervision of Olivier Carré), "Lutte populaire armée. De la désobéissance civile au combat pour Dieu" [Popular Armed Struggle: From Civil Disobedience to the Struggle for God], Université de la Sorbonne nouvelle-Paris III (1989).

9. Sami Zubian, *The Lebanese National Movement* (in Arabic) (Beirut: Dar al-Masira, 1977), pp. 346–347.

10. See Mousbah Rajab, "Le vieux Tripoli, un espace historique en voie de mutation: problématique et perspective d'avenir" [Old Tripoli, a Historical Space in Transformation: Problematic and Future Perspectives], doctoral thesis in urban planning, Paris I-Sorbonne, 1993, p. 379. The figures the author cites are taken from a study conducted by the Tripoli association Makarim al-Akhlaq fi Tarablus.

11. Ibid.

12. See Khalid Dahir's account of events in an interview published in *Hurriyya* (February 2000), no. 20.

13. See the closing speech made by the prosecutor general for the Judicial Council, *al-Nahar,* July 11, 2000.

14. See *al-Nahar,* January 15, 2000. A friend of Basim al-Kanj, Nasir Kabara, explained to the newspaper that he was "mobilizing believers to go fight in Chechnya." This friend conveyed the information by e-mail. He had known Kanj since 1985, when both of them received scholarships from the Hariri Foundation to study in Boston. He added that Kanj had fought in Afghanistan, where he had been wounded by the Russians. He had also fought the Serbs in Bosnia. According to Nasir Kabara, Kanj was killed in Lebanon while mobilizing "true believers" to go fight in Chechnya. Asked why Basim al-Kanj had not gone to fight the occupation forces in the south, his friend replied: "We all know who gives permission to fight Israel there."

15. Roger Naba'a and Souheil al-Kache, "Récits éclatés d'une révolution manquée" [Fragmented Accounts of a Failed Revolution], *Peuples méditerranéens, Liban, remises en cause* (July–September 1982), no. 20, p. 156.

16. Ghassan Salamé, "L'Orient moyen dans un monde en mutation" [The Middle East in a Changing World], *Maghreb-Machrek* (April–June 1992), no. 136.

17. Sermon delivered by Shaykh Jamal Khattab, Ain al-Helweh, 1998.

18. Maher Hammud, who was receiving Iranian assistance, wanted his role in Saida to be equivalent to that played by Shaykh Sha'ban in Tripoli. The two men shared Iranian ties and a common interpretation of Islam.

19. Elizabeth Picard emphasized the difference between "direct knowledge" and "ideological knowledge" in an article comparing two militias and the effect of their actions on their communities in Lebanon (the Lebanese Forces, a Christian militia) and Northern Ireland (the Ulster Defense Association, a Protestant militia), respectively: "From now on, the populations of the regions dominated by the LF and the UDA are replacing the direct knowledge they had of the country's other populations (Muslims; Catholics) by an ideological knowledge, which it is impossible to test empirically, induced through socialization that the militia controls." Elizabeth Picard, "De la domination du groupe à l'invention de son identité. Les milices libanaises et les paramilitaires nord-irlandais" [From Group Domination to the Invention of Its Identity: Lebanese Militias and Northern Irish Paramilitary Forces], in Denis-Constant Martin, ed., *Cartes d'identité: comment dit-on nous en politique* [ID Cards: How to Say "We" in Politics] (Paris: Presses de la Fondation nationale des sciences politiques, 1994), pp. 147–162.

20. See *al-Nahar*, January 8, 2000.

21. Anthony Giddens, *The Consequences of Modernity* (Palo Alto: Stanford University Press, 1990), pp. 18–19.

22. Interview with Shaykh Ahmad, Nahr al-Barid, August 2002. Abu Salim (Chapter 3) speaks of a separate universe in similar terms.

23. Shaykh Ghunaym allegedly told the young preacher: "Because of your violent words, we'll never go further than Tillat al-Sitt" ("Lady's Hill," which marked the location of the Syrian checkpoint at the northern entrance to the camp until the Syrian army left Lebanon on April 26, 2005). Interview with Ahmad, August 2002.

24. Tract by Shaykh Zakariya al-Misri, November 28, 1999. The Lebanese judiciary cleared Samir Geagea of that charge, and to this day no one knows who committed the crime against the Sa'idat al-Najat Church. Once arrested, the leader of the Lebanese Forces was accused of assassinating former Prime Minister Rashid Karami, for which he spent eleven years in jail.

25. According to the Islamists, Ahmad al-Mahmud (Abu Thabit) was killed just after finishing his prayers at Tawar'i Mosque in Ain al-Helweh. In Fatah's version of events, he and twenty other militants

took the offensive, throwing grenades at Fatah's post at the camp's northern entrance, in the Baraksat sector, and he was killed afterward. Al-Mahmud was twenty-one and had finished high school at the Imam al-Bukhari salafist center in Tripoli. At his funeral, held on August 14, 2002, in Tripoli's Bab al-Tabbaneh neighborhood, the crowd shouted slogans that were, to say the least, hostile to Yasir Arafat: "There is no god but God, and Yasir Arafat is His enemy." The deceased's father, whose two other sons were subsequently placed on trial by the Judicial Council for their role in the Diniyeh clashes, accused Sultan Abul-Aynayn of "collaborating with Israel," and added: "We know who killed him at the door to the mosque: Fatah Phalangists, followers of Abu Ammar and Sultan Abul-Aynayn in Ain al-Helweh" (quoted in *al-Mustaqbal*, August 15, 2002).

26. Tract by Zakariya al-Misri, August 16, 2002. The pamphlet ends with a reminder of the role Tripoli played in the clashes between Syria and the PLO: "Don't forget that Tripoli, even as some of you were plotting to hand these youngsters over, took you in, sheltered you, and defended you when you were on the run. This attitude claimed many victims among Tripoli's sons, and caused considerable material damage."

27. The Syrian intelligence services had four centers in Abu Samra, in different parts of the neighborhood: Nazleh al-Khanaq; Sahat Sa'dun; Mafraq Barud; and Tariq al-Shalafa. The main Syrian security center was in Tripoli, in the old city, in Mar Marun center. In Qubbeh, a building in al-Malluleh owned by Syria also controlled access to Tabbaneh and the Palestinian camp of Badawi.

28. See Shaykh Muharram al-Arifi's sermon, for example.

29. See Hasan Nasrallah's declarations in *al-Nahar,* April 5, 2001.

30. Michel Seurat, *L'Etat de barbarie* [The State of Barbarism] (Paris: Le Seuil, "Esprit," 1989), p. 44.

31. The expression "Kurnat Shahwan" refers to the Metn village where various Christian political figures who sought to represent a moderate, legalistic opposition to Syria and its Lebanese allies gathered in April 2001, with the assent of the Maronite patriarch, Nasrallah Butrus Sfayr. The Kurnat Shahwan group has represented Christians in the interconfessional coalition that has headed Lebanon since the summer 2005 elections. The coalition, referred to as the March 14 Group in Lebanese political parlance, is opposed to the reestablishment of Syrian hegemony over Lebanon.

32. "Ruptures et innovations dans l'approche sociologique des relations internationales" [Breaks and Innovations in the Sociological Approach to International Relations], *Revue du monde musulman et méditerranéen* (1993), pp. 68–69.

33. Rumors that circulated in the media usually pointed toward Yasir Arafat; the operation was thereby considered a renewed manifestation of the "Arafatist-Zionist" plot in Lebanon. More surprising is the fact that this rumor was repeated word for word by the correspondent of *Le Monde* in Lebanon, Lucien Georges, in his account of the events of January 2000.

34. See the *Daily Star*, April 18, 2001, for an article on Syria's manipulation of Islamist groups in Tripoli.

35. The Union was created in 1990 at the initiative of Dr. Usama Rifa'i, the president of the Akkar Shari'a court and head of the northern branch of Dar al-Fatwa, al-Azhar's teaching center. Dr. Rifa'i, the scion of an influential family in Akkar religious society, was a graduate of al-Azhar in Lebanon and of the Islamic University in Madina. A member of the Rifa'iyya Sufi order, he sought to establish a religious clientele by giving young Azhar graduates employment opportunities in the region. For instance, he set up a second Shari'a court in the Akkar. Through his actions, the Union experienced an influx of younger members starting in the mid-1990s.

36. Interview with a Palestinian shaykh who preferred to remain anonymous, summer 2002. According to the same source: "In the Nahr al-Barid camp, the Syria *aqid* (lieutenant-colonel or colonel) summoned all the shaykhs. An underling would come to the camp and give a shaykh an appointment, on such a day at such a time. The shaykh wouldn't sleep till then. On the given day, they would take tea, coffee, and the message would be received!"

37. In his chronicle of the Lebanese war, written "in the heat of the action," René Chamussy described the February 6 Movement's disappearance under the combined onslaught of Amal and the Syrian services in the western sector of the capital: "On June 1, 1986, there was talk of a new kind of confrontation: Amal militiamen were clashing with members of Shakir Barjawi's 'February 6 Movement.' The latter, a tiny group, was anchored in the Tariq al-Jadidah neighborhood (between west Beirut and the camps on the city's outskirts); it was Sunni and pro-Palestinian. On June 2, the head of Syrian intelligence arrived

in Beirut with truckloads of weapons. In the evening, the tinderbox caught: it took Berri's militia seventeen hours to take control of Tariq al-Jadidah. Afterward, there were the classic scenes of pillaging and a hunt for 'Sunni combatants' throughout the city." René Chamussy, "La chute. Liban 1986" [The Fall: Lebanon 1986], *Annales de sociologie et d'anthropologie* (1986), no. 3, p. 62.

Conclusion

1. Khalil Chatawi, who served as general director of Palestinian civil affairs in the ministry of the interior from 1994 to 1998, admitted that "Jamil al-Sayyid and Emile Lahoud"—the Syrian regime's two main contacts in the state apparatus—"had priority in dealing with this question." In consequence, Chatawi was prohibited from establishing relations with Fatah leaders in Lebanon. Interview with Khalil Chatawi, Beirut, August 2005.

2. At the Lebanese government's instigation, the PLO opened an office in Beirut, headed by Abbas Zaki, a representative of the Palestinian Authority.

3. Two weeks after Hariri was assassinated, and more than a month before the Syrian withdrawal, opposition to the Syrian regime was already being criticized on al-Risala, Ain al-Helweh's Islamist television station, which broadcasts from al-Nur Mosque. During his weekly program "Spotlight on Current Affairs" *(Qadaya Taht al-Daw),* broadcast on March 1, 2005, Shaykh Abu Dia' and his guest, Shaykh Maher Hammud, denounced "the opposition forces, which showered the Israeli forces with rice and roses when they entered Lebanon, and which now consider the Syrians the occupation troops that must leave the country . . . These forces are also demanding that Resolution 1559 be applied, that the resistance be disarmed, and that the Palestinian presence be eliminated." Camp residents who had access to cable were invited to give their opinion, and one of them made the point that he did not "feel obliged to defend the Syrian regime, for it fought the Palestinians at Tal al-Za'tar, during the war of the camps, and offered them nothing but destruction in Lebanon."

4. The international commission that investigated the assassination of Rafiq al-Hariri suggested this trail in the report it issued on June 14, 2006. The commission, headed by Judge Brammertz, put forth the hy-

pothesis that the assassination was compartmentalized: "This would mean a complex operation, broken down into its constituent parts and conducted by individuals or groups unaware of other aspects of the operation or other participants involved in it." It did not dismiss the possibility that Ahmad Abu Adas was involved. Abu Adas, who hails from the Palestinian refugee camp of Burj al-Barajneh on Beirut's southern outskirts, claimed responsibility for the operation in a videotape broadcast by al-Jazeera.

Acknowledgments

Throughout the research and writing of this book, I benefited from the comments and critiques of Ghassan Salamé. Without his intellectual and moral support, offered at the most difficult times, this work would never have come to completion. I owe the same debt of gratitude to Gilles Kepel, who spared neither time nor effort when receiving me in Paris and sharing his observations and knowledge of radical movements. The late Rémy Leveau encouraged me to follow the first leads I found in the field, by suggesting hypotheses and comparisons that proved both accurate and fruitful. His availability and energy were particularly helpful to me during the crucial early period.

I would also like to thank Selim Abou, S.J., René Chamussy, S.J., and Mounir Chamoun at St. Joseph University. They offered me support and encouragement at the very beginning of this research project. I am grateful to the director of CEMAM (Centre d'Etude sur le Monde Arabe et Musulman), John Donohue, S.J., and to his associate director, Christophe Varin, for granting me access to the center's library, facilities, and wealth of documentation. Similarly, I am most grateful to the former CERMOC (Centre d'Etudes et de Recherches sur le Moyen-Orient Contemporain) in Beirut, now the Institut français du Proche-Orient, which provided an invaluable forum for exchanges and debates among students and researchers. Its directors, Jean Hannoyer, Elizabeth Picard, and then Henri Laurens, were kind enough to read and comment on portions of this work. Their presence was a continual call to intellectual rigor and discipline, and the CERMOC played a crucial role in spreading information and increasing access to high-quality academic publications, whose value should not be neglected in the context of Lebanese intellectual provincialization. I am also grateful to the members of the jury for the Michel Seurat fellowship, offered by the CNRS (Centre National de la Recherche Scientifique), for their faith in this project.

No long-term research project can be successful without the support of patient friends. I am particularly eager to thank all those who supported me—in both French and English senses of the word—for several years. Special thanks go to Joseph Bahout, Annabelle Böttcher, Claudine Harb, Carla Edde, Loula Assi, and, each time I returned to Paris, my family, Adrien Barrot, Frédéric Charillon, Lamia Zaki, and Brian Pierce. Samir Kassir, a historian and journalist, was one of the earliest supporters of this research project, and he kindly shared his hypotheses and insights with me. This book was written in homage to his work, brutally interrupted by his assassination in Beirut on June 2, 2005.

Finally, my gratitude goes to all the refugees, militants, and people of religion who agreed to speak to me, spend time with me, and, sometimes, trust me. Without them, this work would never have seen the light of day.

Index